ABOUT TROUT:

THE BEST OF ROBERT J. BEHNKE

FROM TROUT MAGAZINE

McCLOUD RIVER REDBAND

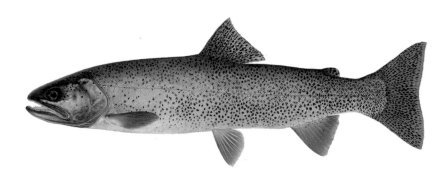

FINESPOTTED SNAKE RIVER CUTTHROAT

BROOK TROUT

THE BEST *of*
ROBERT J. BEHNKE
from TROUT MAGAZINE

ABOUT TROUT

ILLUSTRATIONS BY
JOSEPH R. TOMELLERI

FOREWORD BY
TED WILLIAMS

PREFACE BY
CHARLES GAUVIN
PRESIDENT & CEO, TROUT UNLIMITED

THE LYONS PRESS
GUILFORD, CONNECTICUT

PUBLISHED BY
THE LYONS PRESS
246 GOOSE LANE
GUILFORD, CT 06437
WWW.GLOBEPEQUOT.COM

THE LYONS PRESS IS AN IMPRINT OF THE GLOBE PEQUOT PRESS

PREPARED BY
SCOTT & NIX, INC.
150 WEST 28TH STREET, SUITE 1103
NEW YORK, NY 10011
WWW.SCOTTANDNIX.COM

TROUT UNLIMITED
1300 NORTH 17TH STREET, SUITE 500
ARLINGTON, VA 22209
WWW.TU.ORG

10 9 8 7 6 5 4 3 2 1

LIBRARY OF CONGRESS CATALOG-IN-PUBLICATION DATA IS AVAILABLE.

ISBN 978-1-59921-203-6

PRINTED IN CHINA

CONTENTS

PREFACE

CHARLES GAUVIN
PRESIDENT & CEO, TROUT UNLIMITED

FOR THE PAST 16 YEARS, as Trout Unlimited's CEO, I have had the last word on the editorial content of its flagship publication, *Trout*. In my informal capacity as the magazine's publisher, I have read every one of Bob Behnke's quarterly columns, 86 in number and still counting. More than anything else I have done since joining TU's staff, reading Behnke's writing has increased the depth and the breadth of my knowledge about trout and salmon and their watersheds.

Although it has existed for over 100 years in various forms, often as an appendage to other academic disciplines, fishery science began to come of age in the second half of the twentieth century. For coldwater fish, Bob Behnke's graduate school mentor, Paul Needham, was a critical figure. Where trout and salmon were concerned, Needham was among the first fishery scientists to emphasize the importance of healthy habitat and the need to conserve native gene pools. Before him, the term "trout biologist" too often denoted someone whose principal mission was to churn out fish from hatcheries. After him, thanks to the influence of Bob Behnke and other disciples, the transition had begun from hatcheries to habitat, and from recreational fish husbandry to conservation biology.

The transition continues today, but its progress is more pronounced and its outcome more certain thanks to Behnke's writings, not only his column in *Trout*, but also his many articles in scientific journals and several monographs. Every angler who values wild trout and wild, free-flowing rivers owes Bob Behnke a huge debt of gratitude.

One of Behnke's most important contributions to fishery science has been in increasing our understanding of native trout in the Western United States. With a number of native Western subspecies now so seriously depleted, conserving intact habitats and gene pools has become a matter of life and death, and for some populations at or near the brink, Behnke's work has served as a last firebreak between persistence and extinction. As we contemplate the future of the West's native trout—fish whose habitat is caught in the squeeze play of energy development and climate change—Behnke's work will be ever more important.

For native trout and salmon across North America, Behnke's focus on life history diversity has strengthened conservation and protection efforts and prevented genetics from hijacking biology. Genetics has an important role to play in conservation, but as Behnke recognized long ago, not all biologically significant traits or adaptations have genetic expression (most, indeed, do not). Thus, despite the same genetic profile, steelhead have a vastly different life history from inland rainbow trout, as do sea-run brook trout in contrast to inland populations of the same species. By focusing on what specific populations of native trout do during their life cycles, Behnke has prevented a terrible simplification of fishery science, where evolutionarily/biologically significant populations might be written off because as not worthy of protection because they do not express measurable genetically distinct traits. His deep knowledge of and respect for life history diversity has been a powerful antidote to the hubris that sometimes arises from placing too much faith in technology.

Along with his other contributions, Behnke has given generations of laymen-conservationists an enlightened respect for good science and scientifically responsible management of all coldwater fishes, native and non-native. Although a native trout specialist, Behnke has never been a native trout snob. He was raised in the urbanized zone of the Eastern seaboard and has spent much of his professional career in Colorado, whose rivers have nearly all been over-tapped and "managed" out of a natural flow regime. He understands the role non-native trout have played in fishery management and long ago observed that, in addition to their enormous recreational and economic value, naturalized populations of non-native trout could serve beneficial ecological functions, not the least of which was to be indicators of water quality and other measures of watershed health.

In editing Behnke's columns, I have always enjoyed sharing his interest in exposing the human story behind fishery science and management. His willingness to explore the quiet back roads of our nation's fishery science and management has yielded some interesting results. What lay reader would have known, for instance, that the purest strain of Pyramid Lake's Lahontan cutthroat trout was recovered, decades after the lake's population had been extirpated, in a little stream on the Nevada-Utah border, in which the fish had long ago been stocked? Sometimes, the back roads he has traveled have been those of Europe, where his readers have learned about how brown trout ended up in

America, or how rainbow trout transplanted 100 years ago to Germany from North America may have acquired a resistance to whirling disease that today could help save some North American rainbow fisheries. Other times, they have taken Behnke south of the border, such as when he traced the origin of scientific knowledge of the "Ghost Trout of the Rio Conchos," the recently "discovered" Conchos trout.

In addition to giving lay readers a thorough grounding in fishery science, Behnke has been a powerful voice in objecting to questionable applications of science and any reliance on pseudo-science. He once used soil chemistry to rebut in *Trout*'s pages an anthropologist's claim that tales of Atlantic salmon abundance in pre-colonial New England were greatly exaggerated because no salmon bones could be found in Native American middens. The region's highly acidic soils, he reasoned, quickly destroyed all but the heaviest of fish bones, and later-day commercial fishing records substantiated salmon population estimates.

On another occasion, he railed against the animal rights proponents who were attempting to prove that fish feel pain from angling. After citing the views of a comparative neurophysiologist, Behnke went on to observe:

> "When an issue generates intense controversy, polarization and strong emotion, it can be difficult to determine who has the most scientifically credible, unbiased reasoning…Scientists are not equal in their qualifications and areas of expertise, and the influences of self-interest are pervasive. [A]nglers must remain vigilant about questioning all the information they receive before making a decision."

In a world where scientific expertise is often for sale, where some biologists have mortgaged their principles, Behnke's words represent sound guidance for the perplexed.

I hope you enjoy reading this book as much as I have enjoyed reading its selections when they appeared as Bob Behnke's columns in *Trout*.

FOREWORD

TED WILLIAMS

"I WISH I'D HAD BOB BEHNKE FOR A PROFESSOR." That's a statement I've often heard and often uttered myself. But not until I reread these lyrical yet scientifically precise essays did I realize that he has been and is my professor and the professor of so many of us who love trout and salmon and desperately want to see them saved and restored. It's just that his teachings have come later in our lives, when we are more receptive to learning.

We mourned the loss of these living jewels from so much of their range. But we weren't sure just how we had lost them. And we didn't understand how to get them back, or even that we could.

Shining from every page of this book is Behnke's love for these beautiful and complex works of evolution, his commitment to their conservation and recovery, and his rage at those who would mix, pollute, and waste their genes. He shows how our ceaseless game of musical chairs with species and subspecies has destroyed much of the grand diversity earth was blessed with, homogenizing it into muddy sameness. You will comprehend trout and salmon not just as lovely life forms and splendid quarry but as critical parts of complicated ecosystems. You will understand how they came about, how we have squandered them and, most important, how we can recover them.

Many of the official diagnostic descriptions of the species and subspecies you will read about here were written by Dr. Behnke and published in science journals. One of these fish—the Snake River finespotted cutthroat (*Oncorhynchus clarki behnkei*)—was eventually named after him for his work. After three of them (the greenback, Bonneville, and Lahontan cutthroats) had been written off as extinct, he gave them back to the world by rediscovering them in tiny, remote refuges. Now it appears that he has returned to us the greenback twice. The first time was in 1969 when he found a relict population above an impassable waterfall on a nameless rill near Rocky Mountain National Park. It had to have been started there by a pioneer, a bucket biologist who ironically and accidentally preserved the race from future bucket biologists. The second time was in 2007 when greenback recovery, arguably the greatest success story in the history of the Endangered Species Act, threatened to unravel. Fishery managers had mistaken as a symptom of hybridization what Behnke believes to be remnant and naturally occurring DNA from cutthroat ancestors.

As a reformer of perceptions and attitudes Behnke is to these fish what Aldo Leopold—the forester turned ecologist—was to mammalian predators. And, like Leopold, he differs from so many of his peers by being not just a meticulous and tireless researcher but also a gifted wordsmith, an avid angler, and a fierce advocate for the subjects he studies. This passion and his ability to communicate it are what make him such an effective teacher.

His passion is a function of what Rachel Carson called a "sense of wonder," nearly as commonly lost with age as milk teeth but something Behnke has managed to hang onto. When he cradles a native trout or salmon in the icy flow of its home water he feels as he did when he was ten-years-old and caught his first trout below a Rippowam River mill pond in Stamford, Connecticut. It was barely seven inches long, and it had been reared in a hatchery; but it mesmerized him. "I was in awe," he recalls. "I thought it was the most beautiful thing I had ever seen." He ran home with it and placed it in a pan of water. Later that day it jumped out and died, and he proudly ate it for supper.

Like all great teachers Behnke is gentle. After I had written in *Audubon* magazine that "I'd been hoping" to catch a Lahontan cutthroat in Utah's Logan River, I got a note from Bob, informing me that I was wrong, that the Logan held only Bonneville cutthroats. I countered that my reporting was absolutely accurate, that my abject ignorance did not gainsay my idle hope. My quest had been that of Dr. Seuss' "Marco," patiently fishing the lifeless waters of McElligot's Pool for, among countless other creatures, whales "all spouting their spouts and all thrashing their tails!" Most other scientists would have corrected me via a letter to the editor.

But great teachers know when to be tough, too. For example, you will see throughout this book variations of the wonderful letter to the editor Behnke sent us at *Fly Rod & Reel* and that salmonid advocates now keep on hand for the teachable moment. He was responding to managers I'd quoted who had resisted restoration of coasters (the giant race of brook trout that once patrolled the upper Great Lakes) on grounds that "a brook trout is a brook trout." That kind of statement flings down and dances upon Behnke's life's work. "A grape is also a grape," he wrote us. "One species of grape (*Vitus*

vinifera) is used in virtually all wine made in the world—reds, whites, best and worst. The grape-is-a-grape point of view is the most simplistic and would save money for wine drinkers, because the cheapest wines would be the same quality as the most expensive wines. I wouldn't want some of the managers [you] quote selecting wine for me or, for that matter, being in charge of fisheries programs where subtle genetic differences that may not show up in genetic analysis can be important."

I know of no one who has done more to change public thinking about fish and fish management than Robert Behnke. By commissioning these essays the leadership of TU has learned from this teacher with the rest of us. When Behnke offered his first submission to *Trout* magazine 24 years ago, TU was top heavy, rudderless, confused about its mission. Today I don't know a more streamlined, effective force for the preservation and restoration of native ecosystems, and not just those confined to coldwater habitats. One cannot work for trout and salmon without simultaneously working for forests, prairies, deserts, rivers, lakes, oceans, and air.

Thanks in large measure to what Behnke has written here, more and more anglers are demanding wild trout and salmon instead of what the management establishment calls "the hatchery product"—those hideous, stump-finned imitations selected for tolerance of processed food, crowding, sudden movements, filth, and lack of cover; in short, for everything trout and salmon are not. And, in addition to understanding the value of wild salmonids, anglers increasingly understand the value of pure, native strains.

Yet Behnke's work is far from finished, and he hasn't a prayer of finishing it by himself. Many, maybe most, anglers still follow hatchery trucks like herring gulls. For them a trout is a trout—not part and product of woods, waters, and mountains, but a commodity whose highest and best use is to titillate them by pulling on their lines.

"A mind thus festooned with ignorance is unlikely to inform itself," wrote Tom McGuane in the foreword to Behnke's great book *Trout and*

Salmon of North America (Free Press, 2002). Indeed. But such minds must not be allowed to dictate fisheries policy, as they have done and still do in too many cases. Behnke's essays have helped and will help prevent that. This is why I see them as the most important of the more than 200 scientific and popular articles he has authored. If there is any lingering doubt that he is the world's leading authority on trout and salmon, it dies here and now with the publication of this extraordinary book. Read it. Enjoy it. And, above all, *use* it.

INTRODUCTION

ROBERT J. BEHNKE

I BEGAN WRITING COLUMNS for *Trout* magazine in 1983; the purpose was to interpret my own work and the scientific literature to make it more accessible to a broader audience. In the broadest sense, my columns have been designed to compliment Trout Unlimited's mission as an advocate for cold-water conservation.

In 2007, as I began my twenty-fifth year of columns, I had not fully realized the magnitude of the volume of words produced over this time. For several years I had thought about publishing the columns in a book that might serve as a useful reference source. I began to go over each column for updating and additional commentary. My original plan was to include every column up to the time of going to press. When the word volume of all columns was totaled, it became apparent that we had far in excess of what would be needed to fill the planned number of pages.

Concerning the selection of columns for the "best," I couldn't bring myself to select them because I try to do my best in writing each one. In reality, this book is more of a "reader" than a collection based on a critical rating system of "best." In this regard, the amount of material left over has me thinking about a second volume; it would be called: "The Rest of the Best."

Writing these columns has also benefited my professional career.

An in-depth understanding of various subjects required expanding my interests and research into areas of political science, history, economics, and the human dimension aspects of natural resources management. This has been reflected by new insights and greater information content in my professional publications. I believe Ernest Hemingway advised authors to learn more about a subject than they would use in a book. Accumulate a surplus of information; it can add an authoritative touch to the writing and it might be useful in the future. This attitude created a problem of what to do with the boxes of notes and literature accumulated over many years when I retired from Colorado State University. I had about 60 boxes of "surplus" information that was stored on campus and in my garage and barn. In 2006, The Trout and Salmonid Collection of the Montana State University Libraries, also known as the Bud Lilly Trout and Salmonid Bibliography, transported most of my literature collection to MSU. I had previously visited the trout and salmonid library and was very impressed with the amount and quality of literature that had been obtained during the first few years of their operation. I am deeply indebted to the MSU Libraries for solving my problem for the proper disposition of my information accumulation. I am also indebted to the Monty Bean Museum of Brigham Young University. Two round trips in rental vans transported my fish collection to BYU for proper care and preservation. Although small by museum standards, my salmonid collection consisted of a representation of species and subspecies from around the world, including several "one-of-a-kind" specimens.

In historical perspective, although progress has not been continuous during the past 50 years, the enactment of laws, environmental regulations, and increased influence of conservation organizations during this period, indicate a hopeful future. This is especially true in comparison with how natural resources were exploited in the previous hundred years, beginning in the mid-nineteenth century. The mission of government policy was economic development at any cost. The focus was to maximize single-use commodity values without consideration of any environmental values. There were no such concepts as multiple use management or environmental impact statements.

Prevailing attitudes in regards to fish "conservation" can be found in the old fisheries literature. In 1889, David Starr Jordan, America's leading authority on fish, and first president of Stanford University, addressed the meeting of the American Fisheries Society. Jordan praised the mission of the U.S. Fish Commission to replace "worthless" (native) fishes with "valuable" (non-native) fishes. If Jordan had a concept of "conservation" at the time, it was in accordance with prevailing opinion and government policy. Replacing worthless species with valuable species was for the "public good," therefore, good conservation.

In 1913, J. O. Snyder, an associate of Jordan on the faculty of Stanford, did a survey of the fishes of the Lahontan basin. The best account of the world's largest cutthroat trout of Pyramid Lake is found in Snyder's 1917 publication on Lahontan fishes. In 1907, The Newlands Project was completed. This was the first project of the newly created U.S. Bureau of Reclamation. Derby Dam was constructed on the Truckee River about 30 miles above Pyramid Lake to divert the flow of the Truckee River and convert the "worthless" water flowing to Pyramid Lake to "beneficial" water for agriculture. Perhaps with a touch of cynical frustration, but with an understanding of the reality of the time, Snyder pointed out that the primary use of water was to promote industrial and agricultural development. Or, as Senator Newlands proclaimed at the dedication of his water diversion project: "Fish have no standing in water law." The last spawning run of the Pyramid Lake cutthroat trout occurred in 1938. Their average weight was 20 pounds. The beneficial use of Truckee River water associated with the Pyramid Lake Paiute tribe and their natural resources had no legal standing.

Times have changed, although imperfectly, for the better. The concerted attacks to weaken environmental regulations in recent years can be explained at its most basic level by human nature; most specifically the self-interest aspect of human nature. It can be argued that self-interest has a hereditary basis as expounded in the theory of the "selfish gene." When common self-interests come together, a group interest is formed. With money and organization, a group interest becomes a special interest creating a powerful lobby buying political influence into the highest levels of government. Eventually, when enough people realize that their own self interests in clean air and water and environmental quality are negatively impacted by special interests, a backlash can occur.

Environmental organizations have also learned to form coalitions creating lobbies for a common cause. Because of laws such as the Federal Environmental Policy Act and the Endangered Species Act, legal actions have blunted the effectiveness of the special interests to weaken environmental protection. Looking back over the past 50 years, I've learned that if the mind remains open to new ideas and new information, old or, at least, older age can be the age of enlightenment.

THE McCLOUD RIVER RAINBOW TROUT

SPRING 1983

THE STORY OF THE McCLOUD RIVER rainbow trout might better be entitled: "What is the McCloud River rainbow trout?" The complete story of McCloud River trout is too long and involved to discuss in detail here, and a satisfactory answer to the question is clouded by the fact that there were more than one form of rainbow trout native to the McCloud River in California. The McCloud or "Shasta" rainbow trout gained fame as the source of virtually all stocks of hatchery rainbows. But this legend is only partly true.

The story begins in 1872 when the newly created U.S. Fish Commission sent the eminent fish culturist Livingston Stone to California to initiate the propagation of Pacific salmon. Stone chose a site near the mouth of the McCloud River because a large run of Chinook or king salmon ran up the McCloud. The McCloud is a major tributary to the upper Sacramento River; its headwaters drain from Mt. Shasta, and the wild lands of its drainage were still under the control of the primitive Wintun Indians in 1872. It would be interesting and instructive to devote an entire article on the remarkable and perceptive Livingston Stone, but suffice it to say here that he won the respect and cooperation of the local Indians because he respected them as human beings and exhibited a sensitive understanding of their feelings and way of life.

The great salmon runs had all but vanished in the other major tributaries to the Sacramento—the American, Yuba, and Feather rivers—by 1872 from enormous sediment loads resulting from gold mining operations. Stone realized that the future of salmon abundance in the McCloud River depended on the Indians retaining control of the basin which would, in turn, maintain the primeval environment. He wrote in the first *U.S. Fish Commission Report*:

> "I earnestly hope that the policy which has been pursued with the Modoc Indians, against whom a war of extermination is now going on, just north of the McCloud River, will never be adopted with the McCloud tribe. It would be an inhuman outrage to drive this superior and inoffensive race from the river, and I believe the best policy to use with them is to let them be where they are, and if necessary, to protect them from encroachments of the white men."

Alas, this was not to be, and that Livingston Stone was aware of what the future would hold is apparent by his appending a dictionary of the Wintun language to his report with a comment that this language would soon vanish. In what is now euphemistically known as an environmental "trade-off," the native Indians and most of the native trout and salmon of the McCloud River were traded-off. The site of Stone's first hatchery now lies 300 feet beneath the surface of Shasta Lake.

Stone was a keen observer of nature and he realized that besides the salmon, the McCloud River also contained trout. He noted two kinds—a small trout that mainly lived year-round in tributary streams and a large trout of 5 to 10 pounds that appeared in the McCloud River in December. In 1879 Stone constructed holding ponds, stocked them with trout caught nearby (both kinds) and commenced with the propagation of rainbow trout.

We now know that the large trout that appeared in the McCloud River in December represented a run of steelhead trout. Many years ago I examined museum specimens of the resident (nonanadromous) trout collected by Stone from the McCloud River and realized that they were quite distinct from typical steelhead trout and that they represented a primitive evolutionary line of the rainbow trout species. I have since used the name redband trout for primitive forms of rainbow trout, modified from the name red-banded trout used by Stone in 1872.

Thus, the original McCloud River rainbow trout consisted of two forms—an anadromous steelhead trout and a resident redband trout. Stone clearly stated that he mixed both of these forms in his egg taking operations. Because the steelhead specimens were so much larger and would have contributed relatively more sperm and eggs than the resident redband trout, the first federal propagation of rainbow trout was mainly influenced by the heredity of anadromous steelheads, not resident stream rainbows as was so long assumed. The older angling literature and scientific reports often speculated on the reasons why hatchery rainbow trout often expressed strong migratory behavior when the original source of hatchery rainbows was reputed to be the "Shasta" rainbow of the McCloud River, a nonmigratory fish. The late Paul Needham and I published a paper on the origin of hatchery rainbow trout in 1962, pointing out the long neglected fact of steelhead influence in the original hatchery operation on the McCloud River. We also discussed the fact that the names *Salmo stonei* and *S. shasta* given

by David Starr Jordan in 1894 (Jordan was the world's premier ichthyologist and president of Stanford University at the time), although intended as descriptions for the large (steelhead) and the small resident trout of the McCloud were, in reality, both based on specimens of the resident redband trout. Thus, the native redband trout of the McCloud can be designated as *Salmo gairdneri stonei*. The fact that Livingston Stone's initiation of hatchery propagation of rainbow trout in 1879 was not the first hatchery propagation of the species has also been generally overlooked. In 1872 Stone described the propagation of rainbow trout by the California Acclimatization Society from trout taken from San Andreas Reservoir and San Pedro Brook on the San Mateo Peninsula south of San Francisco. Evidently, in about 1875, California's rainbow trout propagation program was supplemented by eggs sent by J. B. Campbell who began a small hatchery operation on his ranch on the McCloud River, a few miles upstream from the federal salmon hatchery.

The first shipment of rainbow trout eggs from California to the Caledonia, New York, hatchery of Seth Green in 1875, may or may not have been of McCloud River origin. In later years, Green was emphatic that the 1875 shipment was not of McCloud River trout, but was "California mountain trout." It is possible that the 1875 eggs sent to New York represented a mixture of resident rainbow and/or steelhead trout of the San Mateo Peninsula and redband and/or steelhead of the McCloud River. In 1878, the Caledonia Hatchery received the first McCloud River trout according to Seth Green. Last year, Dwight Webster wrote to me about wild rainbow trout he observed below the Caledonia Hatchery in the 1950s that possessed excessively bright red stripes. The older hatchery employees called them the "Lacloud" strain. Although Seth Green claimed that he was the first to import McCloud River trout, Daniel Fitzhugh of Michigan obtained eggs of rainbow trout in 1876 to plant in the Au Sable River. The precise origin of the eggs sent to Michigan, however, is not known.

The mixing of various forms of steelhead, resident rainbow, and the primitive redband trout during the initial stages of establishing hatchery stocks of rainbow trout may have unwittingly provided a broad base of genetic diversity (heterozygosity) that allowed for rapid selection of domesticated hatchery strains of rainbow trout.

In any event, rigorous hatchery selection and later infusion of California and Oregon steelhead trout into most hatchery strains produced a rainbow trout quite different from the original redband trout of the McCloud.

I examined specimens of rainbow trout collected from the McCloud River in the 1950s after the construction of Shasta Dam. They had characteristics more typical of hatchery rainbow trout. I feared the original races of redband trout native to the McCloud River had suffered the same fate as the native Indian tribe.

In 1968, Dr. Donald Seegrist of the U.S. Forest Service called my attention to some peculiar trout that inhabited small headwater tributaries to the McCloud River. We made several collections which I intensively studied and compared with McCloud specimens collected by Stone in the nineteenth century. We found that the native redband trout isolated above a large waterfall in the headwater tributaries were more divergent, with more primitive traits than the redband trout native to the McCloud River further downstream (the redband trout known to Livingston Stone). This is due to the complete isolation of the primitive headwater populations from contact and possible hybridization with the more advanced coastal rainbow and steelhead trout. We may assume that this isolation existed for untold thousands of years because the area around Mount Shasta was a glacial refugium where preglacial relicts of plants and animals were able to persist to the present time.

McCLOUD RIVER REDBAND TROUT
Oncorhynchus mykiss stonei

In tiny Sheepheaven Creek we found what I believe is the purest population of the most primitive living form of rainbow trout in existence. The California Fish and Game Department and the U.S. Forest Service are actively cooperating to preserve the remnant populations of redband trout in the headwaters of the McCloud, but I dream of the wealth of genetic diversity that must have once been found in the McCloud River drainage that would be available for study and perhaps practical use today if only the advice of Livingston Stone was followed and the entire drainage basin left to the Indians.

AUTHOR'S NOTE

In this column I attempted to set right a long history of misinformation that the McCloud River rainbow was the first form of rainbow trout that was artificially propagated—the original rainbow "stockie." They were not. I also pointed out that contrary to popular belief, the propagated McCloud trout was made up of both resident (redband) trout and steelhead.

My current updated assessment of the origins of hatchery rainbow trout is as follows: the first propagation of rainbow trout was by the California Acclimatization Society in San Francisco. The society began its operations in 1870, and obtained rainbow trout, and, likely steelhead, from local sources to stock into their holding ponds. Because the typical spawning period of these trout ran from January through March, the first hatching probably occurred in 1871. As operations expanded, the San Leandro "hatching house" was constructed on San Leandro Creek, a tributary to South San Francisco Bay. The first shipments of rainbow trout outside of California came from the San Leandro hatchery. In 1875, Seth Green obtained rainbow trout from the San Leandro hatchery for his Caledonia, New York, hatchery. The Acclimatization Society called the local rainbow trout, "California brook trout." Green called them "California mountain trout."

In 1876, the San Leandro hatchery shipped eggs to a private hatchery at Northville, Michigan. The first propagation of McCloud River trout occurred in 1877 on Campbell Creek, a McCloud tributary on the ranch of J. B. Campbell. Campbell was assisted by Myron Green, assistant to Livingston Stone, director of the U.S. Fish Commission salmon hatchery on the McCloud, a few miles from Campbell Creek. Campbell and Green supplied eggs from McCloud River trout to the San Leandro hatchery.

In 1878 McCloud rainbow trout eggs from Campbell and Green (probably also steelhead), were shipped to both Seth Green's Caledonia hatchery and to Northville, Michigan. In 1880, the Northville hatchery was leased by the U.S. Fish Commission and became an important source for the distribution of rainbow trout. By 1880, brood stocks of both San Francisco Bay area rainbow trout and McCloud River rainbows were established in hatcheries at Northville, Michigan, and Caledonia, New York.

In 1879, Livingston Stone and Myron Green established the "U.S. trout ponds" on Crooks Creek (later Greens Creek) on the banks of the McCloud River, about four miles above the salmon hatchery. Trout were mainly caught on baited set lines from the McCloud River and maintained in holding ponds until spawned. The first spawning at the U.S. trout ponds occurred in January 1880. Stone mentions that in December, large, silvery trout up to 10 pounds were taken in the McCloud River. Undoubtedly, these were steelhead. The eggs and sperm of both steelhead and resident redband trout were indiscriminately mixed and the fertilized eggs were shipped out to federal and state hatcheries. The facilities at the U.S. trout ponds were constructed to hatch up to six million eggs, but floods, siltation, and disease greatly limited production. From 1880 through 1888, only about 2.6 million eyed eggs were shipped from the U.S. Fish Commission station on the McCloud River. By 1888, federal and state hatcheries had established their own brood stocks. Considering the diversity of parental sources that could have been used to establish brood stocks—San Francisco Bay area trout from the San Leandro hatchery (1871–1876), McCloud rainbows from Campbell Creek at San Leandro (1877–1879) and McCloud steelhead mixed with resident redband trout by the U.S. Fish Commission (1880–1888) makes clear that the origins of hatchery rainbow trout were diverse and the McCloud rainbow was not the first.

In 2002, the *Transactions of the American Fisheries Society* published a paper on a run of steelhead in Argentina. The authors stated: "All early shipments of rainbow trout and Pacific salmon, including those directed to the Santa Cruz Hatchery, came directly from California," i.e. from the U.S. Fish Commission Baird hatchery on the McCloud. The first shipments of rainbow trout to Argentina occurred during the 1904–1908 period. The last shipments of rainbow trout from the Baird hatchery was 1888. I sent in a comment with the correct information as given above. Will my attempts to correct more than 100 years of misinformation on the origins of hatchery rainbow trout eventually succeed? Perhaps, but I wouldn't bet on it.

WESTSLOPE CUTTHROAT TROUT

FALL 1983

THE CUTTHROAT TROUT IS A GOOD EXAMPLE of a poly-typic species. That is, the species as a whole (*Salmo clarki*) is made up of individual parts consisting of numerous geographical races (subspecies). The cutthroat trout once had the greatest distribution of any trout in North America. The coastal cutthroat subspecies inhabited waters along the Pacific Coast from northern California to southern Alaska and various other subspecies extended inland to the South Saskatchewan River system of Alberta (Hudson Bay drainage) southward on both sides of the Continental Divide to southern New Mexico (Rio Grande cutthroat trout). Despite this once great range, the cutthroat trout is one of the least known of our trouts because the subspecies in the interior regions suffered catastrophic declines soon after our ancestors wrought a civilizing influence on Western watersheds and introduced nonnative fishes. In this respect, the cutthroat trout is similar to the canary in the mine—it is typically the first species to go in a disturbed environment.

Salmo clarki lewisi is the scientific name for a subspecies of cutthroat trout that is indigenous to a vast geographical region. Originally, it was the only trout living in the Madison, Gallatin, and Beaverhead rivers and of the whole upper Missouri River drainage above Great Falls, Montana. On the other side of the Continental Divide *S. c. lewisi* is the only trout (considering the bull trout as a char) native to the Flathead, Clark Fork and Bitteroot rivers of Montana. It is also native to the South Saskatchewan River of northern Montana and Alberta, the upper Kootenay River of British Columbia, and Montana, the St. Joe River system of Idaho and the Salmon and Clearwater River drainages of Idaho.

How little is known about this particular subspecies of cutthroat trout is illustrated by the fact that it was only during the past two years that I documented the indigenous occurrence of *S. c. lewisi* in the John Day River drainage of Oregon and as the native trout of Lake Chelan, Washington. The fishery agencies of Oregon and Washington had never realized that *S. c. lewisi* (or any form of interior cutthroat trout) is native to their states. I had long heard stories that cutthroat trout occurred in certain tributaries to the John Day River but it was commonly believed that they were the result of stocking. Mr. Robert Smith, an ardent trout angler from Central Point, Oregon, who now attains his ultimate angling experience by fishing for rare, native trout in their native environments, made several collections of fishes and basic information for me that provided the basis for the verification of the native occurrence of *lewisi* in the John Day drainage.

The fisheries for brook, brown, and rainbow trout and for lake trout and kokanee salmon in large lakes such as Pend Oreille, Priest, Cour d'Alene, and Flathead, in this vast region of the original range of *S. c. lewisi*, are the results of stocking by man during the past 100 years. None of these species is native to the original range of the "westslope" cutthroat trout with the exception that rainbow trout are native to the Salmon and Clearwater rivers of Idaho and to the John Day River of Oregon. With the establishment of nonnative species of salmonid fishes, the westslope cutthroat trout rapidly declined and it now occupies only a tiny fraction of its original range, mainly restricted to small, headwater tributaries.

It was such remnant populations of westslope cutthroat existing in the headwater of the St. Joe River and Kelly Creek in Idaho that first provided conclusive evidence that special angling regulations designed to reduce the numbers of trout killed by anglers can be effective for increasing the abundance and size of trout in a population exposed to angler exploitation. The data gathered by Dr. Ted Bjornn and his students of the Idaho Cooperative Fishery Unit established beyond doubt that, after special regulations went into effect, the native cutthroat trout populations responded by tremendous increases in abundance and in the proportion of older, larger trout in the populations. What is still not generally understood among laymen and biologists, however, is that only the cutthroat trout could have responded so favorably to special regulations in these Idaho waters.

The results of special regulation management of cutthroat trout in Idaho cannot be indiscriminately applied to other waters with other species of trout with expectations of similar success. The cutthroat trout is the species most easily caught by anglers. It takes enormously greater fishing pressure to overexploit a population of brown trout or rainbow trout than it does a comparable population of cutthroat trout under comparable conditions. In most trout populations, overexploitation occurs when anglers remove about 50 percent or more of the catchable-size fish during a year. Brown trout populations are known for their resistance to overexploitation under high fishing intensity. The degree of vulnerability of trout to being caught by anglers, besides hereditary, species-specific differences, also is influenced by the characteristics of individual waters and the degree of expertise of the anglers fishing those waters. Brown trout populations have been known to be exposed to 500 to 800 hours of fishing pressure per surface acre per year with less than 50 percent exploitation rates. Clear-cut examples where brown trout have favorably responded to special regulations include Hot Creek, California, with angling intensity of 3,800 hours per acre per year and the South Platte River near Denver, Colorado, with more than 2,000 hours per acre angling pressure. It has now been documented by U.S. Fish and Wildlife Service biologists that severe overexploitation of the cutthroat trout in Yellowstone Lake occurred at only 5 to 6 hours of angling per surface acre per year even with a 14-inch minimum size limit and a bag limit of three fish. The size-age structure and abundance of cutthroat trout in Yellowstone Lake recovered rapidly after a 13-inch maximum size limit (all trout of 13 inches and larger must be released) was instituted. In the catch-and-release fishery for cutthroat trout in the Yellowstone River below Yellowstone Lake, each fish was caught and released an average of 5–6 times in 1981, with virtually no angler induced mortality according to a U.S. Fish and Wildlife Service study. The total annual catch (and release) of Yellowstone cutthroat trout in the river is about 500 pounds per surface acre per year. No other natural trout fishery in the world sustains such a catch.

Only the cutthroat trout can be expected to respond to special regulations designed to greatly curtail angler kill with a significant increase in the abundance of larger, older fish when exposed to relatively light angling pressure (less than 40 or 50 hours per surface acre per year). Because of this attribute, a stirring of interest and increased recognition of the management potential of cutthroat has emerged in state and federal agencies after a long, sad history of neglect and decline.

I should point out here that the Yellowstone cutthroat trout is not *Salmo clarki lewisi*, but a different subspecies (*S. c. bouvieri*) from the "westslope" cutthroat trout. Most anglers somewhat familiar with fishery literature (and most professional biologists) have learned that *lewisi* is the subspecific name for "Yellowstone" cutthroat trout, but this is incorrect.

Until recently, virtually all references to trout classification were based on the work of David Starr Jordan and B.W. Evermann published by the U.S. National Museum in 1896 and revised for popular consumption in the book, *American Food and Game Fishes*, published in 1902. Jordan assumed that an ancestral trout crossed the Continental Divide from the upper Snake River drainage (Columbia River basin) into the Yellowstone River drainage via Two Ocean Creek—a stream on the Continental Divide that forks with one fork becoming the Pacific Creek, a tributary to the Snake River, and one fork becoming Atlantic Creek, tributary to the Yellowstone River (Missouri River basin). Jordan believed that, once in the Yellowstone River, the ancestral

trout populated the river downstream to the Missouri and then spread throughout the headwaters of the Missouri. Thus, it seemed logical to Dr. Jordan that the Yellowstone trout and the upper Missouri drainage trout should be similar and the name "*lewisi*" given in 1856 to specimens of Missouri trout from near Great Falls, Montana, was applied to both Yellowstone and upper Missouri cutthroat. Jordan did not realize that trout distribution in the Yellowstone River drainage did not extend beyond the Tongue River, in the vicinity of Sheridan, Wyoming (the main army of General Crook was camped on the upper Tongue River enjoying great fishing for "Yellowstone" cutthroat trout on June 25, 1876, while Custer and his regiment were being annihilated on the Little Bighorn, the adjacent tributary to the Yellowstone River to the west). The cutthroat trout native to the headwaters of the Missouri basin originated from a separate crossing of the Continental Divide by

WESTSLOPE CUTTHROAT TROUT
Oncorhynchus clarki lewisi

a different ancestral subspecies than did the Yellowstone cutthroat, and the two subspecies never came into contact.

In the 1960s Montana biologists realized that the native cutthroat trout of the upper Columbia River basin in Montana was distinctly different in appearance from the Yellowstone cutthroat trout and they used the common name of westslope cutthroat trout to differentiate it from the Yellowstone cutthroat. Since then, studies by my graduate students established the fact that the cutthroat trout of the upper Missouri drainage is identical to the upper Columbia basin cutthroat; thus, the name *lewisi* was applied to the cutthroat trout on both sides of the Continental Divide and a different subspecies name was designated for the distinctly different form of cutthroat trout native to the upper Snake River and Yellowstone River.

George Suckley, a surgeon-naturalist and avid lover of trout, collected trout specimens during the Pacific Railroad Survey of 1853. Suckley was aware that Lewis and Clark first encountered "speckled trout" in the Missouri River in the vicinity of the "Great Falls." He made a special trip to the site and caught several specimens on flies. He wrote, "I found them a lively, fine fish jumping readily at the fly." Suckley sent two of these specimens to the Smithsonian Institution and they serve as the basis (type specimens) for the name *lewisi*. Suckley also noted that the trout on both sides of the Continental Divide (upper Missouri and Flathead rivers) were identical, but no one paid attention to his remarks. After 120 years had passed Suckley's observation on the identity of these trout was verified.

It took many years of study and the examination of thousands of trout specimens from Western North America before the evolutionary history and distribution patterns of the numerous subspecies of cutthroat trout became reasonably clear. The subspecies *S. c. lewisi* is differentiated from Yellowstone cutthroat trout by possessing smaller, irregularly shaped spots on the body. The size and shape of the spots are comparable to the spots of the coastal cutthroat trout subspecies, but *lewisi* differs from coastal cutthroat trout by having few or no spots anteriorly on the body below the lateral line. *S. c. lewisi* differs from both coastal cutthroat and Yellowstone cutthroat in the development of brilliant coloration, especially in waters where crustaceans (with carotenoid pigments) contribute to their diet. Spawning males of *lewisi* may have their whole ventral region suffused with a bright crimson color. The westslope cutthroat is probably the least predaceous subspecies of cutthroat trout; it seldom preys on fish even when they are available. This dietary peculiarity is likely the result of a long evolutionary history of coexistence with the predatory bull trout in the upper Columbia River basin. The two species evolved to partition the food resources and avoid direct competition. This proclivity for nonpredatory feeding results in a smaller maximum size typical of *S. c. lewisi* than of other subspecies of cutthroat—about three pounds in all but exceptional cases. However, this hereditary specialization for invertebrate feeding preeminently "pre-adapts" the westslope cutthroat trout to the expectations of fly fishermen. With the wealth of diversity and specializations for different life history types found among the 15 subspecies of cutthroat trout, it is unfortunate for the devotees of wild trout that the fisheries management programs in those states with native cutthroat trout have, historically, placed their emphasis and priorities with the domesticated hatchery rainbow trout to resolve all problems and mitigation disputes. I doubt that big game hunters in those states would willingly accept so many tons of feedlot fattened Herefords in replacement for the loss of deer and elk range.

I recently learned that the westslope cutthroat, the subspecies *lewisi*, should be added to a list of nonnative trout in Colorado. About 25 years ago, two students searching remote areas for greenback cutthroat trout returned with a collection of peculiar trout that I found to be pure cutthroat trout, but certainly not greenback trout. Their spotting pattern was typical of *lewisi*. Trout from this population were genetically analyzed and verified as *lewisi*. I know of no records of westslope cutthroat introduced into Colorado. Who made this transplant? When? From what parental source? Why were they stocked into such a remote headwater site of difficult access? These are questions that baffle me, but they do illustrate the fact that trout have been stocked into the most unlikely places and we may never learn the who, when, or from where answers.

STEELHEAD TROUT

WINTER 1984

A STEELHEAD TROUT IS MOST OFTEN defined simply as a rainbow trout that goes to sea. Although this definition is not wrong, it is a gross oversimplification that leaves much important information unsaid. It is comparable to defining the Mona Lisa as a picture, the pyramids of Egypt as structures. There is a heredity basis for the timing of different runs—spring, summer, fall, or winter, and for the physiological and behavioral differences associated with the distance traveled and time in freshwater of each spawning run. Although all nonanadromous rainbow trout and all anadromous steelhead are considered as a single species, *Salmo gairdneri*, the species as a whole consists of countless races with diverse life history characteristics. Intelligent fisheries management requires recognition and understanding of differences between races of steelhead and rainbow trout. For example, a single river may have summer-run and winter-run steelhead and resident rainbow trout coexisting without hybridization. The three different races may respond very differently to environmental changes and to angler exploitation.

Steelhead trout occur from southern California to southern Alaska. From the Alaska Peninsula northward to the southern tributaries of the Kuskokwim River (Bristol Bay drainages), only resident rainbow trout occur, as far as known. The furthest inland penetration of any steelhead run occurred in the Columbia River into Canada (now long blocked by Grand Coulee Dam) and up the Snake River to near the base of Shoshone Falls, Idaho (run exterminated by Hell's Canyon Dam), distances of almost 1,000 miles. The unique genetic resources contained in these runs have been lost forever.

Rainbow and steelhead trout also occur in Far Eastern waters of the Soviet Union, in the Amur River and in mainland tributaries to the Okhotsk Sea, on the Kamchatkan Peninsula, and on the Commander Islands. I have studied these Far Eastern trout and found them identical to coastal rainbow and steelhead trout of North America. This identity between North American and Far Eastern rainbow trout raises a problem concerning the scientific name of the species. The Kamchatkan rainbow trout was named *Salmo mykiss* in 1792, 44 years prior to the naming of *Salmo gairdneri* from the Columbia River. According to the "rule of priority" of the international rules of zoological nomenclature, when one species has been described at different times with different names, the earliest name is the valid name. I have conveniently ignored this fact for many years by invoking the standard cliché that "further research is necessary" before a decision can be made on the matter, but I have no doubt that *Salmo mykiss* and *Salmo gairdneri* are the same species.

Steelhead trout have been introduced all over the world (the first rainbow trout propagated in hatcheries were steelhead from the Mc-Cloud River, California, later supplemented with steelhead from Redwood Creek, California, the Rogue and Klamath Rivers, Oregon). It is interesting that, despite the establishment of rainbow trout of steelhead ancestry on the Atlantic Coast of North America, Europe, Asia, Africa, South America, Australia, and New Zealand, a true steelhead run, comparable to Pacific Coast rivers, has never developed in introduced populations in marine waters outside their native range. In coastal rivers where ocean temperatures are suitable, sea-run rainbows may be common, but these are fish that have only moved into bays and estuaries for feeding, more similar to the life history of coastal cutthroat trout than to Pacific Coast steelhead. Steelhead in the Great Lakes do have life histories similar to Pacific Coast steelhead. Thus, it may be assumed that thousands of years of evolution have hereditarily programmed steelhead to specifically adapt to the North Pacific Ocean, and they are incapable of fully utilizing other oceans of the world and return to their "home" river.

Steelhead spawn as early as late December–January in the southern part of their range and as late as May–June in northern rivers or in rivers with colder winter flows. After the young hatch, they typically spend two full years (some only one and some three years, depending on growth rate) in freshwater before smolting at a size of 6–7 inches. The smolting process is a physiological preparation for entering seawater where fish must conserve water and excrete excess salt, an opposite process from freshwater existence. The typical juvenile steelhead spends two winters in freshwater and this, I believe, is one of the most severe factors limiting the abundance of wild steelhead populations. It appeared completely logical 30 years ago that this limitation on abundance could be circumvented by raising tremendous numbers of smolts in hatcheries. It does seem logical, but only superficially so—a point I will return to later.

After migrating to the ocean, typically from April through June, steelhead live in the North Pacific Ocean often 1,000 miles or more from shore. They feed on a variety of fish and invertebrates and grow rapidly. Evidently they do not form dense schools or at least do not inhabit the same ocean zone and depths as Pacific salmon because steelhead are taken only singly and sporadically in ocean salmon fisheries. Most steelhead runs are characterized by the bulk of the run returning to spawn in the year following their entry into the ocean. Thus, a steelhead that migrated to sea in June and returned in December of the next year would spend 18 months at sea. A run characterized by smolt migration in April and a return spawning run in February (two years later) would have 22 months of ocean feeding. Size is related to the duration of ocean feeding. Fish living in the ocean for 18 to 24 months will average 5 to 10 pounds. Trophy steelhead in the 15- to 20- pound range typically spend about 30 to 36 months in the ocean. The largest known steelhead are summer-run fish of the Skeena River drainage, British Columbia (Babine and Kispiox rivers are Skeena tributaries). Sizes include a rod and line record of 36 pounds, a line-caught 42-pounder, and a net caught 43-pounder (these last two records were taken in the marine environment near the mouth of the Skeena). Steelhead up to 35 pounds are known from the summer-run up the Snake River, Washington-Idaho, and some winter-run fish of over 30 pounds have been caught in Washington (particularly in the Cowlitz River).

Summer-run fish enter freshwater with immature gonads and may spend 8 to 10 months in freshwater before spawning. Although adult steelhead feed in freshwater, they do not consistently feed (otherwise they would be competing with and consuming their own young) and they must depend on the reserve energy accumulated during ocean feeding to survive until spawning. Steelhead may survive spawning to spawn again (females survive in much greater proportion to males), but most steelhead runs have no more than 10 to 15 percent of the run made up of repeat spawners. Some smaller coastal rivers in the southern parts of the range (southern Oregon, northern California) may have up to 50 percent repeat-spawners in the runs, and Great Lakes steelhead runs consist of about 20 to 50 percent repeat spawners (a more benign environment lacking sharks and sea lions). In general, there is little increase in size between first and second spawning. Virtually all energy goes into repeat maturation of the gonads.

The size-age structure of each native run of steelhead is relatively consistent through time; each particular life history strategy has been evolved through thousands of years of natural selection in each specific environment to optimize those life history traits that result in best survival. Hatchery selection replaces natural selection from the time of spawning to the time of smolting, and this has resulted in hereditary changes in hatchery stocks such as earlier timing of runs, earlier spawning, adaptations to artificial diets, disease resistance, crowding, etc. The end result is that hatchery steelhead, selected for many generations, and usually from a nonnative stock in relation to the river of stocking,

have much reduced reproductive fitness in comparison to any native population. The large-scale stocking of hatchery fish leading to a predominance of hatchery fish in spawning runs may be a major cause in the decline of wild steelhead.

Many anglers and biologists have expressed concern, anger, and frustration in regards to a "gut feeling" they have that hatchery fish are causing the decline of wild steelhead. But more than the emotion expressed from a gut feeling will be necessary to effect a major change in the direction of present-day American steelhead management and its overwhelming reliance on raising millions of hatchery smolts to maintain steelhead abundance. The roots of the hatchery system are deep and firm in ground, nurtured by enormous capital investment and a generation of anglers and chambers of commerce conditioned to the publicized benefits of hatchery programs. It is true that some rivers now

STEELHEAD TROUT
Oncorhynchus mykiss irideus

have steelhead runs numbering in the thousands where natural runs were in the hundreds due to hatchery fish. It is also true that summer-run steelhead have been established by stocking in a few places where no natural summer-run occurred. However, what might be emphasized as the bottom line in any debate on the impact of hatchery fish on wild populations is the fact that, in the 1980s, after 30 years of continually increased hatchery production, from a few thousand smolts in the early 1950s to more than 25 million smolts weighing more than 2.5 million pounds stocked in 1980, the total annual catch of all the Pacific Coast steelhead fisheries is, despite tremendously greater fishing pressure, less in the 1980s than it was 30 years ago when the runs were almost entirely dependent on natural reproduction of wild fish.

The center of action for steelhead anglers in the 1980s is the Great Lakes, where, although mainly dependent on hatcheries, the lake environment gives better survival than the ocean and there is no need to "smolt" before going to "sea." I would also mention that the Province of British Columbia has wisely avoided large-scale hatchery production of steelhead and has emphasized maintaining and improving environmental quality for wild steelhead. A major problem in British Columbia is that some of their prime steelhead runs occur at the same time as salmon runs and thousands of steelhead are taken in the commercial salmon fisheries near river mouths.

Perhaps we need the advice of historians for planning future directions of steelhead management because historians constantly emphasize the importance of learning from the past for intelligent planning for the future. With this in mind, let us briefly review the history of steelhead management—what we have learned—and raise a question concerning delays in applying what was learned to implement better management.

Until the 1950s most hatchery steelhead were stocked as newly hatched fry—to quickly perish in the natural environment with little impact on wild fish. Beginning in the 1940s, Clarence Pautzke and Robert Meigs of the Washington State Game Department compiled

clear-cut results correlating survival of hatchery steelhead with their size at stocking. Raising fish to smolt size could result in ocean survival and return of adults of 10 percent or more of the smolts stocked. Great advancements in hatchery technology, diets, and disease control led to a rapid proliferation of steelhead hatchery programs in Washington followed by Oregon and California. Until the early 1960s, before hatchery production shifted into high gear, the Pacific Coast states were annually stocking smolts at a small fraction of recent levels. The catch at this time was almost entirely dependent on wild fish and averaged about 100,000 per year in California and Oregon and about 150,000 in Washington. As the stocking of hatchery smolts increased in the 1960s to one, two, and three million per year, hatchery fish contributed an increasing proportion to the catch. The annual catch of steelhead increased to 150,000 to 200,000 in Oregon and to 250,000 to 300,000 in Washington. The trend lines plotting smolt stocking and catch induced euphoria. It seemed that the only limit to steelhead abundance was the capacity of hatcheries to produce smolts. Hatchery production increased geometrically in the 1970s to 10, 15, 20, 25 million smolts stocked annually.

In the 1970s it became obvious that something was wrong. As stocking levels increased, survival of hatchery fish decreased dramatically. Where ocean survival once was 10 percent of the stocked smolts, it dropped to two percent or one percent or less. It appeared a "density barrier" was operating. Perhaps the greatly increased density of migrating smolts concentrated predators in the bays and estuaries. By 1980, according to U.S. Fish and Wildlife Service statistics, 8,700,000 steelhead weighing 882,000 pounds were stocked from hatcheries in Washington. Yet the 1980 steelhead catch in Washington (both wild and hatchery) was only 117,000 (more pounds were stocked than caught). Oregon stocked 5,112,000 smolts weighing 763,200 pounds and anglers caught 122,000 steelhead in 1980. The most horrendous disproportion occurred in Idaho where 8,035,409 smolts weighing 737,340 pounds were stocked in 1980 and anglers caught an estimated

9,000 (wild and hatchery) adult steelhead. When it takes 1,000 to 1,500 hatchery steelhead smolts weighing about 100 to 150 pounds to add one steelhead to the angler's catch, each hatchery steelhead caught represents a cost of $200 to $300. It must be recognized, however, that the steelhead hatcheries in Idaho are mitigation hatcheries for dams that export their benefits outside the state but these dams have largely destroyed a once great steelhead and Chinook salmon fishery associated with the Snake River drainage of Idaho. Also, the downstream transportation of the smolts stocked in 1980 below the many dams on the Snake and Columbia Rivers resulted, in 1982, in the largest return in many years of steelhead spawners to the Salmon and Clearwater Rivers of Idaho.

The 1980 statistics for the State of Michigan gives a steelhead catch of 610,900 and hatchery stocking of 1,800,000 fish weighing 21,100 pounds—clearly the situation in Michigan is good. I would raise a question, however, on the authenticity of the Michigan catch statistics. In previous years Michigan relied on mail or phone surveys to estimate catch. Where these data could be compared to actual creel census data, the mail-phone estimates were found to be grossly inflated.

Many readers will be aware of and perhaps angered, at this point, by my neglect to mention Indian tribal fisheries' impacts on steelhead. The Indian fishery currently may harvest more steelhead in Washington than do sportsmen as a result of the 1974 Boldt decision. The Indian river gillnet fishery, selectively removing the larger spawners, can have a particularly harmful impact on wild runs as a result of changing the hereditary basis by favoring the survival of smaller, younger (less ocean growth) fish. In fairness, it must be admitted that for many years Indian tribes were systematically—and frequently illegally—excluded from the bounties of anadromous fish runs promised to them in treaties. The fact remains, however, that the decline of wild steelhead began before Indian exploitation, and the current urgency devoted to resolving the problem of steelhead exploitation by Indians is likely to divert attention from the development of best management practices for the long term.

The negative impacts of stocking increasing numbers of hatchery smolts on populations of wild steelhead (and coho salmon) were documented in the early 1970s.

In 1972 Loyd Royal submitted a report to the Washington Game Department: "An Examination of the Anadromous Trout Program of the Washington Game Department." In this report, substantial evidence was presented to the effect that increasing numbers of hatchery fish were suppressing wild populations. It was found that 20 percent to 50 percent of the hatchery fish were not migrating to the ocean but remaining in freshwater where they would compete for food and space with wild juvenile steelhead. Later genetic research on the Deschutes River, Oregon, and the Kalama River, Washington, left no doubt that the offspring of hatchery fish are less well adapted and suffer higher mortality than the offspring of wild fish native to the river—but until they perish, the offspring of hatchery fish are taking up food and space that could be utilized for the survival of wild fish. How abundant were steelhead before the era of large-scale hatchery production and loss of habitat? Historical abundance is largely unknown, but in 1892 the commercial catch of steelhead from the Columbia River alone was 4.92 million pounds—considerably more than is now caught along the entire Pacific Coast.

If only a small fraction of the funds that have been committed to hatchery production had been devoted to learning more about the proper management of wild steelhead, steelhead trout and steelhead anglers would be better off today. The future of steelhead management should not be polarized into pro-hatchery and anti-hatchery camps, but should be influenced and directed by good business sense—cost-benefit ratios. Should rivers where smolt stocking yields less than two percent survival of returning adult continue to be stocked or should the funds be diverted to improving conditions for wild steelhead, such as overwintering habitat? For example, data on steelhead in the Gualala River, California, reveal that an annual run of about 7,500 native steelhead was supplemented by about 100 fish from a hatchery plant of 20,000 smolts, or a hatchery smolt to adult survival of 0.5 percent. Also, the hatchery fish were significantly smaller than the native fish and only 4 percent of the hatchery adults survived to spawn again versus 38 percent of the native spawners. It is simply good business to reorder priorities in such situations.

In recent years considerable interest has developed in regards to increasing salmonid production by improving or modifying stream habitat. Several symposia have been held and the Pacific Northwest Forest and Range Experiment Station of the U.S. Forest Service is to be commended for their synthesizing, organizing, and evaluating a wealth of information of anadromous salmonid habitat in a series of reports. Many promising studies have demonstrated dramatic increased survival of juvenile steelhead and coho salmon from boulder placements, pool construction, livestock exclusion from riparian zones, etc. Many options for increased production of wild salmonids are suggested—rejuvenation of side channels and sloughs as rearing areas, flow supplementation during low flows, debris and boulder placement, bank stabilization, reducing erosion in watershed.

Some action for improving conditions for wild steelhead has been taken. In 1981, the California Department of Fish and Game committed one million dollars for improvements on northern California coastal rivers to enhance anadromous salmonid populations. In 1981, the Oregon legislature passed the "Salmon and Trout Enhancement Program," which encourages public participation in stream enhancement projects. The U.S. Congress passed the "Salmon and Steelhead Conservation Act of 1980" that calls for "new approaches" to the management of steelhead trout and salmon of the Pacific Northwest. In 1983 the Washington Department of Game prepared a report, "Recommended WDG Fishery Management Goals and Policies for Anadromous Gamefish Species" as a response to the Salmon and Steelhead Conservation Act.

The major priorities are devoted to gaining restrictions on the Indian steelhead fishery. The report emphasizes that the Indian fishery "adversely affects the biological integrity of wild steelhead populations." The sincerity of the report's commitment to preserving the biological integrity of wild steelhead is weakened in a later section that mentions that only six rivers in Washington are to be managed "to maximize wild populations of anadromous fish." Not that stocking of hatchery smolts would cease on these rivers, but the stocking "would not compromise the needs of wild fish." I cannot understand how this statement could possibly be translated into actual management decisions that would prevent the "compromising" of wild fish.

For the future, along with efforts to improve the spawning and rearing environment of wild steelhead, a vigorous and determined effort must be made to use the genetics of hatchery fish and time and place of stocking to attempt a virtual complete separation between hatchery and wild steelhead in the same river system. Angler harvest of hatchery fish should be maximized while minimizing exploitation of wild fish. The typical defense of the present hatchery system is: "This is what the people want." Indeed, in 1977 an angler survey in Oregon revealed the greatest number of anglers chose the stocking of more and larger hatchery steelhead as the top management priority. The majority of these same anglers also said that greater emphasis should be given to wild steelhead—evidently unaware of the contradiction. "The people" are not always informed on history, facts, and figures to make the most intelligent choice of options; enlightened leadership is necessary. A natural resource agency that attempts to justify a degenerating status quo situation as the "will of the people" is analogous to a medical institute that decides on the direction of research and type of treatment based on a vote of the patients.

The official common name designated by the American Fisheries Society is now simply "steelhead." The anadromous form of rainbow trout is so widely known as steelhead, and because there is no confusion with any other species of anadromous trout or salmon, steelhead "trout" is considered superfluous. In this 1984 column I pointed out that *Salmo mykiss* of Kamchatka and *Salmo gairdneri* of North America are the same species and that *mykiss* is the older name. In 1989 the American Fisheries Society recognized *mykiss* as the valid species name for rainbow trout and steelhead, and transferred the western trout from the genus *Salmo* to the genus *Oncorhynchus* with Pacific salmon. *Oncorhynchus mykiss gairdneri* became the subspecies name for the rainbow (or redband) trout native to the Columbia River basin east of the Cascade Mountains and in the upper Fraser River basin.

In this column I stated that the first hatchery propagated steelhead came from the McCloud River. As I discussed in my commentary of the McCloud rainbow trout, the first propagation of rainbow trout by the California Acclimatization Society could have included fish with steelhead ancestry. In 1896, The U.S. Fish Commission began propagating steelhead from runs from Redwood Creek and the Klamath River, California and from Oregon rivers, such as the Rogue and Willamette. The life history between resident rainbow trout and steelhead is so distinct they were considered as separate species. The early hatchery records of the U.S. Fish Commission had separate listings for *Salmo gairdneri* (steelhead) and *S. irideus* (rainbow trout). Modern molecular genetic analysis has verified that not only are steelhead and rainbow trout the same species, the resident rainbow trout and steelhead of the same river basin are more closely related to each other than they are to similar life history forms in other river basins. This close relationship and its implications for conservation were featured in several future columns.

In this column I also stated that no true steelhead run had ever been established outside their native range. There is now good documentation of steelhead established in the Rio Santa Cruz, Argentina. Also, although the Great Lakes are not marine waters, several wild steelhead runs have become established.

I also devoted considerable text in this column evaluating steelhead management and the increasing dependency on hatchery fish. More than 20 years later, what I wrote then still holds true—even more so.

SUNAPEE GOLDEN TROUT

SPRING 1984

THE ARCTIC CHAR IS A FISH THAT GENERATES legends, controversies and complexities. This is particularly true for one relict form of char commonly known as the Sunapee golden trout or Sunapee char. (As noted, char are notorious for causing controversy/not the least of which is the spelling of char—with one "r" or two—and the fact that populations of the same species, *Salvelinus alpinus*, are called both "trout," as in Sunapee trout or blueback trout, and "char," as in Arctic char.)

A better understanding of the Sunapee golden trout, *Salvelinus alpinus oquassa*, is facilitated by returning to the final stages of the last North American glacial period. About 12,000 years ago, great ice sheets had retreated from the lower elevations of New England, and the fresh waters were beginning to be populated by fishes invading from the sea—char, smelt, salmon, as well as strictly freshwater species such as lake trout and whitefish from inland glacial refugia. Environmental conditions at the time were similar to the present Arctic environment. It can be assumed that New England rivers had anadromous runs of Arctic char that gave rise to numerous "landlocked" populations in lakes, similar to the situation presently found in Arctic watersheds.

Glacial ice did not completely retreat from the interior regions of Maine until about 5,000 years ago. At that time, the interior lakes in the headwaters of major rivers were settled by Arctic char. With progress warming, the optimally cold water, preferred by Arctic char, was found only in the depths of certain lakes. Another factor severely limiting char distribution was other fishes, notably lake trout and lake whitefish. A review of all New England lakes known to have native populations of Arctic char reveals that they all lacked lake trout and whitefish. When lake trout were stocked the native char soon became extinct, as was the case in Sunapee Lake. This same phenomenon of Arctic char being pushed south by glaciers and persisting today as relict lake populations can be observed in Great Britain, Scandinavia, and the alpine lakes of central Europe.

Arctic char in lakes are a secretive fish. Typically, they spawn on rocky shoals on the lake bottom. In most lakes they are seldom, if ever, found in shallow water. Thus, they may inhabit a lake yet remain completely unknown to anglers and local people. Several lakes in Great Britain were found to have char only in recent years when the lakes were sampled by gillnets set at proper depths.

By the mid-nineteenth century, the Arctic char in New England was known only from the Rangeley Lakes. The Rangeley populations had the unusual characteristic of spawning in tributary streams where their great abundance became strikingly obvious every autumn, only to disappear into the depths of the lakes for the rest of the year. The Rangeley Lakes char became known as the "blueback trout" and was given the scientific name *Salvelinus oquassa* in 1853.

The Rangeley Lakes were famous for brook trout up to 10–12 pounds. It was commonly assumed that the size of the Rangeley brook trout was due to its feeding on blueback trout; a hatchery was set up to propagate the blueback and distribute it to other lakes. Alas, despite the great brook trout fishery, "well enough" was not considered "good enough" for the Rangeley Lakes, and landlocked salmon and smelt were stocked. Within fifteen years the blueback trout was extinct. The last known specimen was seen in 1904 and the Rangeley brook trout fishery has not been the same since.

Moving on to Sunapee Lake, New Hampshire, we will consider the legends and realities of the Sunapee golden trout. Besides brook trout, the original fish fauna of Sunapee Lake is vague. It is known that land-locked salmon were stocked in the lake in 1866 or 1867, and that smelt were stocked in 1871. In 1878 three thousand blueback trout from the Rangeley Lakes were stocked; this was repeated in 1879 with a plant of 4,000 fish. In 1881, 2 and 3 pound golden trout (commonly called "white trout" or "silver trout" by Sunapee anglers) began to be caught in Sunapee Lake.

The subsequent fame of the Sunapee golden trout in the angling literature of the late nineteenth century was largely due to the writings of John D. Quackenbos, a distinguished angler and writer of the time who was fascinated by native chars and believed the Sunapee char was the most noble of fish. Quackenbos claimed the Sunapee char to have twice the sporting qualities of brook trout. Although they were not caught on the fly, they could be taken by spoons and live and cut-bait by trolling at depths of 60–70 feet. He found the "most exhilarating" of angling experiences to be:

SUNAPEE TROUT
Salvelinus alpinus oquassa

"…trolling from a sailboat with a greenheart tarpon rod, 300 feet of copper wire of the smallest calibre on a heavy tarpon reel, and attached to this a 6-foot braided leader with a Buell's spinner, or a live minnow on a stiff gang.

The weight of the wire sinks the bail to the requisite depth. When the sailboat is running across the wind at the maximum of her speed, the sensation experienced by the strike of a 4- or 5-pound fish bankrupts all description. The pleasure is largely concentrated in the strike and the perception of a big fish 'fast.' The fish holds the coign of vantage; when he stands back and with bulldog pertinacity wrenches savagely at the pliable metal—when he rises to the surface in a despairing leap for his life—the angler is at his mercy. But, brother of the sleave-silk and tinsel, when at last you gaze upon your captive lying asphixiated on the surface, a synthesis of qualities that make a perfect fish—when you disengage him from the meshes of the net, and place his icy figure in your outstretched palms, and watch the tropaeolin glow of his awakening tones soften into cream tints, and the cream tints pale into the pearl of the moonstone, as the muscles of respiration grow feebler and more irregular in their contraction—you will experience a peculiar thrill that the capture of neither *ounaniche*, nor *fontinalis*, nor *namaycush* can ever excite. It is this afterglow of pleasure, this delight of contemplation and speculation, of which the scientific angler never wearies, that lends a charm all its own to the pursuit of the Alpine trout."

Quackenbos obviously had a passion for his favorite fish. The pedanticism of his writing is excusable under nineteenth century standards when a man of education and erudition was expected to display these qualities by an ostentatious style of writing.

Although Quackenbos realized that char were not caught in Sunapee Lake until three years after blueback trout from the Rangeley Lakes were stocked, he was steadfast in his belief that they were native. He reasoned that, after smelt became established in Sunapee Lake, the native char changed its feeding habits, grew to a much larger size and could be caught by anglers. Others, however, were not so certain.

Samuel Garmen of Harvard's Museum of Comparative Zoology pointed out the lack of differentiation of Sunapee char; he believed introduction by man as their probable origin. Others suggested a hybrid origin between introduced char and brook trout. Sam Garmen of Harvard would not describe the Sunapee trout as a new species, so specimens were sent to the U.S. National Museum where Tarleton Bean published the description of a new species in 1887. But the lack of certainty on the origin of the Sunapee species is evident in the title of Bean's paper: "Description of a supposed new species of charr (*Salvelinus aureolus*) from Sunapee Lake, New Hampshire." Quackenbos, perhaps a bit miffed that someone else had the honor to officially designate a scientific name for his favorite fish, went ahead and gave it another name, *Salvelinus sunapee*, in 1889.

The most complete work on Sunapee trout and all New England char was published by W.C. Kendall in 1914. Kendall admitted he could find no consistent differences between Sunapee golden trout and Rangeley Lakes blueback trout in their taxonomic characters. Kendall, however, believed the Sunapee golden trout was native to Sunapee Lake because three other populations of a similar char were found in Big Dan Pond, New Hampshire; Averill Pond, Vermont; and Floods Pond, Maine—and because the golden trout of Sunapee Lake attained a much greater size than did the Maine blueback trout. (This latter contention lacks validity. The studies of Fred Kircheis, Maine Department of Inland Fisheries and Wildlife, have demonstrated that blueback trout in Maine ponds containing smelt for forage can attain weights of at least five pounds.)

If pressed on the matter, I would favor the views of Quackenbos and Kendall: that Sunapee Lake did have a relict native char population—but a relict population of Arctic char, not a distinct species. The facts arguing for native occurrence are: first, Arctic char had access to Sunapee Lake at the end of the last glaciation and they would have found an optimum environment; second, lake trout and lake whitefish are not native to Sunapee Lake; and, finally, the increase in size and abundance of char in Sunapee Lake after landlocked salmon and smelt were established suggests a long period of finely tuned adaption that would not be expected from a first generation of introduced blueback trout. Yet I am not totally convinced. Perhaps the question will always be open.

The golden trout of Sunapee Lake did seem well adapted and maintained its abundance in the face of repeated introductions of nonnative fishes. Besides landlocked salmon and smelt, rainbow trout, brown trout, Chinook, chum and coho salmon were stocked along with the black basses and other warmwater species. Lake trout, which had not been "officially" stocked, began to appear in the Sunapee fishery in the 1930s. By the 1940s golden trout were rare. Lake trout and Sunapee golden trout spawned on the same shoal area at the same time of year, and natural hybridization may have occurred. Reliable reports also mention that, as golden trout became rare and both sexes could not be obtained for fish culture, eggs were fertilized with lake trout milt and the hybrids stocked back into the lake. In any event, in the late 1940s and early 1950s as the golden trout became rare, a few large specimens, larger than heretofore known, appeared in the catch. The world record Sunapee golden trout was caught in 1954; it weighed 11 pounds 8 ounces and was probably a golden trout × lake trout hybrid. Taxonomic data I have seen from large (22–28 inch) specimens of "golden trout" from Sunapee Lake caught during their rapid decline leaves little doubt about their hybrid origin. Trout and char have numerous appendices on their intestines called pyloric caeca. The original Sunapee golden trout (and Maine blueback trout) have about 30 to 50 pyloric caeca. Six large Sunapee "golden trout" caught during the late 1940s or early 1950s have 63 to 91 caeca, or about what would be expected in hybrids with lake trout parents which have 120 to 180 caeca.

The golden trout of Sunapee Lake became extinct due to the impact of lake trout. Lake trout stocked in Dan Hole Pond and Averill Pond exterminated those populations of Sunapee trout, leaving Floods Pond, Maine, with the only population of Sunapee trout (as defined by W. C. Kendall who recognized the Sunapee trout as *S. aureolus* and considered the populations in Big Dan Pond, Averill Pond, and Floods Pond also to be *aureolus*).

No word of blueback trout was heard in Maine after their demise in the Rangeley Lakes until a note was published in 1950 revealing that new populations had recently been discovered in several Maine ponds and lakes. Another group of populations of relict Arctic char is known to occur in lakes of southern Quebec where they are commonly known as "Quebec red trout." The Quebec red trout was given the scientific name of *Salvelinus marstoni* in 1893.

In more recent times, I and other ichthyologists have revived studies of relict Arctic char. We concur that there are no consistent differences in taxonomic characters between Sunapee golden trout, blueback trout, and Quebec red trout. They all should be grouped together and classified as one subspecies of Arctic char: *S. alpinus*. Three names were originally proposed: *oquassa* in 1853 for blueback trout, *aureolus* in 1887 for Sunapee trout, and *marstoni* in 1893 for Quebec red trout. Under the rules of taxonomy, when two or more species or subspecies are combined into one, the oldest of the names is to be used. Thus, Sunapee golden trout, blueback trout, and Quebec red trout are all classified as *Salvelinus alpinus oquassa*. This classification is supported by quantitative genetic studies comparing protein systems which indicate virtually no differences among the relict Arctic char, other than about what would be expected from a relatively few thousand years of isolation from a common ancestor char that gave rise to all of these populations at the end of the last glaciation.

Although the genetic differentiation among Sunapee, blueback, and red trout is slight, and they are all classified today as the same subspecies, isolated populations may evolve different life history characteristics during thousands of years of evolution in different environments and with different combinations of fish species. Contemporary fisheries management recognizes this fact; great importance is attached to the preservation of genetic diversity within a species or subspecies. As such, the extinction of the golden trout in Sunapee Lake is to be considered a significant loss — a point with which I am sure the late John D. Quackenbos would heartily agree. The story of the Sunapee golden trout, however, has a happy ending—they are alive and well in two lakes in Idaho!

This part of the story begins in 1977 when Kent Ball, Idaho Fish and Game Department biologist, was surveying mountain lakes in the state. In one lake, besides the ubiquitous brook trout, his sampling net included specimens of an unusual char, obviously different from the brook trout. Ball returned to the lake in 1978. The 1978 sample was preserved and sent to me for examination. It included 14 specimens identified as brook trout and 14 specimens of the unknown char—unknown but definitely a form of Arctic char.

Critical examination of specimens and the analysis and synthesis of data are time-consuming tasks. For this I must acknowledge the good work of student assistants, Eric Wagner, who helped with examination of specimens, and Steve Culver, who analyzed a vast amount of data by computer. The results left no doubt that the unusual Idaho char were Sunapee or blueback trout. Their occurrence in Idaho must have been the result of stocking by man. There is no conceivable manner an ancestor could have moved westward from New England, crossed the Continental Divide, and gained access above impassable falls into a mountain lake in Idaho without leaving remnants along the way.

The U.S. Fish Commission (now U.S. Fish and Wildlife Service) once propagated both blueback trout and Sunapee trout (from Floods Pond and Sunapee Lake). But a search of U.S. Fish Commission annual reports failed to find any record that Sunapee or blueback trout were ever shipped to the West.

Dr. Richard Wallace, University of Idaho, helped out here by finding a reference in a biennial report of the old Idaho Fish and Game Commission stating that Sunapee trout eggs were received from the New Hampshire Fish and Game Department in exchange for fish eggs from Idaho. Sunapee trout were stocked in five Idaho lakes in 1925.

Subsequent surveys by Kent Ball found the Sunapee golden trout to persist in two lakes. In these high elevation cold lakes, with sparse food supply, the Sunapee trout attains a larger maximum size than coexisting brook trout. The largest brook trout in the collections are about nine inches; my largest specimen of Idaho Sunapee trout is slightly more than nineteen inches.

The cold, deep, high elevation lakes of the Rocky Mountains have environmental conditions similar to Arctic waters where Arctic char are found in maximum abundance. Various forms of Arctic char can probably create greater fish production in these waters than any other gamefish. This is due to their optimal functioning in coldwater (50° F or less) and their great plasticity in feeding on a wide spectrum of organisms from tiny zooplankton, bottom invertebrates (benthos), insects, crustaceans, to fishes. Fisheries in many Rocky Mountain lakes that now contain stunted brook trout populations might be vastly improved if Arctic char could be established.

European biologists have long recognized the Arctic char as an important species for fisheries management. The species has been ignored in the United States. This difference in outlook was made apparent to me in 1981 when I participated in an international symposium on Arctic char in Winnipeg, Canada. Besides myself, only two Americans attended: Bob Armstrong of the Alaska Fish and Game Department, and Ted Cavender of Ohio State University. There were six participants from Japan and a large contingent from Iceland, Norway and Sweden. In my paper written for the symposium, besides the routine disagreements with Swedes and Russians over the correct classification of char, my concluding statement was that the diversity found in Arctic char "…offers a wealth of opportunity for theoretical and practical management studies. I believe the Arctic char is a fish that will become more widely appreciated despite its confused taxonomy."

What other fish can touch the soul of man to the depths that John Quackenbos was touched on Sunapee Lake 100 years ago?

This column disclosed that long after the Sunapee trout was extinct in Sunapee Lake, a population was discovered in a lake in the Sawtooth Mountains of Idaho where they were introduced in 1925. The late Bob Smith was planning a second, revised edition of his 1984 book, *Native Trout of North America*. Now he could add the Sunapee trout from Sawtooth Lake, Idaho, to his text as the forty second and final species, subspecies, and races to be covered in the revised edition (1994, Frank Amato Publications)—if he could catch and photograph a specimen. Bob was an inspiration, especially for older anglers. We first met at an American Fisheries Society meeting in Sun Valley, Idaho in 1975. We discussed his plans for a productive use of retirement. He would travel the continent in search of rare salmonid fishes to catch, photograph and write about. When he began his quest, he was 67-years-old. The story of his expedition to Sawtooth Lake seeking the Sunapee trout, exemplifies his enthusiasm and determination to fulfill his dream. He arranged for a packer to take him and his supplies to the lake, where he would spend the first ten days of October 1989. October was a trade-off. It would be spawning season and the fish should be in shallow water where they might be caught on flies. In this area, it is also the beginning of the winter season. Snow covered the ground around the lake. Bad weather kept him off the lake most of the time. On the third day, Bob celebrated his 81st birthday. The sixth day was clear and calm—a window of opportunity. Bob paddled his raft to a likely spot and caught, photographed, and released a 16-inch Sunapee. His final quest was successful. Perhaps the most memorable trout Bob had caught during his long life. In my summer 2001 column I called Bob Smith a "piscatorial Audubon," who made authentic information on rare, native trout available in the angling literature and greatly stimulated popular interest for their conservation. Bob died in June 2001. In his will, he left funds for the Nature Conservancy to purchase land to protect critical habitat of rare, native trout. A most fitting tribute to an angler who fulfilled his dreams during retirement.

GREENBACK CUTTHROAT

WINTER 1985

THE GREENBACK CUTTHROAT TROUT is one of the rarest and most beautiful subspecies of cutthroat trout. The greenback is native to the headwaters of the South Platte and Arkansas River drainages in Colorado and to a tiny segment of the South Platte drainage in southeastern Wyoming. The greenback and the Rio Grande cutthroat trout, *S. c. virginalis*, in New Mexico, represent the easternmost limits of native trout distribution in the West. The origin of the greenback trout probably occurred several thousand years ago, when one or more extreme headwater tributaries in the Colorado River basin became connected to a headwater in the South Platte and/or Arkansas drainage. This connection allowed the Colorado River cutthroat trout, *S. c. pleuriticus*, to cross the Continental Divide and become established on the east slope of the Rocky Mountains. This headwater transfer must have been very minor because the cutthroat trout is the only species common to the Colorado River basin and the South Platte and Arkansas drainages.

The time since the separation of the Colorado River cutthroat trout from the greenback is not ancient in geological time, and therefore the two forms are little differentiated from each other. They have not had sufficient time to evolve distinct differences. As such, pleuriticus and stomias are not "good" subspecies in the sense of clear-cut differentiation, but these names have been long recognized and they serve a practical function to designate the native trout of two distinct geographical areas. Separate taxonomic recognition has also benefited both subspecies by facilitating conservation programs for the protection and restoration of these rare trout.

The greenback is highly vulnerable to extinction. Apparently it cannot coexist with nonnative species of trout. The cutthroat trout is the only species of trout native to Colorado, Wyoming, and Utah. Thus, the inland forms of cutthroat trout lack an evolutionary history of coevolution and coexistence with other species of trout. The nineteenth century angling literature makes it clear that greenback trout abounded in all mountain and foothill streams along the Front Range of Colorado. By 1878 they were considered "fished-out" around Denver, and city sportsmen had to travel north to Fort Collins to fish the Poudre River, which still had greenbacks in abundance. By the turn of the century greenback abundance drastically declined. They were replaced by brown trout and rainbow trout in the large and medium size rivers. Brown and rainbow trout are better adapted to tolerate pollution from mines, industry and towns, and reduced flows and warmer more silted water due to irrigation diversions, logging and livestock impacts. The widespread stocking of brook trout into headwater streams just about administered the coup de grace to *S. c. stomias*. As brook trout thrived and became dominant in small tributary streams, the greenback was eliminated.

The story of Twin Lakes, Colorado, clearly illustrates the fate of the greenback trout and also typifies the fate of native cutthroat trout throughout the West. The Twin Lakes story also illustrates a moral for fisheries management in regard to man's ill-conceived attempts to improve on nature. In the 1860s and '70s, Twin Lakes swarmed with greenback trout. Parties of two or three fishermen could haul away more than 1,000 trout in two or three days of fishing. Most significant, however, is the fact that Twin Lakes is the only lake known to have contained two distinct forms of cutthroat trout. Besides the abundant greenback, which attained a maximum size of only about 12 inches in Twin Lakes, the lakes also had a much larger cutthroat trout whose silvery coloration and tiny spots distinctly differentiated it from the greenback. The large, silvery trout became known as the yellowfin trout. Its maximum size was given at 12 to 18 pounds. Because of the abundance of greenback trout and the presence of the large yellowfin trout in Twin Lakes, the U.S. Fish Commission in 1890 selected a site near Leadville, Colorado to construct the first federal fish hatchery west of the Mississippi. The Leadville hatchery soon initiated exchanges of fish with hatcheries in other states; within a few years, Twin Lakes was stocked with rainbow trout, brook trout, lake trout, even Atlantic salmon. During this "Johnny Appleseed" era of fish stocking, the addition of nonnative species to an established fish fauna was believed to be entirely beneficial. The concepts of species interactions, environmental limitations, and the probability that new species would eliminate more valuable native species, were not taken into consideration.

The U.S. Fish Commission conducted an intensive fishery and limnological survey of Twin Lakes in 1902 and 1903 led by the distinguished limnologist Chauncey Juday (later gaining fame at the University of Wisconsin but then teaching at the University of Colorado). Juday and his crew could not find a single specimen of the yellowfin trout (and no specimen has been recorded since) during two years of sampling. Rainbow trout was the dominant trout in Twin Lakes by 1902. When I examined the museum specimens of Twin Lakes greenback trout collected by Juday, I found that hybridization with rainbow trout was already underway by 1902. The greenback soon followed the yellowfin trout to extinction in Twin Lakes. The yellowfin trout, however, was known only from Twin Lakes. The entire branch of cutthroat trout evolution and diversity represented by the yellowfin trout was abruptly terminated within ten years after the introductions of nonnative trouts. This valuable resource of a large, lake-adapted cutthroat trout was lost forever.

A later introduction of opposum shrimp (*Mysis relicta*) into Twin Lakes resulted in such a drastic change in the invertebrate fauna that the lake trout is the only salmonid species able to maintain a viable population in Twin Lakes today. Although, by lake trout fishery standards, the present Twin Lakes fishery is considered good (annual catch of about 1 pound of lake trout per surface acre—but the lake trout's diet is subsidized by catchable rainbow trout stocking), the present lake trout catch must be considerably less than the catch of 100 years ago when the fishery was based on the native greenback and yellowfin.

In the twentieth century, the greenback rapidly disappeared from the Arkansas and South Platte River drainages. A bulletin on Colorado trout published by the Denver Museum of Natural History in 1937 considered the greenback extinct. The problem was: How would a greenback trout be recognized if a population was to be found? The original description of the taxon *stomias* in 1872 and all subsequent descriptions were so general and imprecise that no diagnostic characters were known to identify stomias from other subspecies of cutthroat trout. For example, the "back" or dorsal surface of *stomias* is no more green than the backs of any other subspecies of cutthroat trout.

Many years ago I examined all of the nineteenth century museum specimens of *stomias* in the collections of the U.S. National Museum, Stanford University, and the California Academy of Sciences. I recorded data from many characters and compared these data with data from other subspecies. I found that specimens of *stomias* and *pleuriticus* (Colorado River cutthroat trout) were very similar, as would be expected of geologically recent common ancestry. I noted a trend for stomias specimens to have larger spots (about the largest of any cutthroat trout) and to have more scales in a series counted above the lateral line (one population averages 216 lateral series scales, the highest number I have found in any trout of the genus *Salmo*).

After I came to Colorado in 1966, my students and I, assisted by the Colorado Division of Wildlife, initiated a search for remnant populations of greenback trout. This search was greatly expanded in recent years by the Colorado Division of Wildlife's endangered and threatened species program. After several years of effort, three populations judged to be pure greenback cutthroat trout, have been found. One is in the Arkansas River drainage, two in the South Platte. All three populations exist in tiny headwater streams above barrier falls that protected the greenback from invasion by nonnative trouts.

The greenback trout, although only a subspecies, was one of the first fish to be listed as an endangered species by the U.S. Department of Interior. Their status was changed to "threatened" in 1978 to facilitate transplants and management. The greenback will never again become a common fish in its original range, but funding and impetus from the Endangered Species Act has definitely reversed the trend toward extinction. Anglers now have the opportunity to catch—and release— native greenback trout in Rocky Mountain National Park.

Under the Endangered Species Act, a greenback trout "Recovery Team" was established, consisting of representatives of the U.S. Fish and Wildlife Service, U.S. Forest Service, National Park Service, and

GREENBACK CUTTHROAT TROUT
Oncorhynchus clarki stomias

Colorado Division of Wildlife. The effectiveness of such a team is determined by the knowledge and dedication to achievement of its members. Bruce Rosenlund, the U.S. Fish and Wildlife Service's representative, with excellent cooperation from the other agencies, has consistently increased greenback trout abundance from year to year by transplant into new waters. Two small broodstock ponds were established for the remnants of the Arkansas River greenback and a broodstock for the South Platte greenback was established at the Bozeman, Montana National Fish Hatchery. (Sperm from wild greenbacks is used each year to fertilize the eggs from hatchery females to avoid harmful hereditary changes from "domestication.") Headwater streams and lakes with barriers protecting against upstream migration are sought for greenback stocking.

When a suitable site is found, the waters above the barrier are chemically treated to kill all fish (typically stunted brook trout), after which, greenbacks are stocked. In 1983, 22,500 greenback trout were stocked into ten streams and lakes.

One of the early attempts to restore greenbacks was in Hidden Valley Creek in Rocky Mountain National Park. In 1973, the brook trout in Hidden Valley Creek were poisoned and greenbacks were stocked. Hidden Valley Creek, situated along the main road through the Park, had been a popular fishery. The federal endangered status of greenback trout at the time required that Hidden Valley Creek be closed to angling. Many anglers were angry over the fishery closure and perhaps someone restocked some brook trout. In any event, brook trout were found in Hidden Valley Creek in 1976 and they rapidly increased in abundance. Despite efforts to control brook trout by netting and trapping, brook trout became more numerous than greenback trout in the beaver ponds of Hidden Valley Creek. In 1978 fyke nets captured and removed 181 brook trout and captured and released 129 greenback trout. A similar netting operation in 1981 took 191 brook trout and only 55 greenbacks.

The change in status from endangered to threatened allowed regulated angling to occur for greenback trout. In August 1982—and every year thereafter—anglers were invited to fish the beaver pond section of Hidden Valley Creek. Angling was restricted to flies and lures with barbless hooks; all greenbacks caught were to be released, and anglers were urged to keep the brook trout they caught. The goal of this fishery was to favor the greenback trout by differential removal of brook trout. This goal was only partially fulfilled. Trout Unlimited members made up a large segment of anglers on opening day. Most of the TU anglers were so imbued with the catch-and-release philosophy and so believing in the concept of the sanctity of wild trout that they could not bring themselves to keep the brook trout they caught! Of the 171 brook trout caught on opening day, 112 (65 percent) were released. Subsequent creel censuses in 1982 and 1983 showed the same trend—most of the brook trout caught were being released. The catch statistics also further documented the extreme vulnerability of cutthroat trout to angling and their great value for catch-and-release fisheries in which fish are caught again and again to maintain a high catch rate on a limited stock of fish.

If the 1981 net sampling was an accurate indication of the true ratio of the species—and there is no reason to suspect bias for one species or the other—then brook trout predominated over greenback trout by a ratio of 3.5 : 1. On opening day, anglers caught 344 greenback trout and 171 brook trout—greenbacks predominated the catch by 2 : 1. That is, the vulnerability factor (comparative susceptibility to being caught by angling of greenback trout in Hidden Valley Creek is seven times that of brook trout. Another way to interpret these statistics is to conclude that it would take seven times more brook trout than cutthroat trout in a catch-and-release fishery in a given water to support the same catch rate.

When it is realized that the vulnerability factor of brook trout is 5–10 times greater than that of brown trout, some insight and perspective can be had regarding the significance of species differences for determining the success of special regulations. Such enlightenment should also make understandable some of the practical, common sense, reasons to save rare forms of trout from extinction.

This column touted the early success of the recovery of the greenback cutthroat trout. Several new populations had been established; its status under the Endangered Species Act had improved from endangered to threatened, which allowed for regulated angling. Some years later, Bruce Babbitt, when he was Secretary of the Interior, showcased the greenback recovery as an example of how the ESA is working to prevent extinction. Things were going well. Then, progress ceased and the program retrogressed into chaos and confusion. What happened? The recovery program began to fund genetic studies in the belief that this would make the program more scientifically sound. The problem is that the administrators and biologists making decisions based on genetic analysis lack an understanding of the various methods of modern molecular genetics; their limitations and how the data can be open to different interpretations.

A little learning without an in-depth understanding of the subject matter can be dangerous. The genetic data led to an erroneous conclusion that hybridization among greenback, Colorado River, and Yellowstone cutthroat trout was rampant. This caused the recovery program to flounder in confusion. It's a matter of how the genetic data is interpreted. In early 2007, I presented my interpretation to the people involved in greenback recovery. I pointed out that when once widely distributed subspecies such as the greenback and Colorado River cutthroat trout are fragmented into tiny, isolated populations as they are today, genetic analysis will give incomplete and uncertain results. Natural genetic variation once widespread in the ancestor that gave rise to the small, isolated populations was wrongly interpreted as evidence of hybridization.

In my concluding remarks, I expressed my opinion that to get the recovery efforts back on track, it must be simplified and realistically evaluated in the light of the uncertainty of the genetic data. If it looks like a duck, walks like a duck, and quacks like a duck, we should call it a duck. Getting into the molecular structure of a duck can result in confusion and chaos. Now substitute greenback cutthroat trout for duck, and move on.

On March 26, 2007, U.S. District Court Judge Emmett G. Sullivan made a ruling on the proper identification of westslope cutthroat trout (*O. c. lewisi*). A long-standing controversy on *lewisi* identity and hybrid influence from genetic studies was resolved by a ruling that standard taxonomic procedure based on morphology should be the criterion for identification. I was pleased to see that my duck analogy to resolve the identification of greenback cutthroat now has legal standing.

GILA TROUT

EARLY EXPLORERS AND SETTLERS encountered unusual trout in headwater streams of the Gila River Basin of Arizona and New Mexico. These trout were variously called speckled trout, native trout or yellowbelly trout to differentiate them from the later introduced brook, brown, and rainbow trout that became increasingly common after the turn of the century while the native trout faded toward extinction. The earliest notes in the literature about these native trout referred to the trout of the White Mountains, Arizona (Apache trout), as cutthroat trout, and Gila trout of New Mexico and the Verde River drainage of Arizona as rainbow trout.

Detailed studies of the native trout did not begin until they were almost extinct; only remnant populations remained. These studies demonstrated that the Gila trout and Apache trout were distinct from both rainbow trout and cutthroat trout, but they possess several characters that are intermediate between the rainbow and cutthroat species. This intermediacy led to a theory explaining their origin from an ancient hybridization between cutthroat trout and rainbow trout. The unique chromosome complement (karyotype) of both Gila and Apache trout essentially negates the hybrid origin theory. Because these trout could not be confidently assigned to either rainbow trout or cutthroat trout evolutionary lines, they were described as separate species—Gila trout, *Salmo gilae*, named in 1950, and the Apache trout, named *Salmo apache* in 1972.

For many years I and other ichthyologists have pondered and speculated about the evolutionary origins and most correct classification of the native trout of the Gila Basin. As previously mentioned, their distinctive characteristics appear to be intermediate or transitional between cutthroat trout and rainbow trout, but their chromosome number of 56 is lower than any known form of cutthroat trout (64 to 70) or rainbow trout (58 to 64). The Gila trout and Apache trout are much more closely related to each other than to any other species of trout, and, in this respect, I believe they should be considered as two subspecies of a single species—*S. gilae gilae* and *S. gilae apache*. I would suggest that their evolutionary origin is associated with the Gulf of California which gave rise to a common ancestor that migrated into the Gila River Basin. Subsequently, during a glacial epoch the common ancestor separated into a northern branch in the White Mountains (Apache trout) and a southern branch in the upper Gila River (Gila trout). The major distinction between Gila trout and Apache trout is their spotting pattern. Apache trout have fewer and larger spots (similar to inland cutthroat trout) and the Gila trout have smaller, more profuse spots (similar to rainbow trout). Gila trout have tints of yellowish-gold body coloration with pinkish-red hues along the middle of the body. A native trout occurs in the Rio Yaqui, Mexico, which is quite similar in appearance to Gila trout. Since the Rio Yaqui and the Gila River watersheds are contiguous in southern Arizona with opportunities to exchange fish faunas, it would seem logical that the Gila trout is also native to the Rio Yaqui. However, Rio Yaqui trout were found to have 64 chromosomes, which typifies the problems that frustrate attempts to fully understand the evolutionary progressions and correct classification of Western trouts.

Considering all available evidence from morphological characters, chromosomes, protein comparisons (electrophoresis), and distribution (zoogeography), I would speculate that the Gila and Apache trout represent an evolutionary branch arising after a major ancestral division in the evolution of Western trouts. This ancestral separation in Western trout evolution ultimately led to the present two major species groups— rainbow trout and cutthroat trout—but various side branches arising along the evolutionary pathways left remnants such as Gila and Apache trout and native Mexican trout whose relationships are in doubt. I would place the Gila and Apache trouts on the rainbow trout side of this ancient evolutionary divide. As a primitive "side branch" they retain some of the primitive characters assumed for the common ancestor to all rainbow and cutthroat trout.

The Gila and Apache trout and all forms of rainbow and cutthroat trout share sufficiently close relationships that they may hybridize with

GILA TROUT
Oncorhynchus gilae gilae

each other and produce fertile offspring. The impact of hybridization with stocked rainbow trout has been the major cause of the great decline in both Gila and Apache trout.

When White Man first came into the Gila River Basin, Gila trout occurred throughout the whole basin in New Mexico to about the Arizona–New Mexico border (between elevations of about 5,000 to 8,000 feet). They also occurred in some tributaries to the Verde River in Arizona. By the time *Salmo gilae* was officially described in 1950 only five tiny headwater streams, isolated from invasion by rainbow trout and brown trout, still contained pure populations of Gila trout. In this semiarid region, these small streams become intermittent during droughts and trout populations are reduced to those individuals that can find refuge in pools between the dry sections of streambed.

The largest natural population of Gila trout occurs in Main Diamond Creek. This population has benefited from numerous stream improvement dams constructed by Civilian Conservation Corps workers during the 1930s and more recent improvements that have created many refuge pools to carry the population through dry periods. The watersheds of the streams containing Gila trout have some extra measure of protection from potential multiple use abuse of streams on public lands because they occur in wilderness areas of the Gila National Forest (the Gila National Forest had the first national wilderness area thanks to the efforts of Aldo Leopold who was employed by the Forest Service in New Mexico in the 1920s). Wilderness designation, however, inhibits restoration projects for Gila trout. No motorized appliances such as vehicles, helicopters, chain saws, etc. are permitted to assist in the work. Two barrier dams, to protect headwater areas from invasion by brown trout, were constructed by laboriously packing in all equipment and supplies (including cement) for many miles on horses.

Restoration of Gila trout has made steady but slow progress. New populations have been established in three small streams in New Mexico and one in Arizona. All streams with Gila trout are small and subjected to harsh climatic conditions which places severe limitations on total abundance. Because of limited distribution and relatively low abundance, the Gila trout is the only trout still classified as a federally endangered species. All other trout which were formerly classified as endangered have been changed to a threatened classification. Angling, under special regulations, can be permitted for "threatened" species but not for "endangered" species. Thus, a "catch-22" type of situation results from endangered status because, to change the classification from endangered to threatened, several new populations must be established—but to establish new populations of Gila trout, all the brown trout must be poisoned in a selected restoration stream before Gila trout can be stocked. Once the brown trout are gone and the Gila trout are stocked in a restoration site, fishing is prohibited because of the endangered status of Gila trout. The New Mexico Department of Game and Fish understandably is cautious about antagonizing anglers by closing streams to fishing in order to restore Gila trout.

A change in status from endangered to threatened which allows for special regulation angling could speed up restoration efforts and popularize this rare trout as it has with Apache trout and greenback cutthroat trout.

Even with light fishing pressure, special regulations will be needed to protect a Gila trout population from overexploitation if their susceptibility to angling is similar to Apache trout (which I assume to be the case). In two streams in Arizona that had both brown trout and Apache trout, electro-fishing samples revealed the brown trout outnumbered Apache trout by 20 : 1 in one stream and by 4 : 1 in the other. These same streams were then sampled by fly-fishing. The anglers caught 55 Apache trout but only four brown trout!

The Gila and Apache trout represent an evolutionary line leading to the modern rainbow trout. Degrees of relationships based on genetic data show the Gila and Apache trout are much closer to rainbow trout than they are to cutthroat. Their classification as two subspecies of the species *Oncorhynchus gilae* (*Salmo* in the 1985 column) is a compromise.

This column mentions that Gila trout restoration was progressing toward a downlisting from endangered to threatened status under the Endangered Species Act. This change in status was proposed to occur in 1989. Before this occurred, the "perfect storm" of catastrophes hit the upper Gila River basin. A prolonged drought was followed by fires, and then floods washed ash and debris into streams. Recovery efforts suffered a setback. Further information on Gila and Apache trout is found in the winter 1993 column (p. 163) and my commentary.

DOLLY VARDEN

FALL 1985

IF FISHES POSSESSED SUFFICIENT COGNIZANCE, the Dolly Varden would surely suffer from an identity crisis and an inferiority complex. These neuroses would result from man's historical confusion concerning classification of the species and from many years of unjust persecution as a rapacious predator on young salmon—a most foul vermin species to be ruthlessly exterminated with a bounty placed on their heads (actually their tails).

The Dolly Varden's bad reputation was based on a case of mistaken identity and unfortunate myths. The Dolly received a bum rap. Only in recent years has its true character as a fine gamefish been rehabilitated in fisheries literature. The ultimate moral of the story concerns the need to have a correct system of classification and basic information on the life history of the species under consideration before logical management decisions can be made—such as launching into a horrendously wasteful predator control program.

For many years, three species of charr—Arctic charr, *Salvelinus alpinus*; bull "trout," *S. confluentus*; and Dolly Varden, *S. malma*—were all called "Dolly Varden" in Western North America from California to Alaska and inland to Montana and Idaho.

Dolly Varden was a colorful character in the Charles Dickens novel, *Barnaby Rudge*. In America, the name Dolly Varden was given to a popular pattern of green calico cloth with red spots. The appearance of this cloth suggested the common name for the fish. The earliest mention of the name Dolly Varden applied to a fish, that I have found in the literature, concerns the charr native to the McCloud River, California. In 1872 Livingston Stone was on the McCloud River to set up a salmon egg-taking operation for the U.S. Fish Commission. He wrote that anglers called the charr there "Dolly Varden." A minor problem here is that true Dolly Varden, *S. malma*, probably never occurred in the McCloud River. All known charr specimens from the McCloud are bull trout! Since there are no international rules of nomenclature governing the use of common names, as there are with scientific names, it was a simple (but somewhat confusing) matter to transfer the common name Dolly Varden from the McCloud River *S. confluentus* to *S. malma*. In any event, the original "Dolly Varden" or bull trout of the McCloud River is extinct. It rapidly declined after the construction of Shasta Dam which eliminated steelhead and Chinook salmon runs in the McCloud. Salmon eggs and young may have been a major food source for the bull trout of the McCloud.

In the February 1985 issue of *Field & Stream* magazine, Al McClane wrote an article on bull trout and Dolly Varden. Overall, Mr. McClane did an excellent job of keeping his facts straight in describing the confusion between the two species. The artist's illustration of a bull trout and a Dolly Varden for the article, however, evidently fixed on the origin of the name (green cloth with red spots—applied first to the McCloud River bull trout) and his "Dolly Varden" bears more of a resemblance to a bull trout. The "bull trout" in the illustration is more typical of an Arctic charr.

In 1939 the late William Markham Morton was sent to Karluk Lake, Kodiak Island, Alaska, by the U.S. Bureau of Fisheries to study the feeding habits of the Dolly Varden in an attempt to obtain factual data on the Dolly Varden as a salmon predator. Morton examined thousands of charr and realized that he was dealing with two separate species in Karluk Lake—Arctic charr, which lived its entire life in the lake, and Dolly Varden, which was anadromous and overwintered in the lake. Another fact that became obvious after thousands of stomachs were examined was that the anadromous Dolly Varden virtually did not eat fish while in freshwater. They did eat salmon eggs and salmon flesh, but only as scavengers, not predators. When great numbers of salmon spawn in relatively small tributary streams, the successive waves of spawners dig up the redds from previous spawning and enormous numbers of eggs are cast adrift in the river. Once out of the redd these eggs are doomed and scavengers such as the Dolly Varden are only providing nature's custodial services. These salmon spawning streams are also strewn with carcasses of dead salmon (which all die after spawning) which are torn apart by bears and birds. The Dolly Varden acts to clean the stream of the salmon carcass fragments.

Mark Morton's sense of justice was outraged; he spent the rest of

DOLLY VARDEN
Salvelinus malma

his life attempting to reverse the conviction of the Dolly Varden as a vermin species in the court of public opinion. He wrote articles such as, "The Dolly Varden is innocent," and proposed to change the common name from Dolly Varden to "western brook charr" because he believed the name Dolly Varden was too intrinsically burdened with a tarnished image. Mark was also obsessed with spelling charr with two r's instead of char, which is more commonly used in contemporary English and American literature. In honor of Mark's contribution to the rehabilitation of the Dolly Varden's reputation, I will spell charr with two r's here.

How did the Dolly Varden acquire its unjust reputation as a wanton destroyer of salmon?

Mistaken identity is partly to blame. All Alaskan studies documenting considerable consumption of fish by charr in freshwater are now known to be based on Arctic charr, not Dolly Varden. When studies have been made on comparative feeding habits of Dolly Varden and other salmonid species such as cutthroat trout, Arctic charr, or young coho salmon, the Dolly Varden always proves to be the least predaceous species. The predaceous feeding habits of big "Dolly Varden" from large, inland lakes in the Fraser and Columbia river basins are now known to be based on bull trout, a species not officially recognized as distinct from the Dolly Varden until 1978.

From 1921 to 1941 an extermination program on Dolly Varden was undertaken in Alaska—a cooperative effort supported by the Bristol Bay Salmon Packers, the Alaskan Territorial Legislature, and the U.S. Bureau of Fisheries. The hated Dolly was destroyed by trapping at weirs and a bounty ranging in various years from five cents to one-half cent was paid for every tail turned in. Perhaps research data such as Mark Morton's diet analysis played a role in terminating the bounty and extermination program, but when it was realized that the bounty caused the destruction of more valuable commercial species than it did of Dolly Varden, it lost its general popularity. A study on the identification of 20,000 bounty paid tails in 1939 turned up the following results:

14,200 tails came from coho salmon, 3,760 from rainbow trout, and 2,040 from Dolly Varden.

Presently the separation of Dolly Varden and bull trout as two distinct species is not clearly understood, even by most professional biologists. This is also true regarding confusion between Dolly Varden and Arctic charr in Alaska.

Based on current fisheries books, considerable confusion would result from an attempt to derive a clear picture of the most correct classification and distribution of western charrs. For example, in *Inland Fishes of Washington* (University of Washington Press, 1979), under "Dolly Varden" the information is based on a mixture of data from both bull trout and Dolly Varden.

In two widely cited works on northern fishes, *Freshwater Fishes of Northwestern Canada and Alaska* and *Freshwater Fishes of Canada* (Fisheries Research Board of Canada Bulletins 173 and 184, respectively, published in 1971 and 1973), the three species of charr are confused. But the major error concerns classifying the common sea-run charr occurring from the Alaskan Peninsula to the Mackenzie River as Arctic charr when, in reality, they are Dolly Varden.

The Alaska Department of Fish and Game continues to "officially" designate these northern Dolly Varden as Arctic charr, not because anyone disagrees with my classification, but because sport fishing for these Dolly Varden has attracted considerable attention and drawn tourist anglers and tourist dollars from great distances. It is believed that, because of the historically bad reputation associated with the name Dolly Varden, many anglers would not be so eager to make an expensive trip to northern Alaska if they knew they were to be fishing for Dolly Varden rather than Arctic charr which is commonly perceived to be the more exotic and glamorous species.

A logical question is: Considering the confusion in the literature over the classification of Dolly Varden, Arctic charr, and bull trout, why do I consider that my classification is more correct and a better reflection of evolutionary reality than all previous classifications?

Obviously, I cannot provide a fully adequate answer in a few sentences, I can only point out that I have probably spent more time and thought on the subject than has any other person during the past 25 years, surveying the international literature, exchanging information, examining specimens and recording data from all over the Northern Hemisphere. In 1980 a book entitled, *Chars, Salmonid Fishes of the Genus Salvelinus*, was published. This 925-page tome includes contributions from ichthyologists of many nations. In this book I presented my "state-of-the-art" classification of Dolly Varden, Arctic charr, and bull trout, and presented the evidence for the classification. In this volume on charrs, however, some authors continued to mistake bull trout for Dolly Varden and Dolly Varden for Arctic charr; and, a Russian woman, K. A. Savvaitova, of the University of Moscow, wrote a rebuttal.

Savvaitova has long maintained that Arctic charr and Dolly Varden are only variations within a single species, and we have argued over the matter for many years in the literature. Savvaitova could not very well accuse me of insufficient data or provincialism as I had spent almost one year in the Soviet Union examining specimens in their excellent museum collections. So she claimed that my views were somehow distorted because I based my conclusions only on a study of preserved museum specimens.

Since 1980, other Russian ichthyologists working in the Far East have made many detailed studies of charr. Their work leaves no reasonable doubt that Dolly Varden and Arctic charr are two perfectly distinct species. Examination of thousands of specimens demonstrated clear-cut distinctions between the two species where they occur together over a broad geographical area, and with no evidence of hybridization. Despite the mass of new data documenting the validity of the Dolly Varden as a species separate from Arctic charr, Savvaitova refuses to recant her opinions and currently appears to be working on new definitions of "species."

Often a person, either scientist or layman, cannot easily be separated from a long cherished belief by any amount of facts, figures, or logic.

To define the Dolly Varden as a species and its distribution we must begin with specimens from the original locality on which the name malma was based—the common charr of the Kamchatkan Peninsula in the far eastern part of the Soviet Union. Once the Kamchatkan charr is fully characterized, all other charr from other geographical regions which are more similar to Kamchatkan *malma* than they are to any other species, such as Arctic charr or bull trout, are considered to be the same species: *S. malma.*

All of the evidence demonstrates that a charr, essentially identical to *malma* of Kamchatka, occurs northward around the Chukotsk Peninsula in the Far East. On the opposite side of the northern Pacific and Arctic oceans in Alaska, this same charr occurs from the northern half of the Alaskan Peninsula northward and eastward to the Mackenzie River. Throughout this vast area, the Dolly Varden frequently occurs together with various forms of Artie charr. The Dolly Varden can be distinguished by its more slab-sided body, smaller and more numerous spots, deeper caudal peduncle, less forked tail, more pronounced development of the kype at the symphysis of the lower jaws in mature males, and some internal characters.

From the Alaska Peninsula southward to Puget Sound, a differentiated form of Dolly Varden occurs which can be recognized as a southern subspecies. Another southern subspecies occurs in the Far East, south from the Amur River and on the islands of Sakhalin and Hokkaido.

The recent revisions in charr classification caused the International Game Fish Association to vacate the former world record for Dolly Varden of 32 pounds from Lake Pend Oreille, Idaho, when it became obvious that Dolly Varden do not occur in Idaho and the record fish was, in reality, a bull trout. This opened opportunities for new records for Dolly Varden— listed at 4 pounds by the IGFA in 1984, but up to almost 7 pounds by early 1985. For those seeking trophy Dolly Varden, I would recommend the northern subspecies (*S. malma malma*). Maximum size for the southern subspecies appears to be in the 5- to 6-pound range. Sea-run individuals of the northern subspecies may attain a maximum size in the 15- to 18-pound range (Alaska recognizes a 17-pound fish as the state record, but erroneously lists it as "Arctic charr"). I would point out that the average and maximum size of sea-run Dolly Varden can vary greatly between different Alaskan rivers. Perhaps the largest Dolly Varden occur in rivers in the Kotzebue area such as the Noatak, Wulik and Kivalina rivers.

Before seeking a record fish, one should learn the time of year when the largest Dolly Varden return from the sea in any particular area. To those off to seek a new world record Dolly Varden, I wish you luck but warn that proof of identity will likely be required, and this may be a problem.

AUTHOR'S NOTE

The Dolly Varden is an example of the ongoing process for obtaining the most up-to-date information. Considering the vast, mostly remote regions inhabited by the Dolly Varden, it's not surprising that much was yet to be learned. A network of reliable 'informants" is necessary to keep current on new information. In October, 1992, Fred DeCicco, the char expert for the Alaskan Fish and Game Department, provided me with his most recent findings. My Fall 1985 column discussed the confusion over correct identification of Dolly Varden, arctic char, and bull trout. It was known that particularly large char occurred in rivers south of Point Hope, Alaska, southward to northern Kotzebue Sound (Chuckchi Sea basin). This area had produced the Alaskan record for "arctic char" until it was recognized that these large char, were, in fact, sea-run Dolly Varden.

Before 2002, the record size was 19 pounds. During 2002, many Dolly Varden over 20 pounds were caught. Fred DeCicco personally saw a Dolly Varden "just over 27 pounds." It was 41½ inches in length and 21½ inches in girth. A clue to the large size attained by the Dolly Varden of the Kotzebue area is the area of marine waters they use for feeding. Tagged Kotzebue Dolly Varden were found to over winter in the Anadyr River of the Russian Far East; their total migration must have been at least 1,000 miles. Evidently, this super-sized Dolly Varden

also occurs in rivers of the Chukokst Peninsula of Russia, on the western side of the Chukchi Sea.

Russian biologist Igor Chereshnev related that Dolly Varden of 1 meter (almost 40 inches) are relatively common in several rivers of the Chukokst Peninsula. There is a second hand report of a Dolly Varden of 1.2 meters (47 inches) caught by a Russian commercial fisherman. Considering that up to 1984, the "world record" Dolly Varden recognized by the International Game Fish Association, was only 4 pounds, one can understand why, until Dolly Varden and arctic char could be clearly identified from each other, no one had any idea about the maximum size attained by Dolly Varden. And, this is still true. A most significant discovery made by Canadian geneticist, James Reist, identified Dolly Varden in the Coppermine and Tree rivers which extended their known range, about 500 miles to the east. All previous literature gave the Mackenzie River as the easternmost distribution of Dolly Varden. The world record arctic char of 32 pounds, 9 ounces was caught from the Tree River in 1981; but, it could have been a Dolly Varden. Both sea-run arctic char and Dolly Varden occur in the Tree River and they both attain a large size. The former "world record" Dolly of 32 pounds caught in Lake Pen Oreille, Idaho, in 1949, was "disqualified" when the Pend Oreille char was found to be a bull trout, *Salvelinus confluentus*. Perhaps a new 32-pound or larger Dolly Varden record will be established now that they are known to occur at least as far east as the Tree River. American, Canadian, and Russian research on the genetic relationships of members of the genus *Salvelinus* indicate a rather startling conclusion that the northern and southern subspecies of Dolly Varden do not share a most recent common ancestor. Each subspecies appears to be more closely related to subspecies of arctic char than they are to each other. All species definitions imply that all members of a species are more closely related to each other than they are to any other species. This does not seem to be true of the Dolly Varden species, *S. malma*. If the genetic data are verified beyond reasonable doubt, then the two subspecies of *malma*, each arose independently from *S. alpinus ancestors*, not from a single common ancestor. An important point is that both the southern and northern Dolly Varden coexist with arctic char and do not hybridize. They conform to the definition of "biological species" whereby reproductive isolation is maintained in coexistence with closely-related species. This reproductive isolation is reinforced by the distinctly different life histories and ecology between Dolly Varden and arctic char (they occupy different niches). The southern Dolly Varden coexist with bull trout over much of its range and hybridization between the two has been documented in the Skagit River of British Columbia. Although some hybridization occurs under certain circumstances, both species maintain their identity (they do not merge into a "hybrid swarm").

I wouldn't lose much sleep over the most correct classification of Dolly Varden. It simply demonstrates the complexity of evolutionary divergences and how they can be misinterpreted. We can still call the char conforming to the characteristics of the northern and southern subspecies (or species) as Dolly Varden. After all, *S. malma* usurped the name Dolly Varden from the bull trout of the McCloud River where the common name was first used, and, the bull trout, in turn, usurped the 32-pound world record Dolly Varden as its own world record. Common names are not governed by a code of nomenclature; it's more a matter of popular preferences.

BROWN TROUT

⟶

WINTER 1986

THE BROWN TROUT MIGHT BE CONSIDERED as the "archetype" species of trout. *Salmo trutta* is the first species of trout described in Linnaeus's 1758 edition of *The System of Nature*, the origin of scientific zoological nomenclature (whereby all species are denoted by two words, a genus name and a species name). Linnaeus, however, also described two additional "species" of trout in this same volume: *Salmo fario* and *S. lacustris* (for river and lake forms of brown trout). Thus he initiated a long history of controversy and confusion concerning the most correct classification for all of the enormous diversity contained within a species evolving innumerable separate races over a vast geographical area.

Since 1758 about fifty new species have been described for variations found in the species I call *Salmo trutta*. The matter of the most correct classification to encompass all forms of brown trout has not been settled and probably never will be because it concerns interpretations of definitions of "species."

One reason for the taxonomic confusion concerns the wide distribution of brown trout and its evolution of geographical races (subspecies) throughout its range. The natural distribution of brown trout extends from the Arctic Ocean of northern Norway and the northeastern part of the U.S.S.R. (White Sea drainage) southward to the Atlas Mountains of North Africa (Algiers and Morocco). The westernmost limit of native brown trout is Iceland and the easternmost limit extends to the headwaters of the Amu Darya drainage (Aral Sea basin) of Afghanistan and Pakistan. Introductions have subsequently established brown trout into almost all suitable trout waters of the world.

I should mention a new distribution record for brown trout that does not appear on any present distribution map of the species. In 1974, I conducted a fishery survey in Iran. Barry Nehring (presently a fisheries biologist with the Colorado Division of Wildlife) took me to a small stream, the Ligvan Chai, southeast of Tabriz in the Rezaiyeh Lake desert basin to collect specimens of a peculiar trout he had previously encountered. The Rezaiyeh basin trout is derived from the Caspian basin subspecies of brown trout, but it has been isolated for a long time and is considerably differentiated by a profusion of small black and red spots. The Rezaiyeh basin trout represents an undescribed subspecies and is known only from one small stream.

Throughout this great area of distribution, the brown trout species is made up of subspecies associated with particular regions or drainage basins. The boundaries between subspecies, however, are not sharply defined; intergradation or intermediate forms between one subspecies and another is the rule. More fascinating are the complexities among brown trout populations within a geographical region ("intrasubspecific" diversity) that have evolved during or since the last glacial period—within the last 50,000 years. There are specializations for anadromy (sea trout), for life as resident populations in rivers and small streams ("bachforelle" or "brook" trout) and adaptations for large lakes ("seeforelle" or "lake" trout). The basic question concerning the recognition of separate species or even subspecies for different life history forms is: are all sea, brook, and lake forms of brown trout derived from single common ancestors? That is, are all of these three distinct life history forms attributable to three separate common ancestors? If so, there would be no question that we are dealing with three separate species. All studies on brown trout morphology, biochemistry and chromosomes agree that this is not the case. Only one common ancestor is involved which gave rise to different life history forms in each geographical region. For example, the sea, brook and lake forms of Great Britain are more closely related to each other than they are to similar life history forms of other regions such as the Baltic Sea basin or the Black Sea basin. Even more complex and a gray area for classification are situations where two or more specialized life history forms of brown trout live together in the same lake and do not hybridize with each other. The distinct populations behave as separate species.

The older English angling literature is full of odd names for trout such as "gillaroo" (small size, snail eating trout), "ferox" (large, predatory trout), and "sonaghen" (intermediate size, mainly invertebrate feeder). At one time all of these forms were described and recognized as separate species. In modern times it has been assumed that the differences noted in appearance, growth and maximum size are due to the environment not heredity (nurture not nature) and all are Salmo trutta. Studies of protein patterns of Irish trout by Andrew Ferguson and his associates at the Queen's University, Belfast, produced some most interesting findings. The old timers were right: the gillaroo, sonaghen

and ferox of Lough Melvin are real entities, not figments of an active imagination or due to something they ate. Ferguson demonstrated that Lough Melvin contains at least three distinct groups of brown trout, long known to anglers as gillaroo, sonaghen and ferox. The three differ in feeding habits, growth rates and maximum age and size, and they do not interbreed with each other. The implications of such situations go far beyond simplistic taxonomic arguments over lumping versus splitting. Populations with different life histories and ecologies that live together without hybridizing should be managed as separate species. The problem or gray area for classification is the fact that, among salmonid fishes, the occurrence of closely related populations living together in the same lake is such a common phenomenon that, if we recognized every such population as a separate species, names would proliferate and classification would become chaotic.

In my studies of European trouts, I found some trout that are so distinct from any form of brown trout that they should be recognized as separate species. The marble trout, *Salmo marmoratus*, a large predatory trout (maximum size to about fifty pounds) found in the larger tributaries to the Adriatic Sea in Yugoslavia and northern Italy, has no black or red spots on the body, only light colored marbled markings similar to char (genus *Salvelinus*). The marble trout is a true trout and is known to hybridize with *S. trutta*.

In 1967 I received three specimens of trout collected in Turkey by a Hamburg University expedition. The bodies of these specimens completely lack spots or markings, and their other characters are so different from any known form of brown trout that I did not hesitate to describe a new species: *Salmo platycephalus*. These three specimens are all that is known about *S. platycephalus*; none have been collected since 1967. If anyone has fished in Turkey in streams draining the Taurus Mountains to the Mediterranean Sea, and caught a peculiar trout, obviously different from brown trout, please let me know.

There are also borderline cases for recognition of separate species. The trout native to Lake Ohrid, Yugoslavia–Albania, and to Lake Sevan, U.S.S.R., are generally recognized as *Salmo letnica* and *S. ishchan* respectively. *S. letnica* and *S. ishchan* represent ancient divergences from a primitive brown trout ancestor and both species have several distinct ecological forms that live together without hybridizing in their respective lakes. A trout was named *Salmo pallaryi* from Lake Algueman, Morocco in 1924. I once examined four preserved specimens from Lake Algueman at the British Museum. The specimens showed no spots or markings on the body but had mottled markings on the head—quite distinct from *S. trutta*. With environmental changes and introductions of exotic fishes, I suspect that Lake Algueman is now devoid of trout and is, perhaps, a carp pond. If anyone can tell me more about Lake Algueman and its peculiar native trout, I would also like to hear from you.

Why is the brown trout "smarter" than other species of trout? That is, why is it more difficult to catch?

Comparisons quantifying catch per hour, catch per unit area, or proportion of brown trout in the catches of many different fisheries unanimously agree that the brown is the most difficult species to catch followed by rainbow, brook and cutthroat, in that order. Yet the anatomy of the brown trout brain provides no indication of a greater intelligence or reasoning ability compared to other trouts. Perhaps the answer lies in evolutionary specializations for ecological and physiological adaptions. The retina of the eye of brown trout is better adapted to optimally function in dim light. Thus, browns are more oriented to dense cover and shaded areas such as deep undercut banks, and more prone to nocturnal feeding.

The current rod and reel caught record brown trout recognized by the International Game Fish Association is a specimen of 35 pounds 15 ounces caught in Argentina in 1951 (the 1866 record of 39½ pounds

BROWN TROUT
Salmo trutta

from Loch Awe, Scotland was ruled invalid). The maximum size attained by brown trout is probably about twice the official record size. The large Alpine lakes of central Europe and the Caspian Sea historically were known to produce brown trout in excess of fifty pounds. In the early 1900s a commercial fisherman trolling lures from a winch was known to have taken several trout of more than fifty pounds from the large lakes of the Alps. His largest was a trout of 31 kilogram (68 pounds) from the Wolfgangsee (Lake Wolfgang). Even larger brown trout probably once occurred in the Caspian Sea.

The sea-run trout of the Caspian exhibited life history variations similar to our steelhead trout. They consisted of seasonal spawning runs up tributary rivers (winter, spring, and fall runs) and the average and maximum size varied greatly between the different runs and different rivers. The largest of the Caspian trout was the winter run up the Kura River. Considerable information on Caspian trout (*Salmo trutta caspius*) is found in L. S. Berg's book, *Freshwater Fishes of the U.S.S.R.*. Berg cites an 1897 report of a 33 kilogram (72 pounds) Kura River trout and an unverified report of 51 kilogram (112 pounds). No doubt the winter run fish of the Kura were large. In 1916, the average size of the fish in the commercial catch was 15 kilogram (33 pounds). The winter run in the Kura River entered the river from November to February, proceeded far upstream and did not spawn until the following fall, 8–11 months after leaving the Caspian Sea. They first spawned at six to eight years of age. With such a life history, it would be advantageous to attain a large size and have great energy reserves before undertaking a long spawning run.

The races producing the largest known brown trout may now be extinct. The ecology and fish fauna of most of the large Alpine lakes of Europe have been drastically altered by pollution and introductions of exotic fishes. None of these lakes has produced exceptionally large trout—thirty pounds or more—in many years. Dams have blocked spawning runs on most of the major tributaries to the Caspian Sea. Pollution and water diversions have ruined other former trout spawn-

ing tributaries. The Caspian trout now exists only as rare, remnant populations. Russian fishery agencies have about given up on them and have stocked Pacific salmons and American striped bass and steelhead trout to replace the native brown trout as the top level predators in the Caspian. The major food for the Caspian trout are species of alewife, shad, and herring. I have often indulged in a game of "ifs"—if some of the winter run Kura River race of Caspian trout still exist, and if the U.S. could have obtained some of them from the Russians in exchange for steelhead and striped bass, and if the Caspian trout had been stocked into Lake Michigan during the height of alewife abundance—might Lake Michigan have produced 60- to 70-pound brown trout?

Considering the great diversity in brown trout, I have often wondered how much of this diversity was incorporated into our North American brown trout. Obviously, the brown trout in North America has been a huge success. They thrive in small and large rivers, lakes and reservoirs. Some populations utilize marine bays and estuaries (but I do not believe a true "sea trout" population, with a long duration of ocean life, exists in North America).

I consider our North American brown trout to be an "all purpose, generic" type of trout resulting from the mixing of several different life history forms. Perhaps because of this early mixing of different forms, the brown trout stocked so widely in North America had a broad base of hereditary diversity (heterozygosity) that facilitated adaptations to new environments.

Most anglers are familiar with the history of the introduction of brown trout in America: from Germany in 1883 and from Loch Leven, Scotland in 1885. Actually, several shipments from Europe were made in the 1880s and the original 1883 shipment from Baron von Behr contained the eggs of two distinct forms of brown trout.

Wherever Englishmen settled in foreign lands, they attempted to import their beloved brown trout. Australia and New Zealand were real challenges for the shipment of viable eggs with a sea voyage of six months or more required. After several futile attempts it was discovered that, if a room on a ship was filled with ice and converted into a giant icebox, eggs could be maintained just above the freezing point. The low temperature slowed development and the time to hatching could be extended to six to eight months. The first successful shipment of brown trout eggs to Tasmania occurred in 1864. With this technique—and faster ships—transoceanic shipments became a relatively simple matter. American brook trout were shipped to Great Britain in 1868, but it was to be several years before brown trout made the return trip.

In 1874, Fred Mather, a pioneer fish culturist, was appointed as a special assistant to Spencer Baird, the U.S. Fish Commissioner. Mather made several trips to Europe to learn European techniques and to keep an eye out for new species to import to the u.s. In 1880 Mather was in charge of the United States exhibit at the International Fisheries Exhibition in Berlin. While there, Mather met Baron von Behr, president of the German Fisheries Society. Von Behr took Mather fishing for brown trout in the Black Forest. Mather was impressed by the potential this new trout might have for American waters and the wheels were set in motion for their eventual introduction. Mather later pointed out that brown trout had been privately brought to America to the Old Colony Trout Ponds in Plymouth, Massachusetts, about 1880, prior to the government shipment. Evidently, this first brown trout shipment was not propagated and distributed, thus, the 1883 shipment from von Behr to Mather can be considered as the first source of brown trout that contributed to the present genetic make-up of American brown trout.

On February 23, 1883, the German ship Werra arrived in New York with 80,000 brown trout eggs. Five days later, Mather brought the eggs to the Cold Spring Hatchery on Long Island. The hatchery did not have adequate facilities to handle all of the shipment so Mather divided the eggs, sending some to Northville, Michigan, and some to his arch rival, Seth Green, at the Caldonia, New York, hatchery. Later, Green claimed that his hatchery had the greatest survival rate and he attempted to garnish most of the credit for the introduction of brown trout in America, which caused near apoplexy in Fred Mather. After Mather applied the common English name "brown trout" to the new import, Green began to call them "German trout." The resulting compromise, "German brown trout," is still widely used in America.

Mather explicitly stated several times that the original shipment from von Behr contained 60,000 eggs from a large lake form of brown trout and 20,000 eggs from brown trout living in a small mountain stream in the Rhine River drainage. Thus, it is apparent that the original shipment contained the diversity of two very different life history forms of brown trout. On February 5, 1884, an additional 70,000 brown trout from von Behr arrived in New York. These eggs were also sent to the Northville, Michigan, hatchery and to the Caldonia, New York, hatchery. Some of the 1884 shipment became the first brown trout stocked into an American public stream. On April 11, 1884, the U.S. Fish Commission railroad car took on 4,900 newly hatched fry from the Northville hatchery and deposited them from a railroad bridge into the Baldwin River, a tributary to the Pere Marquette River. The Pere Marquette originally contained grayling and the 1884 stocking of brown trout initiated a history of brown trout contributing to the replacement of native American salmonids—grayling in Michigan and Montana, brook trout in many Eastern rivers, and especially cutthroat in the West.

The first shipment of "non-German" brown trout to contribute to genetic diversity was from Loch Leven, Scotland. The Loch Leven eggs arrived in New York on January 1, 1885. Other shipments from Germany, England and Scotland soon followed. A great variety of life history forms—large lake forms, resident river forms, and sea trout—probably all contributed to the formation of the American brown trout. Despite this diversity, I consider all of these forms that contributed to the establishment of the American generic brown trout to represent a single subspecies, *Salmo trutta trutta*, the North European brown trout.

Depending on the time of introduction and the hatchery source, the brown trout stocked around North America represented a range of genetic diversity. Natural selection operating in new environments for the past 50 to 100 years, fine tuning adaptations to these new environments, has likely produced an array of differentiation so that hardly any two populations of American brown trout are exactly alike. It is possible that some of the original shipments from von Behr or from Loch Leven were stocked into waters that were never stocked with brown trout again and the original "pure" form still exists. The records of trout shipped from the Northville, Michigan hatchery to Yellowstone Park, in 1890, state that the shipment included both von Behr trout and Loch Leven trout.

The Loch Leven trout was stocked into Lewis Lake with lake trout from Lake Michigan (Lewis and Shoshone lakes and the Lewis River above the falls were barren of fish at the time). Supposedly, brown trout were never stocked again into the upper Lewis-Shoshone drainage and the present brown trout of the upper Lewis River and Lewis and Shoshone lakes represents an undiluted stock of Loch Leven trout. If so, the "Loch Leven" trout in Yellowstone Park attain a considerably greater size than they do in Loch Leven—a common phenomenon in America where immigrants have been known to flourish to a much greater extent than did their ancestors in their native land.

AUTHOR'S NOTE

By the late 1880s and into the 1890s, brown trout were propagated and distributed to most cold waters of the continental United States. They soon were widely established as naturally reproducing populations. By about 1900, brown trout, similar to an earlier highly successful European import, the common carp, fell out of favor. Anglers found them difficult to catch and they were accused of being a serious predator on other trout. Some fly fishers, however, were stimulated by the challenge to fool the wary brown. They perfected flies to imitate the insects on which trout fed. The last 25 years of Theodore Gordon's life (1890–1915) was the period when brown trout became the dominant species in the Catskill area where Gordon developed his thinking on fly patterns and techniques. The levels of sophistication and innovation found in contemporary American fly-fishing literature owe a debt of gratitude to the importation of brown trout.

My information source on *Salmo trutta* and related species is Johannes Shöffmann of Austria. Over many years, Shöffmann made field trips to distant lands, collecting, analyzing and publishing on rare, and little-known forms of trout. I consider Johannes the world's authority on the brown trout and its relatives. This is all the more remarkable because he is a baker by profession with no formal education in ichthyology. Over the years he and James Prosek have traveled together to learn more about trout. For those wanting to learn more about the range of variation found in brown trout and their relatives, in their markings, coloration, large-spotted, fine-spotted, and non-spotted forms, I recommend James Prosek's book, *Trout of the World* (Stewart, Tabori, and Chang, 2003). It's more than just a book with colorful trout illustrations. The text contains a wealth of authentic information, a reflection of what James has learned from Johannes.

ALVORD CUTTHROAT TROUT

SPRING 1986

ONE OF THE MOST EXCITING EVENTS in the history of trout taxonomy occurred in 1985 when the rediscovery of the Alvord cutthroat trout was verified after fifty years of "extinction." The continued survival of the subspecies depends on a few old fish and the possibility of transplanting them to new waters to establish a new population. Otherwise this special race of cutthroat trout will be lost forever to hybridization with rainbow trout. The situation is precarious. We must await the outcome of the next act to discover if this drama has a happy or tragic ending.

The Alvord Basin of northwest Nevada and southeast Oregon is one of several desert basins that make up the Great Basin of the western United States. These basins, all isolated from one another, are characterized by drainages from surrounding mountains that go out onto desert floors—no water escapes to drain to the ocean. Some of the separate basins have had relatively recent (12,000–15,000 years) contact with the Columbia River Basin, and share common Columbia River fish species, including the redband form of rainbow trout. In others, such as the Alvord and Lahontan Basins, connections to the Columbia River are much more ancient; the differentiation of the fish fauna tells of their long isolation. In these long-isolated basins the cutthroat rather than the rainbow is the native trout. This distribution pattern, with cutthroat trout as the native of the longer isolated basins, tells us that a cutthroat ancestor inhabited the Columbia River Basin long before rainbow trout were on the scene.

During cooler and wetter climatic periods—periods when precipitation and accumulation of water exceeded evaporation—the Alvord Basin and others of the Great Basin contained large lakes. A narrow lake about one hundred miles long filled the floor of the Alvord Basin until its final desiccation about 8,000 years ago. The isolation of the Alvord Basin to invasion by fishes was almost complete. Only two ancestral fish species gained access to the entire basin: a minnow which evolved into a distinct new species in the basin, the Alvord chub, and a cutthroat trout which evolved into a new subspecies. The transfer of both ancestors was most probably by way of the Lahontan Basin which forms the southern boundary of the Alvord Basin.

Little was known of Great Basin fishes until 1934 when the eminent ichthyologist Carl Hubbs of the University of Michigan and his family collected fishes from many localities and brought the specimens back to Michigan for study.

The 1934 collections of cutthroat trout from Virgin and Trout

Creeks were the first and, until very recently, the last record of the Alvord cutthroat trout.

In arid regions, streams are mainly intermittent. Only two major drainages, Virgin Creek and Trout Creek, maintained perennial flows adequate to serve as refugia for the persistence of the Alvord cutthroat trout after the ancient lake desiccated. Professor Hubbs collected cutthroat trout in Virgin Creek in 1934, but also collected rainbow trout that were first stocked the previous year by a local rancher. In Trout Creek, cutthroat trout and cutthroat × rainbow hybrids were found in 1934. Cutthroat were also found in Willow and Whitehorse Creeks, which drain out onto the desert floor immediately east of the Alvord Basin. Willow and Whitehorse Creeks are part of a separate basin, the Whitehorse Basin, and the cutthroat trout, probably derived from the Alvord Basin, is the only fish species native to Whitehorse.

In the late 1950s, as a graduate student, I began studying Great Basin trouts. I borrowed the specimens collected by Hubbs in 1934 from the University of Michigan's Museum of Zoology. I recognized that two distinct subspecies were involved: one for Virgin and Trout Creek specimens (Alvord Basin) and one for Willow and Whitehorse Creeks (Whitehorse Basin). Nothing more was heard of the Alvord cutthroat trout for many years. A collection made in 1970 in Virgin Creek, from the same locality where cutthroat trout were found in 1934, were typical rainbow trout—I could find virtually no trace of cutthroat ancestry in the specimens. In 1972 I explored the Alvord Basin in an attempt to find a remnant population of the native cutthroat. The greatest amount of trout habitat in the basin is found in the two forks of Trout Creek, which drains from the Trout Creek Mountains, just north of the Nevada border. I sampled trout to the uppermost headwaters of both forks and found only rainbow trout. I felt defeated and discouraged. The Alvord cutthroat trout appeared to be extinct. I did find native cutthroat still occurring in Willow and Whitehorse Creeks, although they had suffered a great loss of habitat from impacts of livestock grazing.

Before a final declaration of extinction I requested that interested persons search out remote areas of the Alvord Basin on the slim chance that a remnant population still existed. Adventurous anglers Bob Smith of Central Point, Oregon, and John Perry of Eugene, Oregon, each made several trips, seeking out any waters that might maintain trout. All to no avail. All streams they checked were barren of fish or contained brook or rainbow trout. Professional ichthyologists Carl Bond and Jack Williams of Oregon State University carried out surveys of the Alvord Basin in 1978–1979 and again in 1982. In their 1983 publication of the results of their study they concluded that "…the Alvord cutthroat trout is now extinct in pure form." In several of my own publications of recent years, I also declared the Alvord trout to be "…almost certainly extinct."

In 1984, fisheries biologists with the U.S. Bureau of Land Management and the Oregon Department of Fish and Wildlife wanted to obtain more habitat protection for the native cutthroat trout of Willow and Whitehorse Creeks under multiple use management of federal lands. There was a particular conflict with livestock management. They realized that if the Whitehorse Basin trout was officially described as a unique subspecies, their arguments for habitat protection would carry more weight.

I was requested to prepare a formal original description of the Whitehorse Basin cutthroat. While preparing the description of the Whitehorse cutthroat as a new subspecies, I thought it only logical to include a formal description of the "extinct" Alvord cutthroat in the same paper. In my description of new subspecies I expressed a hope that formal recognition of the Whitehorse cutthroat would benefit this rare fish by facilitating better multiple use management of the watershed and by eventual designation of the headwater area of Willow and Whitehorse Creeks as a Wilderness Area. I added that, unfortunately, formal recognition of the Alvord cutthroat trout was too late to save it from extinction—no living specimen had been documented for a half century.

Before submitting the paper for publication I sent several copies out for review and comment. I received a letter from Pat Coffin, Chief of Fisheries of Nevada, telling of a strange red trout Nevada biologists found in a remote headwater area of Virgin Creek in the summer of 1984. Pat sent me two photographs of the fish. I was elated to see two cutthroat trout with a spotting pattern identical to the type specimens collected in 1934 from lower Virgin Creek: spots relatively large, roundish, sparsely distributed above the lateral line. I could not be certain that the trout found in 1984 were truly native Alvord cutthroat until I examined specimens to compare their characters with data from the 1934 collection. It was possible that the fish in the photographs represented introduced nonnative cutthroat or a hybrid combination. I tried not to build my hopes too high, only to court another disappointment.

I relayed the latest information and photographs to Bob Smith in Oregon, whose greatest angling experience is to find rare native trout.

After an unsuccessful attempt in June because of impassable roads, Smith and his angling friend Jack James made it to the Wilson Ranch near the headwaters of Virgin Creek in July. Rancher Harry Wilson gave them permission to fish on his land and they descended into the Virgin Creek Gorge in an attempt to find the Alvord cutthroat trout. They caught about forty trout. Most appeared to be rainbow trout or rainbow × cutthroat hybrids. Smith selected three large specimens of 15, 17 and 20 inches, which resembled pure cutthroat trout, to preserve and send to me.

When I examined the three specimens and compared their characteristics with the specimens collected in 1934, I found them to be identical—the Alvord cutthroat trout still existed! Their prospects for continued survival, however, are extremely precarious. Hybridization with rainbow trout has been going on for several generations. The

ALVORD CUTTHROAT TROUT
Oncorhynchus clarki alvordensis

origin of the rainbow trout is most likely from a 1942 stocking of an upstream irrigation reservoir. Evidently only a few of the oldest fish remain pure. I aged the three specimens at five, six, and seven years.

The hope for survival of the Alvord cutthroat in its pure form rests on the possibility of removing pure specimens and transplanting them into a new stream, barren of other fishes. Such a stream has been selected on the U.S. Fish and Wildlife Service's Sheldon Antelope Refuge. I had hoped that a transplant would be made in 1985 because there may not be a sufficient number of pure cutthroat left in 1986 to establish a new population (the Virgin Creek Gorge area is generally inaccessible to vehicles before spawning season, thus any fish transplanted in 1986 would not spawn in their new stream until 1987).

No transplant was made in 1985. Pat Coffin has assured me that a 1986 transplant will be a high priority item. Nevada biologists did electrofish the gorge area in late summer 1985, and verified that not many pure cutthroat remain. A sample of five fish that appeared to be cutthroat trout were selected by the Nevada biologists and sent to the University of California, Davis, for electrophoretic analysis of enzymes. Enzyme patterns of rainbow trout were found by electrophoresis—the specimens were hybrids! There are four diagnostic gene loci that produce four distinct types of enzymes by which Lahontan cutthroat trout can be distinguished from rainbow trout and most other subspecies of cutthroat trout. In the five Virgin Creek specimens, both rainbow and Lahontan cutthroat types of enzymes were found, verifying a hybrid influence in the specimens and also indicating the origin of the Alvord cutthroat from an ancestor invading from the Lahontan Basin. In addition, a completely distinct form of enzyme was found in the Virgin Creek specimens, never before seen in any species or subspecies of trout. This supports the evidence based on morphological differentiation that the cutthroat trout of the Alvord Basin and of the Lahontan Basin have been separated from each other for a very long time, and each has proceeded along its own evolutionary pathway.

Can the Alvord trout be saved from extinction?

If the five specimens selected by Nevada biologists for electrophoresis had been transplanted to start a new population, the new population would be a hybrid and not pure Alvord cutthroat trout. Pure specimens must be recognized live, in the field. For verification of purity, the specimens must be killed. Thus, a large element of doubt will remain in regard to the purity of any transplanted fish. A transplant must be made and a new population established; only then can the offspring of the parent stock be critically analyzed to evaluate the success of preserving the Alvord cutthroat in its pure form. A valuable observation is that, of the 1934 specimens and the three pure specimens taken by Smith in 1985, all have only a relatively few spots, almost entirely restricted to an area above the lateral line (a few spots may occur below lateral line on caudal peduncle area). The five hybrid specimens used for electrophoresis had more profuse spots, many occurring below the lateral.

The distinct branch of cutthroat trout evolution that flourished for eons in the Alvord Basin—and believed extinguished fifty years ago—sputters with a bare spark of life. Its survival depends on the assumption that spotting pattern accurately reflects the genetic composition of the specimens, and that the correct spotting pattern can be accurately selected from visual observation.

I believe more is at stake here than the extinction of a rare and beautiful subspecies of trout. The "costs" of preservation are far less than the costs of extinction. Useful attributes associated with life history and ecology of unique local races acquired by natural selection over thousands of years can never be fully replaced by nonnative races of the same species or subspecies once the original native race is extinct. For example, the stocking of Pyramid Lake, Nevada, with nonnative races of Lahontan cutthroat trout has resulted in a noteworthy fishery. But the survival, growth, abundance, and maximum size of the nonnative trout are only a shadow of the performance of the original native trout of Pyramid Lake, which was lost in 1938.

Any trout that can produce 20-inch specimens in a harsh desert environment must have something going for it.

AUTHOR'S NOTE

This column was written on a hopeful note that the Alvord cutthroat trout, long believed to be extinct, might yet be saved. Unfortunately, the transplant made into a fishless stream in 1986 was never seen again. Hope springs eternal, however, and there is some circumstantial evidence that, long ago, Alvord cutthroat were transplanted into Guano Creek of the Northern Great Basin. Although it is unlikely that the present trout population in Guano Creek represent a pure line of Alvord cutthroat, some specimens accurately duplicate the external appearance of the original Alvord. These could be selected and transplanted into a fishless stream and the Alvord phenotype, if not genotype, could be resurrected.

ATLANTIC SALMON

SUMMER 1986

OF MORE THAN 20,000 KNOWN SPECIES of fish, the one species that, by general acclimation, has been proclaimed as the "king of fishes" since before the time of Izaak Walton is the Atlantic salmon. Admired and esteemed above all species by the Romans and all other people fortunate enough to have intimate contact with this noble fish, no other fish has attained the degree of awe, mystery, glamour and excitement comparable to that endowed upon Atlantic salmon.

This superlative description can be translated into more materialistic and quantifiable economic terms by consideration of the price that anglers are willing to pay per day, week, or season to rent a beat on a prime salmon river in Scotland, Norway, or Iceland. No other species can compare with the expenditures generated by merely renting the opportunity to fish for Atlantic salmon. What other species but Atlantic salmon could have possibly stimulated the spending of about $100 million in recent times in an attempt (with very limited success) at restoration of the species to New England rivers?

Also, more than any other single species, the Atlantic salmon has historically stimulated more intense and emotional controversy regarding various aspects of its life history. For example, landlocked or lake resident salmon versus anadromous or sea-run salmon—are they two different species? Which came first? How far do salmon migrate in the ocean? Do they "home" to the river of their birth? Do returning spawners feed in freshwater? If they do not feed, why can they be caught on flies, lures, live bait, cut bait?

We now have relatively sound answers to all of these questions except to the one most fascinating to anglers: why do adult salmon take a fly, lure, or bait in freshwater if they do not feed? I wish I could provide some new insights into this age-old question, but I can only point out that such behavior is not unique to Atlantic salmon, nor to salmonid fishes in general. Most fish species cease feeding or greatly reduce feeding prior to spawning and during spawning migrations. Behavior patterns change. Odd things may occur. For example, fish such as shad and carp can be caught with flies and lures during their prespawning behavior change, but rarely later when they return to active feeding.

The ocean fishery for salmon off of Greenland, although devastating to some runs of salmon, particularly to those of New Brunswick and Scotland, did reveal a wealth of information about ocean migration that was previously unknown.

Landlocked salmon are native to many lakes of Maine and Canada (also native, but now extinct, to Lake Ontario and Lake Champlain) and to a few lakes of Norway, Sweden, and the Northwestern U.S.S.R. Examining the distribution of landlocked salmon reveals a common pattern: all of the lakes that contain native landlocked salmon occur at relatively low elevation, about 300 feet above sea level or less. These lakes were covered by, or broadly connected to, the ocean during the maximum postglacial rise in ocean levels several thousand years ago.

The smelt, also an anadromous species, has a distribution pattern of landlocked populations very similar to that of Atlantic salmon. Almost all lakes with native landlocked salmon also have native populations of smelt. It seems obvious then that, when ocean levels receded, some anadromous runs of salmon began to utilize large lakes with optimum environments and adequate food supplies as permanent habitats in which to complete their life cycle. They gave rise to "landlocked" populations. The implications are that different populations of landlocked salmon, in different river drainages, originated from different ancestral anadromous populations. This lack of a single common ancestor for all populations of landlocked salmon (their polyphyletic origins) argues against separate taxonomic recognition for landlocked and anadromous populations of Atlantic salmon—all Atlantic salmon, throughout their total range are recognized as a single species: *Salmo salar*.

An argument could be made, however, that North American and European groups of *S. salar* should be classified as two separate subspecies because of differences in chromosome numbers (typically 56 in North American populations and 58 in European populations) and some slight protein differences.

The original distribution of Atlantic salmon in North America extended from the Housatonic River, Connecticut, northward in all suitable rivers of New England and Eastern Canada to Ungava Bay, northern Quebec. A 1968 report of a salmon taken at the mouth of the Kogaluk River, northeastern Hudson Bay, is the westernmost record of Atlantic salmon in the northern part of their range. The discovery of landlocked salmon above waterfalls in the Hudson Bay Drainage suggests that *S. salar* gained access to Hudson Bay by crossing an Atlantic Ocean drainage divide rather than by movement through the sea. Atlantic salmon also occurred as landlocked populations in Maine, Quebec (ouananiche), Newfoundland, and Lake Ontario. The salmon of Lake Champlain may have consisted of both landlocked and anadromous populations. (A historical note of interest, called to my attention in a publication by Dwight Webster, Cornell University, concerns one of the earliest records of angling for salmon in North America. A British officer, Lieutenant John Enys, caught great numbers of Lake Champlain salmon in the Chazy River and in the Saranac River by fly-fishing in 1768. The local people were amazed; they used nets, clubs, spears, and pitch forks.)

Salmon are native to a few rivers of southwestern Greenland, many—about 60—rivers of Iceland, and to Great Britain and Ireland. On the European mainland, the original southernmost distribution of salmon probably was the Douro River, Portugal (the river where port wine is barged to "port"). From Portugal the species occurred in all suitable rivers northward to the North and Baltic seas, around Norway in the Norwegian Sea and Arctic Ocean drainages, then eastward in rivers of the Soviet Union tributary to the White and Barent seas (such as the North Dvina, Menzen, and Pechora rivers). The easternmost recorded distribution in the northern part of the range is the Kara River. Lake Vänern, Sweden, and Lakes Ladoga and Onega, U.S.S.R., have been known for particularly large landlocked salmon, to about 40 pounds. (Probably the world's largest landlocked salmon were once found in Lake Ontario—to about 45 pounds.)

Erroneous references may be found in the literature pertaining to landlocked glacial relicts of Atlantic salmon occurring in tributaries to the Adriatic Sea in Yugoslavia and Albania, and in the Atlas Mountains of North Africa. The Adriatic trout confused with *S. salar* is not even closely related. It is classified as a distinct genus and species: *Salmothymus obtusirostris*. The North African trout is the brown trout: *Salmo trutta*.

Some of the older Russian literature frequently classified the large sea-run trout of the Caspian Sea and Black Sea as Atlantic salmon. Anatomically, brown trout and Atlantic salmon are so similar that positive identification of the large Caspian and Black sea trout as *S. trutta* was not possible until modern techniques of chromosome analysis (80 chromosomes in *S. trutta*) and protein electrophoresis were developed.

Throughout the range of Atlantic salmon considerable differences are found in life history patterns—duration of parr-smolt stage, duration of ocean life, percent grilse in spawning runs, riming of spawners entering rivers, survival to repeat spawning.

Atlantic salmon, like brown trout, are fall spawners. Most runs, however, enter the rivers well before spawning time, typically in May and June, with the oldest, largest fish entering first (April–May) and grilse running later (June–July) There is great variation, however, in timing of the runs of the different races of salmon. A large river system may have several distinct runs, representing different races homing to different tributaries. Particularly towards the northern part of the range, some salmon enter the rivers in the late summer, fall and winter, a year or more before they spawn (the Serpentine River, tributary to the Saint John River, New Brunswick, had such a run of salmon before it was exterminated by a dam).

The young typically spend two or three years in freshwater before smolting and migrating to the ocean in their third or fourth year of life. There is a general trend for extended duration of the juvenile stage in rivers toward the northern extreme of distribution because of a shorter growing season and slower growth. In rivers of the U.S.S.R. (White and Barent sea drainages) smolts are more typically three- or four-years-old. And, in Ungava Bay tributaries of northern Quebec, smolts are typically five or six—some up to eight—years of age. Adult size is related to how many years are spent in the ocean. Thus, different rivers are known for different average sizes of their spawning runs. In some runs grilse (one year in ocean) predominate or are in high proportion; average weight in the run will be about three to eight pounds. Runs predominantly with

ATLANTIC SALMON
Salmo salar

two- and three-year ocean fish will have fish averaging ten to fifteen pounds. The largest fish spend four or five years in the ocean, and are typically repeat spawners.

Of all anadromous salmonid fishes, the life history of steelhead trout most closely approximates that of sea-run *salar*. The major differences are between "jack" steel-head and salmon grilse, and in the growth of repeat spawners: jacks are all males and return before winter; Atlantic salmon can add considerable growth between spawnings whereas steelhead typically do not increase in weight to any extent after first spawning.

World-class size salmon of 60 to 80 pounds are only known from Europe. The angler caught record salmon of 79 pounds 2 ounces from the Tana River, Norway, was caught in 1928. Very large salmon have been historically reported from the Pechora River, U.S.S.R. The rivers of the Northwestern U.S.S.R. represent the greatest area in the distribution of the species where the runs have been virtually untouched by anglers. The Soviet tourist industry is missing a good bet.

The largest known salmon from North American waters is a fish of 55 pounds caught in the Grand Cascapedia River, Quebec.

The maximum known size of Maine anadromous salmon was about 40–45 pounds. Historically, the salmon runs in Maine rivers contained very few grilse. Canadian rivers are highly variable in the percent of grilse in the runs.

No doubt the virgin abundance of Atlantic salmon was very great. But just how abundant, in millions of pounds of fish, we'll never know, because many of the most productive rivers such as the Seine and Rhine in Europe, and the Connecticut and Merrimack of New England, lost their salmon before catch records were kept. Originally, 28 rivers of New England were known to have salmon runs. A dam across the Connecticut River in 1798 eliminated the native runs (and also the adapted genetic diversity crucial for successful restoration). Henry Thoreau paddled down the Merrimack River in 1839 and reflected on the sad fate of its shad and salmon. He wrote: "Perchance after a thousand years, if the fishes will be patient, and pass their summers elsewhere, meanwhile nature will have leveled the Billerica dam, and the Lowell factories, and the Grass-ground River run clear again, to be explored by new migrating shoals." Thoreau might be pleased to know that at least meager runs have been restored to the Connecticut and Merrimack rivers from massive stockings of nonnative hatchery salmon, which have poor survival and are enormously expensive to maintain.

Currently, 15 New England rivers are part of the Atlantic salmon restoration project. From millions of fry and smolts stocked annually, runs estimated at about 7,000 fish are maintained (about 6,000 from hatchery fish and about 1,000 from natural reproduction). A major problem confronting restoration attempts is the minute amount of genetic diversity, once contained in the original runs of the 28 New England rivers, that is left to work with. One New England river after another lost its salmon. By the early 1900s only residual runs remained in a few Maine rivers. The largest Maine salmon river, the Penobscot, lost all of its native runs by 1958 when Penobscot Bay became so polluted that its waters had no oxygen for fish survival. When conditions in the Penobscot improved sufficiently for stocking salmon again, eggs were taken from residual runs that still occurred in the Narraguagus and Machias Rivers. The establishment of the "new" Penobscot salmon—from Narraguagus and Machias stocks—has been the most successful restoration of any of the New England rivers stocked with salmon, but they are not the native Penobscot salmon. Historically, the Penobscot had an early run of salmon, in March and April, whereas the introduced salmon run peaks in June and July.

The tragic point is this: the great range of adaptive genetic diversity once represented in the various races of the Housatonic, Connecticut, Merrimack, Penobscot, Androscoggin, and Kennebec Rivers, which was the very basis of historical salmon abundance, is gone.

All kinds of Atlantic salmon stocks have been used in hatchery propagation for stocking in New England rivers—Miramichi and other Canadian stocks, landlocked salmon, hybrid combinations, etc. "Penobscot" salmon (of Narraguagus and Machias origin) have proved the most successful, but returns have been low—less than one percent of the smolts stocked. An example of the maladaptiveness of nonnative stocks was apparent a few years ago when smolts leaving the Connecticut River, instead of migrating north in Long Island Sound to colder waters, turned south to be trapped in warm water. Many of these sought refuge by entering small southern Connecticut coastal streams such as the Mianus River. It is highly doubtful that any of these wayward salmon survived to maturity.

In contrast, I would point to the example of Sweden's attempt to maintain its native runs in tributaries to the Baltic Sea after the rivers were blocked by dams. Each major river has its own hatchery (17 in all) propagating the native runs of each river in an attempt to preserve a significant amount of the original genetic diversity. Smolt to adult survival (sport and commercial catch plus return to hatcheries) has typically ranged from 10 to 20 (average 14) percent over many years.

Another crisis for the continued survival of Atlantic salmon began in the 1960s when Danish commercial fishermen found an ocean feeding ground where salmon congregated off southwestern Greenland. Through the early 1970s the annual catch increased to almost six million pounds. No other species of fish could have stirred such emotions over a relatively small commercial fishery. Statements of outrage and threats of retribution emanated from the United States Congress and from the leading statesmen of salmon-producing nations.

In 1972 the annual catch quota for the West Greenland fishery was set at 2.6 million pounds, and reduced to 1.9 million pounds by 1984 with a phasing out of the offshore fishery. The inshore fishery in 1984 took less than 600,000 pounds.

In 1983, the North Atlantic Salmon Conservation Organization (NASCO) was formed. It consists of three separate commissions—a North American Commission to represent Canada and the United States; a West Greenland Commission to represent the United States, Canada, and the European Economic Community (EEC); and the Northeast Atlantic Commission to represent Denmark (Faroe Islands), Finland, Iceland, Norway, Sweden, and the EEC. The goal of the Commission is to control and reduce the ocean catch of salmon. The problem is that unanimous agreement must be reached by all three commissions before any new regulation is adopted. When dealing with Atlantic salmon, it appears that emotional debate among representatives of friendly nations can become more acrimonious than with nuclear weapons control negotiations between the U.S. and the U.S.S.R.!

As an example, at the February 1985 meeting, the United States representatives provided factual evidence that a relatively high proportion of the small stocks of salmon returning to New England rivers is taken in the Canadian commercial fishery off Newfoundland. The U.S. requested that Canada close this fishery from September through December to save these valuable American fish. It was also pointed out that this closure would have very little impact on the Newfoundland salmon fishery, which could be fully compensated by extending the June season by only one day.

The proposal certainly seemed reasonable. The U.S. data were examined and verified by an independent committee. But the Canadian representatives demanded further reductions in the Greenland catch before agreeing to the American proposal. Greenland refused unless reductions were also made in the Faroe Islands catch. Thus, American fish did not receive the needed protection from the Newfoundland fishery in 1985. Again outrage was expressed in Congress with hints of a ban on importation of Canadian fishery products (annual trade of almost one billion dollars). Secretary of State Shultz registered a strong protest to the Canadian Government and, in the fall of 1985, the Canadian Minister of Fisheries, John Fraser, resigned. Let's hope for an amicable resolution of the problem so that a few hundred American salmon might be saved from the Canadian commercial fishery in 1986 and return to New England rivers—they need all the help they can get.

During the 1960s enormous reductions in salmon abundance resulted from DDT spraying of whole watersheds in Canada in an attempt to control the gypsy moth (which follows natural boom-and-bust cycles with or without insecticides). The DDT did not kill the salmon directly; juveniles starved to death after their insect food supply was virtually eliminated. Recently, the threat of acid deposition has become a reality. Natural reproduction of salmon in many rivers of southern Nova Scotia has already ceased because the pH is now less than 4.7.

For the future, I believe it is only a matter of common sense economics that Atlantic salmon will be managed like big game animals: The species' value is much greater when harvested by sportsmen than when commercially harvested and marketed—and the market and restaurant trade can be met with pen-reared animals. Already, most of the market and restaurant trade in Atlantic salmon is supplied by pen-reared salmon, especially from Norway, where salmon are selectively bred for market.

By the year 2000, I predict that 100 million pounds or more of Atlantic salmon will be produced and sold, entirely from intensive fish culture—probably more than twice the maximum commercial catch ever made in the best years from North America and Europe combined.

AUTHOR'S NOTE

In recent times the name "Atlantic" salmon, has been tainted in a way, because it is the dominant salmon species raised in fish farms across the world. The salmon farming industry has attracted negative publicity concerning pollution and dispersion of parasites and pathogens. Wild and farm-raised Atlantic salmon are the same species but create very different economic values and perceptions as an icon. The 1985 column predicted that the rapidly growing salmon farming industry would be producing "100 million pounds or more" of Atlantic salmon by the year 2000 and the farmed salmon would essentially replace wild Atlantic salmon on the market. The latter part of the prediction was correct, but the production volume prediction was off by at least 10 fold. The industry exceeded one billion pounds by 2000, and the magnitude of this growth resulted in problems of pollution, parasites, and pathogens caused by the tremendous densities of salmon concentrated in large rearing sites in bays and estuaries.

After many years, the world's commercial catch of Atlantic salmon has been substantially restricted, but the expected increases in wild populations were not realized. This is explained by cycles in the North Atlantic ecosystem. Similar to the cycles of changing temperatures and nutrient levels that control productivity from phytoplankton to zooplankton, to forge organisms, to salmon in the North Pacific, the North Atlantic has similar cycles that ultimately, control the abundance of wild Atlantic salmon.

The restoration of Atlantic salmon to some New England rivers has been the most intensive and expensive fish restoration in American history. The 1986 column offered some hopeful expectations for New England salmon restoration. The annual returns had been increasing although about 80 percent or more were hatchery fish. Total returns included 15 rivers, but the run in the Penobscot River in Maine made up about 75 to 80 percent of the totals. It had been calculated at the time that 60 percent of the salmon returning to New England Rivers were caught in the commercial fishery off of Newfoundland. It seemed logical to assume that when this fishery ceased, returning spawning runs should increase by about 60 percent. It didn't happen. The factors determining changes in productivity of the North Atlantic Ocean are non-negotiable. Despite increasing hatchery production and the cessation of commercial fishing, the total return of about 6,000 New England salmon in 1986, hasn't been matched during the next 20 years. In the

1990s, returns dropped below 2,000, fluctuated slightly and reached the lowest total of 803 in 2000. I'll finish up with an encouraging word. During the past five years, with protection from commercial fisheries, salmon runs in Canadian rivers have generally showed moderate increases. Salmon counts in the Penobscot increased from 985 in 2005 to 1,046 in 2006: this was only a five percent increase, but it was enough to celebrate with a one month catch-and-release fishery for anglers on the Penobscot. The Penobscot count in 1986 was 4,541.

REDBAND TROUT

⤻

FALL 1986

THE REDBAND TROUT HAS LONG CONFUSED ichthyologists, fisheries biologists, and knowledgeable anglers. In the past it was recognized as several different species or subspecies, sometimes aligned with cutthroat trout, *Salmo clarki*, sometimes with rainbow trout, *S. gairdneri*. I did not designate a scientific name for the redband trout in the painting for this article because the redband trout, in my assessment, consists of several distinct evolutionary lines. It is not a single entity.

The 1980 edition of the American Fisheries Society's *List of Common and Scientific Names of Fishes* includes an annotation for rainbow trout (*S. gairdneri*) that reads: "The redband trout has been recognized as a species distinct from rainbow trout and has been included on recent published lists"—several citations are then listed—"The systematic status of this species is unresolved and no specific scientific name was applied to it by the authors cited above." The Endangered Species Committee of the American Fisheries Society has designated the redband trout as a "species of special concern."

Some readers may recall the redband trout featured on an *American Outdoors* television program or may have read about them in magazines, especially their ability to thrive in waters too warm for other trout. The late Ted Trueblood, an outdoor writer widely recognized as well above the average in his ability to accurately observe and interpret nature, once wrote a story for *Outdoor Life*, "Cutthroats of the Cattle Country." The "cutthroat" trout he wrote about from southwestern Idaho were, in reality, redband trout. In the 1969 edition of *True's Fishing Yearbook*, Mr. Trueblood provided a color photo of the southwestern Idaho "cutthroat" with the caption: "Native throughout the interior West, cutthroat, like these offer some of the most exciting small-trout action." The photo illustrates three beautiful redband trout which I recognize by their distinctive parr marks, yellowish colors, spotting pattern, and fin markings. I would point out that for many years I tracked down sources of "native cutthroat" reported to me by professional biologists in this same region (Owyhee River drainage and other tributaries to Snake River below Shoshone Falls), and they all turned out to be brightly colored redband trout.

Is the redband trout for real? If so, why hasn't it been properly classified?

To regular readers of this column, confusion regarding trout classification should, by now, be accepted as a fact of life. The redband trout, however, is a special case—not only in regard to the level of complexity and controversy, but also because, among the diversity of forms I include as redband trout, there are some unique adaptations potentially of great value to modern fisheries management.

The confusion concerning redband trout classification began in 1892 when the U.S. Fish Commission sent C. H. Gilbert and B.W. Evermann to survey the fishes of the Columbia River Basin. In the upper Snake River drainage of Wyoming and Idaho, above the great Shoshone Falls, typical cutthroat trout (Yellowstone subspecies) were the only trout found. From the mouth of the Columbia River to the Cascade Mountains, both rainbow trout (coastal rainbows) and cutthroat trout (coastal subspecies) were found together; each was perfectly distinct. Between Shoshone Falls on the Snake River and the Cascade Range, the Columbia River Basin produced a confusing array of native trout that seemed to bridge the gap between the rainbow and cutthroat species. Gilbert and Evermann wrote: "With every additional collection of black-spotted trout it becomes increasingly difficult to recognize any of the distinctions, specific or subspecific, which have been set up . . . we think it not unlikely that the coastal form should be recognized as *Salmo mykiss gairdneri*, though the question is sadly in need of systematic and thorough investigation." The cutthroat trout at that time was mistakenly classified as *Salmo mykiss*. Gilbert and Evermann suggested that all rainbow and cutthroat trout might be lumped into a single species (*mykiss*) because the trout of the middle Columbia River Basin appeared to represent a complete intergradation between the two.

In their 1896 classic text *Fishes of North America*, Jordan and Evermann classified the middle Columbia River redband trout as a subspecies of cutthroat, *S. mykiss gibbsi*.

In 1872 Livingston Stone set up the first salmon hatchery for the U.S. Fish Commission on the McCloud River, California. He pondered over the question of how many species of trout occurred in the McCloud. Besides the large, silvery trout (steelhead), Stone mentioned smaller, more colorful trout that lived in headwater areas and tributary streams. He called this trout the "red-banded" trout. I adopted the name

from Livingston Stone, modifying it to "redband" (as there is only one band). D. S. Jordan proceeded to describe two subspecies of rainbow trout, *shasta* and *stonei* for forms of redband trout sent to him from the McCloud River by Stone. Jordan also described the two basic forms of golden trout from the Kern River drainage, California, *aguabonita* and *gilberti*. At first Jordan classified *aguabonita* as a subspecies of cutthroat trout, then changed it to a subspecies of rainbow trout. He finally concluded that the California golden trout represented a transition from the cutthroat species to the rainbow species.

Around the turn of the century, J. O. Snyder, an associate of Jordan, studied the trout in a series of desert basins in southern Oregon that lie between the Columbia River and Sacramento River Basins. Snyder expressed uncertainty about the origins of these desert trout but he classified them as cutthroat trout. About 25 years ago, aware of the confusion in the literature, I began to study the museum specimens collected by the surveys and expeditions mentioned above. Most of the specimens did indeed appear to be quite intermediate between cutthroat trout on one hand and rainbow trout on the other. In my first publication on the subject I concluded that the origin of redband trout was from an ancient hybridization between rainbow and cutthroat trout in interior waters. Such a conclusion certainly seemed logical to me at the time. But I was wrong.

After many years of additional studies, supplemented with new evidence based on chromosomes and protein comparison, it became clear that redband trout represent a diversity of primitive evolutionary lines associated with the ultimate evolution of the typical modern rainbow (coastal rainbow trout).

Although all the details are far from complete, my explanation of redband trout, in an evolutionary sense, is as follows. In the early stages of evolution leading to the typical rainbow trout, various side branches appeared. One of these early branches became established in the Sacramento River Basin, another in the Columbia. They were characterized by traits possessed by a primitive common ancestor to both rainbow and cutthroat trout. Within each basin diversification occurred; for example, the evolution of golden trout in the southern end (Kern River) of the Sacramento Basin, and the more typical red trout in the northern end (McCloud and Pit Rivers). In the Columbia River Basin, redband trout spread inland as far as all the major barrier falls on the Kootenay, Pend Oreille, Spokane, and Snake Rivers. Above these falls, the cutthroat is the only native trout. Below the falls, the redband trout replaced the earlier established cutthroat westward to the Cascade Range. The redband trout also invaded the Oregon desert basins during a glacial epoch when these basins contained large lakes.

In the Columbia River Basin the ancestral redband trout evolved into lake-adapted populations (the Kamloops trout, which is also found in large lakes of the Fraser River Basin), anadromous populations (steelhead trout native to tributaries east of the Cascades, such as the Salmon and Clearwater Rivers of Idaho), and resident stream populations. Many of these resident stream populations have evolved for the past several thousand years in hot, desert-like country of northern Nevada, southwestern Oregon and southwestern Idaho (Ted Trueblood's "cutthroats" of the cattle country). As such, many populations have evolved adaptations to survive and thrive in extremely harsh and highly fluctuating environments.

In each of several separate desert basins in southern Oregon the redband trout evolved differentiated populations. In the Upper Klamath Lake Basin, Oregon, the redband ancestor evolved into two distinct

REDBAND TROUT
Oncorhynchus mykiss gairdneri

forms—a specialized lake form which attained a size of 20 pounds or more, and a resident stream fish restricted to the smaller tributaries.

With such diversity, the problem of devising a classification scheme that would accurately reflect evolutionary reality—and still encompass all of this diversity—is enormously difficult. The problem of classification is further compounded by mixing and hybridization between the diverse evolutionary lines. The more recently evolved coastal rainbow trout later invaded the Sacramento and Columbia Basins and hybridized with the earlier established redband trout. Today no sharp line of separation between interior redband trout and coastal rainbow trout is possible. Only in areas isolated from the later invasion by coastal rainbow trout, such as the Kern River and the headwaters of the McCloud above barrier falls, did the original ancestral redband trout persist, more-or-less, in its original form. In the Pit River, California, mixing of "Columbia redband" (via Goose Lake to Pit River headwaters), "Sacramento redband" (the original native trout of Pit River), and the later-invading coastal rainbow trout evidently occurred to produce a mosaic of diversity that defies any attempt at logical classification. The famous Eagle Lake rainbow exemplifies a trout which cannot clearly be classified as either a coastal rainbow trout or a redband.

The human mind seeks orderliness. Nature, however, is seldom orderly.

Bureaucracies may need a classification of rainbow and redband trout to base decisions in regard to the protection of rare native fish. For such purposes they can arbitrarily declare any population to be a coastal rainbow trout or a redband trout by fiat. It must be recognized, however, that, in many cases, all diversity within a species cannot simply be pigeon-holed into categories in a manner that accurately reflects ancestral origins and relationships. My advice concerning the classification of rainbow and redband trout is that we must learn to accept and live with a certain amount of natural disorder—and eventually learn to appreciate and enjoy it. The problems created for classification by disorder or "noise" in nature extend beyond the classification of organisms (taxonomy). The philosophical and logical limitations of classification of any aspect of nature equally applies to models of habitat classification. Biologists who do not comprehend these limitations are susceptible to entrapment by the illusion of technique and seduction by mindless methodologies.

I have recommended that the coastal rainbow trout (both steelhead and resident populations) be classified as *Salmo gairdneri irideus*, and the redband trout of the Columbia and upper Fraser River Basins (steelhead, Kamloops, and resident stream trout) should be *S. g. gairdneri*. Under this broad scheme, the California golden trout would be *S. g. aguabonita* (South Fork Kern) and *S. g. gilberti* (Kern and Little Kern golden trout).

The trout native to the McCloud and Pit Rivers (northern Sacramento Basin) and to the Oregon desert basins reflect a hodgepodge of differentiation for which I can envision no simple breakdown into neat sub-specific units. The common name "redband trout" as here discussed implies a more inclusive name of "golden-redband-Kamloops complex" which encompasses diverse evolutionary lineages. As such, the term "redband" can be applied to Sacramento redband, Columbia redband, or Oregon desert basin redband.

Much more important, however, than any debate over scientific and common names is the fact that the natural diversity produced during redband trout evolution is a natural resource of great potential value. Such traits as specialized lake predation (some Kamloops trout or upper Klamath Lake trout), or survival under extreme environments (some desert lands redband), offer opportunities to utilize these resources in fisheries management. This is especially true in situations where stocking of domesticated hatchery rainbows gives poor results.

Several years ago, the Oregon Department of Fish and Wildlife established a broodstock of redband trout in a small impoundment. The original source of this broodstock was Three Mile Creek, a tiny stream draining the west slope of the Steens Mountains into Catlow Valley, one of the Oregon desert basins. The U.S. Fish and Wildlife Service obtained eggs from this broodstock for propagation, and Catlow Valley redband trout have been sent to Texas and Missouri in expectations of establishing a trout resistant to high temperatures in waters unsuited for other trout.

A problem I find with the current propagation of redband trout concerns the "typological" approach to fisheries management, whereby all redband trout are considered to be similar—if some populations of redband trout thrive in warm water, any redband trout can do the same. My personal experience with redband trout that live in streams where daily summer water temperatures may reach 85° F concerns the Owyhee River drainage of northern Nevada and southeastern Oregon. I once caught one redband after another on dry flies in Chino Creek, Nevada, when the water temperature was 83° F. These trout put up a good fight and appeared to be in excellent condition. In these desert areas, nights are cold, and stream temperatures may drop 25 to 30 degrees below the daytime maximum.

In an experiment performed at a Texas hatchery, Catlow Valley redband trout, rainbow trout from the Firehole River, Yellowstone Park, and a standard hatchery rainbow were subjected to constant warming of their water by 1° F per day until they perished. The redband trout perished at 81° F and the two groups of rainbow trout perished at 82° F.

Perhaps the Catlow Valley redband trout is less heat-tolerant than some rainbow trout, at least under the conditions of this experiment, but I would raise a question concerning the pertinence of such experiments to natural conditions. What must be kept in mind is the selective pressures exerted by the environment during the evolutionary history of a particular common group of fish. No fish, in nature, is subjected to constantly increasing temperatures, but rather to daily and seasonal variations. Evolutionary survival adaptations reflect the natural conditions of the evolutionary environment. Thus, the heat-tolerant redband trout I caught in the Owyhee River drainage might not demonstrate survival at higher temperatures than ordinary rainbow trout in laboratory studies. But I would expect that they evolved physiological adaptations to allow normal functioning for a few hours per day at temperatures that would severely stress other trout. Such a temperature criterion might be called maximum functional temperature—the maximum temperature (with diurnal variation) at which the fish continue to feed and do not lose weight.

Another problem in the use of desert redband trout is that, for the past several thousand years, they have been confined mostly to small, intermittent streams, essentially subjecting them to selection for life history traits similar to Eastern brook trout. They tend to spawn at a small size and die at an early age; few live to spawn again. In small, highly unstable environments such a life history is advantageous for the survival of a population, but not favorable for stocking into waters where it is desirable to have the life-span extend five or six years or more.

Life history traits such as age at maturity and maximum life span can be artificially selected for by continually choosing the oldest spawners and repeat spawners for propagation. Artificial selection may be difficult with the present stock of Catlow Valley redband trout, which were derived from a small population native to a tiny rivulet. They can be expected to lack a broad base of genetic diversity (heterozygosity) needed for selection or to adapt to new environments.

Yet mixing of several distinct stocks should provide the diversity for "improvement" and increase adaptability to new environments.

There is virtually unlimited diversity for life history types and specializations among the redband trout as I define them. In Kootenay Lake, the giant Kamloops trout (Gerrard strain) has specialized to feed on kokanee salmon. It does not sexually mature until it is four- to six-years-old. One of these Kootenay Kamloops stocked in Lake Pend Oreille, Idaho, weighed 37 pounds when it was caught at five years of age. Another, from a broodstock in Jewel Lake, British Columbia, attained a weight of 52 pounds. The Eagle Lake, California, trout derived from the Pit River specialized to feed on tui chub, a large minnow. The upper Klamath Lake trout probably also specialized to feed on tui chub and a variety of non-game fishes.

A point to be emphasized is that there can be no "trout for all seasons" or for all waters. But creative and innovative fish culturists working in an experimental hatchery, drawing on the wealth of natural diversity found in redband trout, could produce new races. Viable trout populations might then be established in waters that do not now support trout. Specialized predators might be developed for lakes and reservoirs, trout that could convert a trash fish problem into a forage fish asset.

Pat Coffin, now Chief of Fisheries for the Nevada Department of Wildlife, accompanied me in 1972 when I caught redband trout in 83° F water. Pat was impressed by this remarkable fish and wrote an article on redband trout in a 1975 issue of *Nevada Outdoors* magazine. He concluded that the redband trout "may have eventual fisheries management implications when fisheries management becomes sophisticated enough to appreciate this unique trout."

I'm afraid that neither Pat nor I will live long enough to see the fisheries management potential of redband trout fulfilled if we must wait for management to become "sophisticated enough." This is a situation where judicious use of common sense, innovation, creativity, and determination to carry out an action-oriented program would be much more important than sophistication. Such a program would be similar to aspects of agricultural plant breeding where wild races of propagated species are constantly sought to establish a base of diversity necessary to incorporate new, desirable traits into specific strains for specific environments.

AUTHOR'S NOTE

A most obvious change from 1986 is the classifications of all rainbow and redband trout from *Salmo gairdneri* to *Oncorhynchus mykiss*. *O. m. gairdneri* is now the subspecies name for the redband trout of the Columbia River basin east of the Cascade Mountains and the upper Fraser River basin of British Columbia. What I call redband or redband-rainbow trout display a great range of diversity. This is a reflection of their evolutionary history. There is no single common ancestor that gave rise to all redband trout, but rather they represent several lines that independently branched off the stem leading toward the "modern" or coastal rainbow. The diversity of independent origins creates problems for classifying redband trout into subspecies. More important than the most correct classification, however, is the diversity of life history and ecologically adaptive forms produced under different selective factors. The large size and predatory feeding associated with the Kamloops form of redband trout can be cited. Also, redband trout adapting for thousands of generations in semi-arid regions with warm summer temperatures, have the ability to actively feed and grow at temperatures considerably higher than found in typical rainbow and redband trout that lack this evolutionary history.

YELLOWSTONE CUTTHROAT

WINTER 1987

YELLOWSTONE LAKE AND THE YELLOWSTONE RIVER downstream to the two spectacular falls in Yellowstone National Park contain the greatest concentration of inland cutthroat trout still in existence. Thus, the common name "Yellowstone cutthroat" seems appropriate, although the origins of this subspecies are associated with the Snake River on the other side of the Continental Divide.

The Yellowstone cutthroat trout is characterized by relatively large, roundish spots, less brilliant coloration (in comparison with other subspecies) and 64 chromosomes. The presence of cutthroat trout in the Yellowstone River is due to a crossing of the Continental Divide in recent geological times from the headwaters of the Snake River (Columbia River Basin) to the headwaters of the Yellowstone River (Missouri River Basin). This transfer occurred after the end of the last glacial epoch and the melting of the glacial ice from the Yellowstone Plateau about 6,500 years ago.

After the common ancestor to all cutthroat trout became established along the Pacific Coast of North America there was an inland movement of the species in the Columbia River. This inland invasion led to the eventual separation of the coastal subspecies from interior subspecies with the Cascade Mountains forming the line of demarcation. The an-

cestral inland cutthroat trout soon divided into a northern Columbia River group associated with the Kootenay, Pend Oreille and Spokane River systems, which evolved into the westslope cutthroat trout, *S. c. lewisi*, and a group associated with the Snake River system, which evolved into the Yellowstone cutthroat trout. Based on the degrees of divergence as interpreted from morphological differentiation, protein patterns, and chromosomes (karyotypes), I estimate that the original separation of a common ancestral cutthroat trout into three major evolutionary lines—coastal, westslope, Yellowstone—may have occurred about one million years ago or more.

The ancestor to the present Yellowstone cutthroat gave rise to all other inland subspecies by successive invasions from the Snake River system into the Lahontan, Bonneville and Alvord Basins (separate desert basins of the Great Basin), and into the Green River drainage of the Colorado River Basin and subsequent radiation into the South Platte, Arkansas, and Rio Grande drainages. The formation of Shoshone Falls on the Snake River near Twin Falls, Idaho, isolated the cutthroat trout in the drainage above the falls and protected them from a later invasion of rainbow trout in the Columbia Basin.

After rainbow trout became established in the Columbia Basin, they completely eliminated the Yellowstone cutthroat from the Snake River drainage below Shoshone Falls wherever they came into contact. Rainbow trout also virtually eliminated the westslope cutthroat subspecies from the Columbia Basin up to barrier falls on the Kootenay, Pend Oreille, and Spokane Rivers. During the past 100 years, stocking of rainbow trout into almost all areas of the upper Columbia Basin and the upper Missouri and Yellowstone drainages has demolished the isolation that had protected the native cutthroats from rainbow trout for thousands of years. Hybridization and replacement by rainbow trout and replacement by brook, brown, and lake trout has resulted in the present survival of pure populations of both Yellowstone and westslope cutthroats in only a tiny fraction of their native range. This same phenomenon of hybridization and replacement has occurred with other inland

subspecies so that Yellowstone Park has become the greatest stronghold for any of the interior subspecies of cutthroat trout.

There is a record of 20,000 rainbow trout stocked into the Yellowstone drainage above the falls many years ago. Evidently their survival was very low or nil. No trace of the effects of rainbow trout hybridization can be found in the cutthroat trout in Yellowstone Lake or in the river above the falls today.

In 1985 Eastern brook trout were found in Arnica Creek, a tributary to Yellowstone Lake. Perhaps an angler caught some brook trout in another part of the park and kept them alive in a bucket until disposing of them in Arnica. If so, he couldn't have realized the potential ecological catastrophe his action might trigger.

I doubt that brook trout could successfully compete with the native

YELLOWSTONE CUTTHROAT TROUT
Oncorhynchus clarki bouvieri

cutthroat in Yellowstone Lake, but they would be expected to eventually spread to most or all of the lake's 68 tributary streams used by cutthroats for spawning. Their presence could severely impact cutthroat spawning success and recruitment. To head off such a catastrophe, the National Park Service and the United States Fish and Wildlife Service mobilized a counter-offensive by chemically treating Arnica Creek to kill the brook trout and nip the threat in the bud. This treatment was repeated in 1986.

The older literature designates Yellowstone cutthroat trout as *Salmo clarki lewisi* because the name *lewisi* was assigned to cutthroat trout native to the Missouri River near Great Falls, Montana. It was assumed that the cutthroat trout of the Yellowstone and upper Missouri Rivers were the same subspecies. Actually, the upper Missouri River cutthroat trout is derived from a separate crossing of the Continental Divide by westslope cutthroat from the headwaters of the Flathead River drainage. The two subspecies never came into contact, although they occurred within a few miles of each other in headwaters of the Yellowstone and Madison Rivers. The downstream environment of the Yellowstone and Missouri Rivers in eastern Montana is too warm and turbid for trout. This environmental barrier enforced isolation between the Yellowstone and Missouri River (westslope) cutthroat trout.

Several years ago it became obvious that the cutthroat trout of the upper Missouri and Yellowstone drainages represented two distinctly different subspecies.

The subspecies name *lewisi* must be assigned to the cutthroat native to the upper Missouri and upper Columbia River drainages. Thus, a new subspecies name had to be found for Yellowstone and upper Snake River cutthroat trout. I searched the literature to find the oldest available name that described the large-spotted cutthroat of the Snake and Yellowstone Rivers. I decided on *Salmo clarki bouvieri*, a name given in 1883 to the cutthroat trout native to Waha Lake, Idaho. Waha Lake is located near the Washington border, far downstream from Shoshone Falls. The lake is isolated from direct connection to the Snake River. This isolation blocked rainbow trout from Waha Lake and the na-

tive cutthroat persisted unmolested until impacted by the influence of Caucasian civilization. The Waha Lake watershed was degraded and rainbow trout and a hodgepodge of nonnative fishes, including carp, were stocked. *S. c. bouvieri* has been long extinct in Waha Lake, the type locality for the name, but the name survives to be used for the remaining populations of the subspecies in the upper Snake and Yellowstone drainages.

Fortunately, the native cutthroat persisted in the upper Yellowstone drainage in Yellowstone National Park, although the native westslope cutthroat is long gone from the Madison and Gallatin Rivers in the park. Native Yellowstone cutthroat existing in a near-pristine environment have been the subject of many studies to provide a better understanding of population dynamics, exploitation rates and effects of special regulation fisheries.

Knowledgeable and observant anglers familiar with Yellowstone Lake and its cutthroat trout are likely to raise questions based on their experience with other trout fisheries. These questions may seem to lack reasonable answers. For example, where are the young trout? Why are fish less than 12 inches long so rarely seen? Why might two fish of the same size look so different? Why is their flesh red like that of a salmon?

Cutthroats in the lake typically reach maturity at four or five years of age and 14–16 inches. They run up tributaries from late May through early July for spawning. Their eggs hatch in about 30 days and almost all of the young move into the lake soon after hatching. Movement of the juvenile cutthroat once in Yellowstone Lake is not well understood. They must spend their early years in deeper, open waters, segregated from larger, older trout. Cutthroat are rarely taken in net samples with large fish and are not found in the stomachs of large fish (though large cutthroat, given the opportunity to intercept the lakeward run of newly hatched fry, will gorge on them; they have no inhibitions against cannibalism). Typically, in their third or fourth year of life, averaging 12 inches, the trout move into shallow water to join the adult population.

There are insects in Yellowstone Lake—midges, mayflies, caddisflies—but the main cutthroat diet consists of Crustacea: water fleas (daphnia) and amphipods (freshwater shrimp or scuds). This diet imparts the salmon-red color to their flesh.

Because of a great depletion of energy reserves from spawning and a relatively short growing season in Yellowstone Lake, most of the surviving spawners must wait out a full year before their gonads can mature again for repeat spawning. That is, they wait to spawn again two years after first spawning. This is why some fish, caught in midsummer soon after spawning, appear sickly and emaciated, while others, having spawned the previous year and now fattening for next year, are plump and bright.

With a 13-inch maximum size limit to protect the older fish, Yellowstone Lake has experienced a resurgence of older age classes of its cutthroat trout. Formerly, under heavy angling exploitation, fish of more than five years were extremely rare. In recent years trout of seven to eight years have become increasingly common. Some nine-year-olds have been found.

It is now well known that cutthroat trout are extremely susceptible to angling; they are easily overexploited. Because of this vulnerability, however, cutthroat also respond to special regulations much better than other trout species. Although I have a long familiarity with all aspects of cutthroat trout biology, I am still amazed at some of the data developed from studies of the native cutthroat in Yellowstone Park.

Yellowstone Lake has a surface area of more than 87,000 acres. At an elevation of slightly over 7,700 feet, it is the largest high lake over 7,000 feet in North America. The cutthroat trout and a small minnow, the longnose dace, are the only fish species that crossed the Continental Divide at Two Ocean Pass from the Snake River and became established in the Yellowstone Lake Basin. (Redside shiner and longnose sucker have been established in recent times by illegal introductions). The cutthroat trout essentially had Yellowstone Lake and its tributaries all to itself for several thousand years. They flourished in great abundance.

Until 1970, angling regulations allowed three trout of any size to be creeled from Yellowstone Lake. From 1970–1972 a minimum size of 14 inches was initiated, and the bag limit was reduced to two fish per day in 1973. Despite these restrictive regulations, the population in the lake drastically declined. A most astonishing fact is that this decline occurred when angling pressure was no more than four to five hours per surface acre per year. I have never heard of a documented case of overexploitation—overfishing—occurring at such low angling pressure. I am quite certain it could occur at such low pressure only if cutthroat trout is the species being exploited.

In 1975 a new regulation was instituted requiring the release of all fish of 13 inches and larger, a two-fish daily bag limit, with only flies and artificial lures allowed. This regulation was designed to protect the older, mature fish. It has proven highly successful.

By the 1980s the size of the spawning run in Pelican Creek had doubled from counts made in the 1960s, from 12,000 to 24,000. In Clear Creek, spawning runs had dropped below 10,000 fish by the 1950s, but recovered rapidly under the 1975 regulation; the 1978 run peaked at about 70,000. In regard to trophy-size fish, only 3 fish per 1,000 caught in 1973 and 5 per 1,000 in 1974 were more than 18 inches. In 1983 this ratio had increased to 80 per 1,000. The proportion of fish spawning for the second or third time (repeat spawners) increased from only a few percent of the spawning runs to 25 to 30 percent.

From the lake, the Yellowstone River flows for about 20 miles through gentle terrain before plunging over the upper and then the lower falls into Yellowstone Canyon. About nine miles of the river below the lake is presently open to catch-and-release angling. This section supports the greatest cutthroat trout fishery in the world. It is also probably the greatest completely natural fishery for any species of trout in the world as expressed in annual catch of large fish (14–18 inches) per unit area of river. A fishery of such quality is only possible because of the susceptibility of cutthroat trout to be caught again and again.

Fishery regulations on the river became increasingly restrictive by the 1950s in an attempt to prevent overexploitation. By the 1970–1972 period, regulations prohibited bait fishing and had a 14 inch minimum size and a three-fish-per-day limit. Yet overexploitation still occurred. Electrofishing sampling made in the fall of 1971 compared a section of the river closed to angling with the open section. The results left no doubt that the cutthroat in the river were severely overexploited. The trout in the closed section averaged 17.6 inches, with fish up to 22 inches. The trout in the open section averaged 14.2 inches, with virtually no fish more than 16 inches—almost every trout was being removed upon attaining (or nearly attaining) the minimum size of 14 inches!

In 1973 the catch-and-release (no-kill) regulation was instituted with only flies and artificial lures allowed. The results were dramatic. Average age and size of fish in the catch jumped. By 1974–1975 the total annual catch was two- to two-and-one-half times the annual catch in the 1970–1972 period. Catch-per-hour had tripled to an average angler catch of more than two trout per hour—which has since declined to slightly more than one per hour in the 1980s due to a great increase in fishing pressure.

In 1980 and 1981, a graduate student at Idaho State University, Mr. Daniel Schill, and his professor, Dr. J.S. Griffith, conducted research on the Yellowstone River fishery to provide some insights into how a finite population of cutthroat trout can consistently sustain such a high total catch.

A section of river about three miles in length in the Buffalo Ford area—which is subjected to the greatest fishing pressure—was selected for critical analysis. During a six-week period from July 15 to August 25, 1981, an estimated 7,500 trout provided an estimated catch of 72,698 during six weeks of angling—that is, each trout was caught and released an average of 9.7 times. The total mortality of trout during this period was estimated at 236. If all this mortality was due to hooking or handling mortality, it figures out to be 3 fish killed per 1,000 caught and released, or 0.3 percent (236 died from 72,698 caught). This section of the river probably contains less than 100 surface acres. The trout caught averaged about 16 inches. Thus, during a six-week period the native cutthroat trout provided a catch (and release) of about 1,000 pounds per acre with angling pressure of about 700 hours per acre.

The results from the Yellowstone cutthroat trout fishery should not be cited to indiscriminately demand catch-and-release trout fisheries all over the country. Thoughtful consideration of a few facts should make it evident that the same results would not be expected in other rivers with other species of trout.

For consideration of catch-and-release regulations a useful comparative indice is the number of hours of angling per unit area it takes to catch each fish in the population an average of two or three times. The Yellowstone River cutthroat trout were caught an average of 9.7 times with about 700 hours per acre angling—or the population was "turned over" with every 70 hours per acre of angling. The rapid drop in total catch and catch-per-hour soon after opening day demonstrates that even cutthroat trout learn from experience—they become progressively more difficult to catch with successive catching. I estimate that only about 20 hours of angling per acre was required to catch each Yellowstone cutthroat an average of two times.

The brown trout stands at the other extreme in angling vulnerability. In the South Platte River, Colorado, it took 1,900 angling hours per acre to catch each brown trout in the population an average of two times. To catch each brown trout in Hot Creek, California, an average of three times required 3,800 angling hours per acre! Special regulations governing angling in the Madison River in Yellowstone Park have produced no detectable changes in the brown trout population.

Besides considerations of angling pressure and vulnerability to being caught, it is important to know life history characteristics of trout populations considered for special regulations management. Are they relatively long-lived—general maximum age of about five to eight years? Do they continue to exhibit good growth throughout their life (average about 3 inches per year increase), or do environmental limitations place severe restrictions on growth and longevity?

The Yellowstone River cutthroat trout represent an exceptional situation. Evidently, soon after hatching they migrate into Yellowstone Lake to grow and mature. They do not return to the river until they are adults—about 95 percent of the population in the river are fish of more than 12 inches. Thus, virtually none of the habitat or food supply is utilized by young, small fish. To my knowledge the combination of circumstances that is responsible for the phenomenal fishery in the Yellowstone River is not duplicated anywhere else on earth.

The fisheries research studies in Yellowstone Park have also helped to dispel some long-established beliefs.

Contrary to popular opinion, it is not necessary to restrict catch-and-release fisheries to barbless flies only. A large proportion of Yellowstone anglers have only casual interest in fishing and are not highly skilled or experienced. Many use large treble hook lures. The trout they catch are frequently left flopping on the bank while a camera is dug out and photos taken. Yet survival of the released trout is exceedingly high (97 percent) based on the 1981 study. Almost all detailed comparative studies on hooking mortality have demonstrated no significant differences in mortality between trout caught on single, treble, barbed, or barbless hooks. There is, however, a slight but consistent increase in mortality due to barbless hooks.

John Deinstadt, a California Fish and Game Department biologist with long experience with catch-and-release fisheries, believes this is due to what he calls the "stiletto effect." Barbless hooks have the tendency to penetrate more deeply. Although mortality of released trout rapidly increases with warmer water temperatures (especially as temperatures approach 70° F), under normal conditions, almost all mortality of trout caught on flies or artificial lures is due to rupture of the respiratory filaments of the gills or puncture of the carotid artery in the roof of the mouth. Because of their greater penetration power, barbless hooks are more prone to puncture the carotid artery. Large treble hooks often cause the least mortality because, unless the trout is quite large, the hooks cannot be engulfed into the mouth.

Another long-entrenched belief is that regulations that promote the selective removal of large trout, such as a 14-inch minimum size limit, will cause dwarfing of the population. That is, the continued removal of larger, faster-growing trout leaves the slower-growing "runts" to breed, and a hereditary change for slower growth will occur in the population. This certainly seems logical. It is theoretically possible or even probable until the matter is looked into in greater depth and the right questions are asked.

For such an effect to occur, the larger or faster-growing fish must be eliminated before they reproduce—otherwise they have already passed their hereditary information on to the next generation. Many, perhaps most, of the Yellowstone cutthroat trout had already spawned before they were removed from the population in former times under the 14-inch size limit. Also, opposing selection factors acting against slow growth must be considered, such as lower fecundity and increased vulnerability to predation. In any event, the adult populations of cutthroat trout both in Yellowstone Lake and River were exposed to extreme levels of exploitation for many years—probably higher than any other major wild trout fishery in the country. If a hereditary change for slower growth and a smaller adult size is a consequence of high exploitation rates of larger adults, then the Yellowstone cutthroat would be expected to show this effect. All of the empirical evidence, comparing the average and maximum size of cutthroat trout caught in "the old days" before high exploitation occurred with what is found in the present populations protected by special regulations, demonstrates that no detectable change has occurred. Edward R. Hewitt, in his book *A Trout and Salmon Fisherman for Seventy-five Years*, recounted a fishing trip to Yellowstone Park in 1881 before the park was open to the public. Hewitt caught thousands of Yellowstone cutthroat trout and commented that none exceeded four and one-half pounds, which is about the present general maximum size.

For history buffs, the Yellowstone cutthroat is richly associated with the lore of the Old West. When documenting the easternmost natural range of Yellowstone cutthroat trout in the Tongue River, a tributary of the Yellowstone River immediately east of the Little Bighorn drainage, I found reference to General Crook's army encamped in the upper Tongue River drainage in June, 1876.

Crook had retreated after the battle of the Rosebud, where his army met fierce resistance from a surprisingly large number of Indians led by Crazy Horse. Crook's army found the streams full of large, easily caught cutthroat trout. The men so enjoyed this wilderness paradise that General Crook decided to spend a few extra days for the morale of his men. When the main army finally moved westward to the Little Bighorn they found the remains of Colonel Custer and his troops. Perhaps if the range of the Yellowstone cutthroat trout had terminated with the Little Bighorn River and not extended to the Tongue River, names such as Little Bighorn, Custer and Sitting Bull would not have such common familiarity today. If the Indians had had their way there would still be native cutthroat trout in the Little Bighorn and Tongue Rivers. The taming of the West was bad news for cutthroat trout.

Fortunately for *Salmo clarki bouvieri*—and for *Homo sapiens*—a large area of the untamed West, including the headwaters of the Yellowstone River, was set aside in 1872 to become our first national park.

AUTHOR'S NOTE

This column highlighted the great rebound of cutthroat trout in Yellowstone Lake and in its outlet, Yellowstone River, after new angling regulations were implemented. A 13-inch maximum size limit was instituted in the lake and no-kill regulations on the river. I pointed out that no other trout species would have shown such dramatic response to special regulations as the cutthroat. Even with a 14-inch minimum size limit and a two-fish bag limit, the cutthroat trout population of Yellowstone Lake was severely depressed with annual angling pressure of only four to six hours per surface acre. I thought that demonstrating how soundly based angling regulations can be a powerful conservation tool to protect and enhance populations of wild, native trout would be good news to wild trout anglers.

I was somewhat surprised when an angry letter was sent to *Trout* magazine accusing me of "selling out," as if I had endorsed a gold mine using the cyanide leach process to be sited in Yellowstone Park. The angry protest concerned my comment that the new angling regulations required artificial flies or lures, but did not restrict the types of hooks, barbed, barbless, single or treble hooks could be used. This was based on "sound science." A doctoral research project had anglers catch hundreds of trout barbed and barbless on single and treble hook flies and lures and hold them in live boxes for up to 30 days. Water temperature, the length of time the trout were played before landing, and the hooking site were all factored into the data. The conclusion was that there were no statistical differences in mortality of fish caught and released on the four different combinations of hook types.

This conclusion agreed with several other published studies. Such evidence would be of no consequence to the angry letter-writer and like-minded fly fishers, who firmly believe that to conform to their ill-conceived moral value system, trout must be caught and released only with barbless flies. To do otherwise is blasphemy.

In 1984, the future of the cutthroat trout native to Yellowstone Park seemed secure. The watershed was in a national park and angling regulations had restored abundance. In the spring 1994 column on Yellowstone fishes, the future outlook for maintaining a thriving cutthroat population was positive. That year, however, was the year when a large population of illegally introduced lake trout was documented.

The lake trout had a devastating impact on the cutthroat. Without an intensive lake trout removal program, the cutthroat trout of Yellowstone Lake would have been reduced to a tiny remnant population. In 2006 alone, about 60,000 lake trout were removed from Yellowstone Lake. After the lake trout discovery, another catastrophe occurred due to an introduction of a nonnative parasite (probably via fish-eating birds). Whirling disease is now well-established there.

In recent years, whole year classes of young cutthroat trout have been eliminated from Pelican Creek, one of the most productive spawning tributary to Yellowstone Lake. As the newly hatched trout migrate toward Yellowstone Lake they must pass through low gradient areas with sediment substrate hosting millions of tubifex worms. The worms release billions of whirling disease spores. Virtually no young trout survives passing this gauntlet. It is sad to update the information on Yellowstone cutthroat trout on such a bleak note. It does clearly illustrate the dangers of the introduction of nonnative species. And, the most deadly of these alien organisms can be the smallest, even of microscopic size.

PAIUTE CUTTHROAT

SPRING 1987

LAST LABOR DAY WEEKEND I JOINED about 50 people on a nine-mile hike to the headwaters of Silver King Creek to participate in a Trout Unlimited–sponsored habitat enhancement project to help the threatened Paiute cutthroat trout. Although the scenic setting of Upper Fish Valley on the east slope of the Sierra, Alpine County, California, where the headwaters of Silver King Creek are located, is magnificent, the lure of the rare Paiute trout, *Salmo clarki seleniris*, must have been a factor to attract so many volunteers.

It is doubtful that any Paiute trout would still exist if they had not been officially endowed with their own sub-specific name. This demonstrates a practical aspect of subspecies taxonomy—having a unique name can help save a special form of life from extinction. Official taxonomic recognition facilitates listing under the Federal Endangered Species Act. Such recognition promotes active management and protection programs by federal and state agencies, and also can stimulate volunteers to participate in enhancement activities such as the expeditions to Silver King Creek over the Fourth of July and Labor Day holidays in 1986.

The Paiute cutthroat trout was discovered and named in 1933 when J.O. Snyder of Stanford University received some specimens of trout collected in Silver King Creek above Llewellyn Falls (named after Mrs. Lynn Llewellyn, who caught the specimens). Snyder realized that Silver King Creek is a tributary of the East Carson River of the Lahontan Desert Basin. He knew the trout found above the waterfall represented an isolated population derived from Lahontan cutthroat trout (*Salmo clarki henshawi*), but he was so impressed by their distinctive characteristic—the absence of spots on the body—that he originally described them as a new species, *Salmo seleniris*. The name *seleniris* for the new trout was selected because it suggested a "fanciful resemblance of its evanescent tints to the lunar rainbow." Similar to the Lahontan cutthroat, the Paiute trout lacks brilliant colors. The body is typically a pale silvery color with yellowish and greenish tints. The absence of spots on the body distinguishes the Paiute from the Lahontan and all other subspecies of cutthroat trout.

About 25 years after the 1933 description of *seleniris*, I examined the specimens of the original collection and compared them to Lahontan cutthroat trout. I found the Paiute trout to be identical to Lahontan trout in every character except for the spots on the body.

Obviously, Paiute trout are extremely closely related to Lahontan cutthroat, and their isolation in Silver King Creek from the parent stock in the East Carson River is only a matter of a few thousand years. Subsequent electrophoretic analysis of Paiute trout showed them to be identical in their protein patterns to Lahontan cutthroat. Because of such close relatedness between the Paiute and the Lahontan, some biologists have questioned the validity of the subspecies *seleniris*. I would point out that the subspecific category in taxonomy is a practical device for classifying geographically unique populations or races of a species. There are no rules or standards of quantifiable genetic differentiation to qualify as a subspecies; only that a subspecies should possess one or more unique characters which differentiates it from all other subspecies of a species. Thus, the lack of spots on the body of Paiute trout "validates" the subspecies *seleniris*.

No unique life history or behavioral attributes have been discovered for Paiute trout. They typically spawn when they are two years old. In the small mountain streams where Paiute trout live at elevations of 8,000 feet and higher, spawning occurs from May to July at water temperatures of about 42° F–48° F. An 8-inch female will spawn from 250 to 400 eggs. The eggs will incubate in the redd for about 35 days before hatching. Evidently mortality is high after spawning and few fish in the population attain an age of four years or older. Feeding is opportunistic, on a variety of aquatic and terrestrial insects.

The major limitation for the continued survival of the Paiute trout concerns their evolutionary heritage (or burden) that makes them imperfectly adapted to survive in small streams in competition with other trout species. Their ancestral origins are with the Lahontan cutthroat trout, which specialized as the top level predator in ancient Lake Lahontan. About 12,000 years ago Lake Lahontan was 8,500 square miles in area and had a maximum depth of 880 feet. Except for its remnant, Pyramid Lake, Lake Lahontan dried up about 8,000 years ago. At that time, an ancestral population of Lahontan cutthroat trout was established in the East Carson River. Subsequently, a fraction of this population became isolated in Silver King Creek to evolve into the present Paiute trout. This most recent evolution, however, occurred in isolation from all other fish species. This evolutionary history leading to the present Paiute trout, first with selection as a large lake predator and then in isolation in a small stream, makes the Paiute extremely vulnerable to extinction when other species of trout gain access to their habitat.

The real benefit to the Paiute of having its own subspecies name was the listing of *S. c. seleniris* under the Endangered Species Act, stimulating large-scale federal and state restoration efforts to save this fish from extinction. When I first visited Silver King Creek in 1964, the continued existence of Paiute trout was doubtful. Rainbow trout had been stocked into Silver King Creek above Llewellyn Falls and the population had thoroughly hybridized. The only pure populations at that time existed in two tiny isolated tributaries of Silver King Creek (Four Mile Canyon and Fly Valley Creeks) and a small introduced population in the North Fork Cottonwood Creek, a minuscule rivulet in Mono County, California.

To understand the precarious situation of the Paiute trout in 1964, it is necessary to review some historical events. Sometime after the 1933 description of the Paiute trout, testimony obtained by the California Department of Fish and Game revealed that no trout occurred above Llewellyn Falls in Silver King Creek until they were stocked by a sheepherder in 1912, who transplanted fish he caught below the falls. Thus, the original habitat of the Paiute trout was about six miles of Silver King Creek, from Llewellyn Falls downstream to a canyon area near the confluence with the East Carson River. A 1933 collection of specimens taken below Llewellyn Falls is made up of hybrids of rainbow trout and Paiute trout. If it were not for that early transplant the world would never have known that a unique spotless form of cutthroat trout ever existed.

An early transplant from Silver King Creek also established Paiute trout above a falls in Coyote Valley Creek, a tributary of lower Silver King Creek, and in its tributary, Corral Valley Creek. In 1946, Paiute trout were transported to the White Mountains of Mono County and stocked into the North Fork of Cottonwood Creek, a tiny, fishless stream near the Nevada–California border. In 1947, some Paiutes were moved above a falls in Fly Valley Creek, the uppermost tributary of Silver King Creek, to establish a new population in this formerly fishless stream. This proved to be a most significant transplant, because the Fly Valley population became the ultimate source to re-establish Paiute trout in the Silver King drainage after the hybridization tragedy occurred.

During the dark ages of fisheries management, when state fisheries programs consisted almost entirely of setting regulations, stocking lots of hatchery fish, and law enforcement, pack trains of mules and horses carrying eyed eggs and fry became a popular method of stocking mountain streams in the West. This is an example of the "Johnny Appleseed" mentality—to seed all headwater streams with eggs and baby trout in hopes that they would be fruitful and multiply. It seemed like a good idea but, in actual practice, these small headwater streams, with good habitat, were already overseeded from natural reproduction. Besides being a wasteful practice, headwater stocking of nonnative trout in the West was responsible for the virtual extinction of the native cutthroat trout throughout vast areas—such as the entire Lahontan Basin.

In 1949, a California Department of Fish and Game pack train, a lingering vestige from the dark ages, headed out with its cargo of baby rainbow trout. In the Carson River drainage the pack train took a wrong trail and Silver King Creek above Llewellyn Falls was mistakenly stocked. Coyote Valley and Corral Valley Creeks were also stocked with rainbow trout, and by 1964 all Paiute trout in the Silver King drainage were thoroughly hybridized with rainbow trout except for the small population isolated in Fly Valley Creek and a small population in Four Mile Canyon Creek, where a beaver dam had blocked access to the hybrids.

In late summer 1964, Silver King Creek, Coyote Valley Creek, and Corral Valley Creek were poisoned with rotenone to remove the hybrids. Pure fish from Fly Valley Creek were used to reestablish pure

PAIUTE CUTTHROAT TROUT
Oncorhynchus clarki seleniris

populations. Unfortunately, the eradication was not complete. After a few years, hybrids again appeared in Silver King Creek and Coyote Valley and Corral Valley Creeks. Intensive electrofishing to remove all hybrid specimens (those with more than five spots on the body) failed to reverse the tide of hybridization. Chemical treatment and restocking was again carried out in 1976 in Silver King Creek and in 1977 in Coyote Valley and Corral Valley Creeks. Again the hybrid eradication efforts failed. In recent years, hybrid specimens have been found in Silver King Creek and Coyote Valley Creek.

During my visit to Silver King Creek last summer, I estimated that 8.5 percent of the population appeared to be pure Paiute trout (including some of the largest Paiute specimens I had ever seen—11–12 inches) and 15 percent were hybrids. It can safely be predicted that hybridization will continually increase and Silver King Creek will have to be treated again if the goal of re-establishing a pure Paiute population is to be achieved.

Even in small streams, a complete fish kill from chemical treatment is extremely difficult. For the next treatment program, it will be essential to have a crew experienced in eradication techniques and the treatment done twice, in successive years, to ensure complete elimination of hybrids.

In the meantime, besides the pure populations in Fly Valley and Four Mile Canyon Creeks and in the North Fork Cottonwood Creek, a few small populations have been established in tiny, isolated streams in California. Paiute cutthroat trout are presently protected by angling closures, but I would suggest that an active propagation program be instituted to stock small lakes with Paiute trout for special regulation or no-kill fisheries. The opportunity for catching and perhaps photographing this rare and beautiful trout should stimulate increased public awareness and support for restoration programs. Paiute trout once stocked in Bircham Lake, Inyo County, attained a size of 18 inches (the world record for Paiute).

Many might wonder why habitat enhancement would be needed in Silver King Creek, so far from civilization. Silver King Creek is in a wilderness area of the Toiyable National Forest, where domestic livestock grazes on Forest Service lands. Cattle destroyed the riparian vegetation, caved in streambanks, and initiated erosion to degrade the habitat of Silver King Creek. Even protection granted by the Wilderness Act or the Endangered Species Act is not sufficient to overcome the forces of the powerful Western livestock lobby when conflicts between livestock and endangered species' habitat arise. Forest Service employees are well aware of political realities and the best they can hope for is a workable compromise.

In the case of Silver King Creek, the Forest Service worked out a revised grazing program with the livestock operator which will greatly lessen the cattle's impact on the creek. To more fully restore the habitat to near-pristine conditions and revegetate the streambanks, it was necessary to construct fencing to exclude the cattle from the stream in a critical meadow area of Silver King and to initiate erosion control measures. This is expensive, labor-intensive work. The Forest Service lacked the funds and manpower to get the job done. Thus, the cooperative venture between the Forest Service, California Fish and Game, and Trout Unlimited resulting in the volunteer task force to accomplish what needed to be done.

The diverse group of TU volunteers consisted of men, women, and children from all over the state. They all deserve a round of applause for devoting their holiday time to the Silver King Creek project. I would single out for special commendation a key individual as an example of the type of person necessary to make such projects successful.

Fred Divita was the first one up in the morning, before sunrise, to get the fire blazing and the coffee brewing. He took charge of preparing three hearty, gourmet meals each day for more than 50 people. After mealtime Fred was the most tireless worker, installing logs to protect an eroding streambank. I tried to keep up with him but ended up with a sore back. I couldn't keep up with him on the job or on the trail. I would be embarrassed to reveal Fred's age so I will only provide a clue with the term "three score and ten plus." All habitat enhancement projects should have people like Fred!

I found the Silver King project to be a learning experience regarding habitat enhancement methods. Since my return home, I have devoted some time to thinking and reading on the subject. Habitat improvement of trout streams is still much a trial-and-error, learn-by-doing type of activity—more of an art than a science. Present methods for protection of eroding streambanks, consisting of gabion baskets, large boulder rip-rap, or log revetments, is extremely labor-intensive and expensive. Thus, I have been learning more about the river restoration techniques of George Palmiter and of trout stream enhancement projects conducted by Allen Binns of the Wyoming Game and Fish Department, where the goal is to understand river hydrology and to work with the river to manipulate and dissipate the energy of flowing water with strategically placed brush and trees. I plan to participate in a U.S. Forest Service stream habitat workshop to be held at Colorado State University in 1987.

It's stimulating and exciting to learn new things and get involved in new and varied aspects of fisheries work. One can never tell where participation in a TU habitat project might lead.

AUTHOR'S NOTE

Despite supposed protection under the Endangered Species Act and the Paiute's occurrence in a wilderness area on U.S. Forest Service lands, the Silver King watershed suffered from a long history of livestock grazing—the cows had de facto priority over an endangered trout under multiple use management as practiced by federal agencies at the time. Livestock were eventually removed and the Paiute trout appeared to be sufficiently secure to change its ESA status from endangered to threaten. The entire distribution of Paiute trout, however, occurred outside its native range in Silver King Creek below the barrier falls. Several years ago, biologists of the California Department of Fish and Game and the U.S. Forest Service, began to plan an ambitious restoration program to chemically treat about eight miles of Silver King Creek below the falls to eliminate rainbow trout and hybrids and restore the Paiute trout to its original range. Meanwhile, a determined group of anti-chemical treatment people fought the proposed restoration at every step of the way. The chemical treatment was scheduled for September 2005. The last hurdle seemed to be approval by the California Water Board.

The restoration project had the backing of conservation organizations and all federal and state agencies involved, including the California Attorney General. I went to Sacramento in July 2005 to testify at the hearing. All went well and the water board granted the permit for chemical treatment. Was this success at last? Not by a long shot. The "chemophobes" as Ted Williams labels them, went to a federal judge who granted an injunction against the chemical treatment until a full environmental impact statement could be performed. The federal judge, with little understanding of the background of this case, thought it not unreasonable to require a complete environmental impact statement. The facts of the matter are that several years of surveys had demonstrated beyond any reasonable doubt that no protected or rare species of vertebrate or invertebrate animals would be affected by the treatment. Some aquatic invertebrates would be killed, but these species would rebound to their carrying capacity within weeks or months after treatment. That is, nothing new would be learned from an environmental impact statement that was not already known. The injunction effectively killed the project. After many years of study and expenditure of about $250,000, the agency people realized the implications of the injunction calling for further, needless studies (paralysis by analysis). Considering the costs and time involved to conform to the requirements of a complete environmental impact statement, they threw up their hands and threw in the towel; the chemophobes had won. This is unfortunate because fish restorations can't be done without chemical treatment. Essentially, there are no alternatives for eliminating nonnative species.

It's one of those situations that stir fond memories of the "good old days" of restoration. More than 35 years ago biologists with the U.S. Fish and Wildlife Service and National Park Service at Rocky Mountain National Park began to restore the greenback cutthroat trout in small streams above barriers after chemical treatment to remove all nonnative trout. My students and I would assist in the transplants. At the time, with about two dollars worth of rotenone, we could treat a mile or two of a small headwater stream. Nowadays, it is not so simple. Environmental assessments must be performed and public hearings held. It is at the public hearings that the chemophobes come to work their scare tactics by ranting and raving over irrelevant issues. The bottom line is that there are no feasible options to chemical treatment for restoring native trout and other native fishes threatened by nonnative species.

BROOK TROUT

SUMMER 1987

A BOYHOOD IMPRESSION INDELIBLY FIXED in my mind is the first trout of my life—a brook trout caught in the Rippowam River in Stamford, Connecticut. The elegant form and total beauty of the seven-inch fish in my hand induced such awe, wonder, and complete fascination that I ran home as fast as I could and placed the little fellow in a basin of water so I could observe the living fish and prolong my ecstasy. Undoubtedly, this imprint learning experience was a strong influence in determining direction in my life.

The brook trout, *Salvelinus fontinalis*, is a char, the common English name given to all members of the genus *Salvelinus*. Char can be spelled with one "r" or two (originally "charre") and the word is derived from the Gaelic "ceara"—red, blood-colored. The first English and European immigrants to America were probably only vaguely familiar with the Arctic char, *S. alpinus*, in their homelands because it is restricted to deep lakes. The brook char they encountered in North America was ecologically and morphologically more similar to the European brown trout, *Salmo trutta*, than to other species of char; thus, it would logically be called "trout" by the first European settlers. No inviolate rules or protocol can be invoked to determine the most correct common name of *Salvelinus fontinalis*; "brook trout" or "brook char" is equally correct so long as the scientific "Latinized" name leaves no doubt what species is being referred to.

Species in the genus *Salvelinus* are distinguished from species of the other genera of the family Salmonidae by the absence of black spots on the body. *Salvelinus* species also lack teeth on the shaft of the vomer bone in the roof of the mouth and have tube-like lateral line scales. These two traits are shared with the genera Hucho and Brachymystax, with which *Salvelinus* evidently shares common ancestry. *S. fontinalis* differs from other species of *Salvelinus* by the mottled, worm-like markings (vermiculations) on their back and on the dorsal fin and tail.

The brook trout has been one of the most intensively studied fish species in the world in regard to its life history, ecology, behavior, and physiology. Yet its intraspecific taxonomic structure is not well-defined. For example, should subspecies of brook trout be recognized for northern and southern races? What are the aurora trout of Ontario and the silver trout of Monadnock Lake, New Hampshire? Are they only "color varieties" of *S. fontinalis*, subspecies of *fontinalis*, or distinct species?

The native distribution of brook trout in northeastern North America covers a vast area from tributaries of Hudson Bay (to northeast Manitoba) and James Bay in the north, continuously southward throughout Ontario, Quebec, Labrador, the Island of Newfoundland, New England, the Great Lakes and upper Mississippi drainage of Minnesota and Wisconsin (and the Iowa River of Iowa), and on both sides of the Appalachian Mountains to northeast Georgia and northwest South Carolina.

There are some unusual and unexplainable aspects of the original distribution of brook trout, such as its native range in Michigan.

Brook trout occurred naturally only in rivers of the northern tip of the Lower Peninsula, north of a line drawn from Traverse Bay (Lake Michigan) to Thunder Bay (Lake Huron). South of this area, the Michigan grayling was native. Many of Michigan's most famous trout streams—the Pere Marquette, Manistee, Muskegon (Lake Michigan tributaries), and the Au Sable River (Lake Huron tributary)—lacked brook trout before they were stocked. These rivers had native grayling,

which soon became extinct after brook, brown, and rainbow trout were introduced. Why didn't brook trout establish natural populations in the rivers of lower Michigan by movement along the coasts of Lake Michigan and Lake Huron? Superficially, it would appear that brook trout and grayling are incompatible (competitive exclusion), but both species naturally occurred together in the Jordan River (Traverse Bay area) and in Otter Creek of the Upper Peninsula (tributary to Lake Superior). Brook trout became readily established in Lower Peninsula drainages after they were introduced by man.

In Ohio, brook trout were native to only two streams (Lake Erie Basin), but were absent from Cold Creek, Ohio's best trout stream (Castalia Trout Club waters). The first artificial propagation of fish in the United States was with brook trout near Cleveland, Ohio, by Theodatus Garlick and H. A. Ackley in 1853. Garlick traveled almost

BROOK TROUT
Salvelinus fontinalis

600 miles to Sault Ste. Marie to obtain large specimens in the outlet of Lake Superior, for their broodstock.

With such a vast range, exposure to evolution in diverse environments, and the rearrangements of the landscape during the last glacial period, it would be expected that a great amount of intraspecific diversity is contained in *S. fontinalis* which can be applied in modern fisheries management. A simple example concerns the proclivity for benthic feeding in brook trout and pelagic feeding in rainbow trout, which suggests that if both species are stocked in a lake, the total food supply (benthic invertebrates and pelagic zooplankton) will be more fully utilized and total trout production will increase. Ecologically, brook trout can be divided into three major groups: those evolving in large lakes with specialization as lacustrine predators; sea-run populations that use the marine environment for feeding and rapid growth for a few months of the year; and the "generalist" type of brook trout whose evolution since the last glacial period has been associated with small streams and ponds.

The most common and widely distributed type of brook trout is of the generalist ancestry. They rarely live much more than three years or attain a size much larger than 12 inches. Recognizing the genetic basis for different types of life histories and the limitations of hatchery stocks of brook trout imposed by their evolutionary history and domestication, many years ago the late Dwight Webster of Cornell University imported the Temiscamie and Assinica strains of brook trout from Canada as representatives of the large predatory form. Webster and Bill Flick studied the performance of the Canadian strains in Adirondack lakes for years. They conclusively demonstrated a great advantage in survival, longevity, maximum size, and total return to the fishery of the wild Canadian strains over hatchery strains. In recent years, the Assinica and Temiscamie brook trout have been raised and stocked in several states, but we have barely scratched the surface in regard to innovative uses of the genetic diversity of *S. fontinalis* in fisheries management.

It should be understood that Flick found the Temiscamie and As-sinica brook trout to be extremely susceptible to angling. Even with light angling pressure, it is necessary to impose restrictive regulations if the inherent longevity and growth potential of these strains are to be realized in a fishery. There are numerous races of brook trout with the genetic potential to produce a new world record if introduced into a new lake with optimum environmental conditions and abundant forage.

The 14½-pound brook trout caught by Dr. J.W. Cook in the Nipigon River has been the world record for the species since 1916. The Nipigon River was famous for large brook trout. Nineteenth-century reports include fish up to 17 and 19 pounds. I suspect that the Nipigon no longer produces record brook trout because the original race that produced these giant fish was lost. A dam was constructed on the Nipigon River which blocked fish movement between Lake Superior and Lake Nipigon. It is likely that the great size of the Nipigon brook trout was related to feeding and spawning migrations between the two lakes. When the migration route was blocked, this particular race was lost.

The Rangeley Lakes of Maine, a most significant area in the lore and history of brook trout, was noted for large brook trout in the nineteenth century. Specimens of 12 and 12½ pounds were recorded. In the Rangeley Lakes, brook trout originally coexisted and preyed on relict populations of Arctic char, locally known as blueback trout. About 1890, Atlantic salmon and smelt were stocked and became established, which led to the extinction of the blueback trout and a change in the feeding relationships of brook trout. Since then, brook trout in the Rangeley Lakes have never attained their former maximum size.

Brook trout of world record size on Long Island, implied in the legend of the brook trout and Daniel Webster, is a myth similar to the story of the devil and Daniel Webster. When Samuel Mitchill described the species *fontinalis* in 1815, based on the fish known to him in the vicinity of New York City, he discussed the excellent trout fisheries known on Long Island at that time. Long Island trout averaged less than one pound and the largest specimen Mitchell had heard of weighed 4½ pounds.

Brook trout have been introduced all over the world, although not with the success of brown and rainbow trout introductions. Some exceptionally large brook trout are known in some South American lakes. I can recall a photograph in an Ashaway Line catalog of many years ago of a brook trout from Argentina reputed to be 15 pounds.

Concerning geographic variation in brook trout, populations native to the southern Appalachian Mountains differ from typical northern brook trout by their more profuse, smaller spots. Biologists at Pennsylvania State University published a paper in 1981 on an electrophoretic analysis of enzymes of brook trout from three populations from Pennsylvania, two from New York, two from Tennessee, and one from Great Smoky Mountains National Park in North Carolina. The three southern samples clearly differed from the five northern samples at a level typical of subspecies differentiation. A problem is that there are no comparisons of brook trout in the intervening area of Virginia and West Virginia. If a complete transition occurs between northern and southern brook trout, then the case for separate subspecies recognition is weakened.

During the past 100 years, the distribution of the southern Appalachian brook has been drastically reduced by environmental changes and the introduction of rainbow and brown trout which have pushed the remaining brook trout populations back to the uppermost headwaters. Several protection and restoration programs are attempting to halt and reverse this decline. In Great Smoky Mountains National Park, certain streams, in which rainbow trout distribution overlaps with brook trout, are systematically electrofished to remove the rainbow trout (which are transplanted downstream in public angling waters).

It is ironic that the most massive abundance of brook trout now occurs in the West, where they are a nonnative species. Brook trout dominate most headwater streams of the Rockies, Sierras, and Cascade Mountains, where they have replaced native subspecies of cutthroat trout. A common practice for cutthroat restoration concerns poisoning brook trout and restocking with the native cutthroat.

The "aurora trout," known from three lakes in the headwaters of the Montreal River (Saint Lawrence River Basin), Ontario, was described as a new species, *Salvelinus timagamiensis*, in 1925. At first it was believed to be related to Arctic char rather than brook trout, but subsequent studies have clearly demonstrated that the aurora trout was derived from a brook trout ancestor. The aurora trout differs from brook trout by the absence of vermiculated markings. Currently, the aurora trout is recognized as a subspecies of brook trout, although it did occur together with brook trout without hybridizing in one of its native lakes.

The most interesting and mysterious variety of char related to the brook trout is the silver trout of Monadnock Lake, Dublin, New Hampshire. The local people of the area had long known that large numbers of "silver trout" would suddenly appear in shallow water for spawning each October, and they would be snagged and snared for human and hog food. The first written account of the Monadnock silver trout appeared in 1850 when it was already mentioned that their abundance had declined from former times. In the 1870s and '80s, fishermen claimed that because the silver trout was not a brook trout ("normal" brook trout also occurred in Monadnock Lake and spawned about two weeks later than the silver trout), they were not protected under brook trout regulations in regard to season and bag limits. This caused the New Hampshire Fish Commission to send specimens of silver trout to Harvard and to the U.S. National Museum for identification. It was first identified as a form of lake trout and then as a variety of brook trout. In 1885 the silver trout was described as a new species, *Salvelinus agassizi*. W. C. Kendall studied the silver trout, and the results of his study, including a color painting, are included in his monograph of New England chars published in 1914. Kendall concluded that the silver trout was related to the Arctic char rather than the brook trout because their body shape and tail are more similar to Arctic char and they lacked vermiculated markings on the body.

Not much more has been said about the silver trout of Monadnock Lake since Kendall's 1914 monograph.

About 20 years ago I was studying trout specimens in the National Museum's fish collections and I came across 13 specimens of silver trout collected from Monadnock Lake in the 1870s and '80s. When I examined them I realized that the silver trout was derived from a brook trout ancestor—markings on dorsal fin and tail and numbers of vertebrae, gillrakers, and pelvic fin rays are characteristic of brook trout and of no other species of char. But they were quite distinct from brook trout. I found 8 of the 13 specimens to have basibranchial teeth (tiny teeth in throat between gill arches) and the structure of the gillrakers was highly distinctive. Most of the protuberances on the gill arches were rudimentary knobs bearing tiny teeth, similar to gillrakers of highly predacious fish such as northern pike.

The differentiation of characters in the silver trout specimens I examined is outside the range of variation of *S. fontinalis*. Undoubtedly, the silver trout of Monadnock Lake represented a significant divergence from a brook trout ancestor—perhaps evolving to fill the "lake trout niche" outside the range of lake trout. It is improbable that this significant evolutionary divergence could have occurred in Monadnock Lake during the past few thousand years. More likely, the silver trout of Monadnock Lake is a relict of an ancient lake system. As the last glaciers retreated from the Connecticut River Valley, a series of large glacial lakes formed. One of these, Lake Hitchcock, was more than 150 miles long, extending from Connecticut into New Hampshire and Vermont, and persisted for 4,000 years. Kendall also found a form of silver trout in Christine Lake, Stark, New Hampshire. Both Monadnock and Christine Lakes are in the Connecticut River Basin; both have similar characteristics   deep, clear, cold, well oxygenated. The evidence suggests that the silver trout diverged from a brook trout ancestor, its evolution directed toward specialization for pelagic life in large glacial lakes. When the large glacial lakes disappeared the silver trout persisted in the most suitable environments to which they had access—Monadnock and Christine Lakes.

The silver trout is presumed extinct. In 1939, the New Hampshire Fish and Game Department published the Biological Survey of the Connecticut Watershed. The results of sampling Monadnock and Christine Lakes were given in this report. No silver trout were found and they were believed to be extinct due to stocking of nonnative fishes such as rainbow, brown, and lake trout, salmon, and smelt.

I would prefer not to finish a story on the dismal theme of extinction, so I will mention that the January 1939 issue of *Outdoor Life* contained a story entitled "Warriors in Silver," with the intriguing heading, "As mysteriously as it had disappeared, a scrappy species of trout returns to a mountain lake." The story concerns catching silver trout in Monadnock Lake and has a photo of an angler holding four silver trout of about two to three pounds. Are they indeed *S. agassizi*? I cannot tell from the photo; I would have to examine their gillrakers for positive identification.

If anyone believes he has caught a true silver trout, I request that the specimen be preserved and I be notified. Until then, I will consider that *S. agassizi*, the most interesting divergence in brook trout evolution, is most probably extinct. But, based on the lessons of the return from "extinction" of the original Pyramid Lake and Alvord Basin cutthroat trout, there is always hope.

I was partly in error when I stated that a dam blocked access of coaster brook trout from Lake Superior to Lake Nipigon. A natural barrier falls on the Nipigon River had blocked this access long before the dam was constructed. The world record brook trout of 14½ pounds caught in the Nipigon River in 1916 is one of the longest standing fish records. A flurry of excitement occurred in late 2006 when a story with a color photograph appeared in the media of a brook trout caught, measured, and released on Barbe Lake, Manitoba. The angler claimed it was 29 inches in length with a girth of 21 inches. Its weight was estimated at about 16 pounds. This giant brookie lacks the required documentation to officially be recognized as a new world record, but it suggests, that after more than 90 years, a new world record brook trout might be caught and properly documented.

KAMLOOPS TROUT

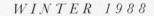

WINTER 1988

KAMLOOPS TROUT CAN BE MOST SIMPLY DEFINED as a form of rainbow trout native to the upper Columbia and upper Fraser River Basins of British Columbia. The problem with such a definition is that it is too simple to be informative. Burgundy can be defined as a form of wine, but such a simple definition is not at all useful to someone seeking an in-depth understanding and appreciation of wines.

My first exposure to the Kamloops trout was in the summer of 1957 when the late Paul Needham and I made a trip from California to Alaska. Our aim was to collect and preserve specimens of rainbow and cutthroat trout which we believed would provide the basic evidence to resolve the confusion surrounding the evolution and classification of Western trouts. I must admit that I had a more naive faith then in the orderliness of nature, in the ability of "research" to provide a clear understanding of how evolution works, and how we could interpret evolutionary diversity for an unambiguous system of classification.

One of the confusing forms of rainbow trout in need of study was the Kamloops trout, which had, at various times, been considered as a distinct species, a subspecies, and a "form" of rainbow trout. (The Kamloops trout was first described by David Starr Jordan in 1892 as *Oncorhynchus kamloops*, under the mistaken belief that it represented a landlocked species of Pacific salmon.) On our return trip, we made several collections of trout from the upper Fraser River Basin to obtain material to characterize the Kamloops trout. Although nets were sometimes used during our 1957 collecting trip, most of our specimens were collected with a fly rod. The most distinctive attribute I recall about Kamloops trout was their spectacular fighting ability—of all the "forms" sampled, the Kamloops were the most fun!

On our way down the Fraser River, we stopped for a few days to visit Tommy Brayshaw and his wife Becky at Hope, British Columbia. Tommy Brayshaw was a friend of Roderick Haig-Brown (he did the illustrations for Haig-Brown's book, *The Western Angler*.) Both Brayshaw and Haig-Brown represented an extremely rare form of angler: anglers who have an obsession for learning about all aspects of their beloved fish—their biology, life history, evolution, and classification. Haig-Brown and Brayshaw avidly sought out scientific literature on trout biology. They read it, discussed it, and exchanged information.

Tommy Brayshaw was the first person I met who had first-hand, in-depth information on Kamloops trout, and I asked his opinion on the question: What exactly is a Kamloops trout? Much of what we discussed can be found in Haig-Brown's book, *The Western Angler*, and concerns attempts to delineate the relative roles of nature and nurture for a decision on the status of Kamloops trout.

That is, how much of the differences that have been used to characterize Kamloops trout are the result of heredity (nature) and how much are due to direct environmental influence (nurture)? The question of formal taxonomic recognition as a separate species or subspecies concerns the origin of Kamloops trout. Can all the rainbow trout native to the upper Fraser and upper Columbia River Basins be traced to one common ancestral divergence from all other evolutionary lines of rainbow trout? If so, then are there hereditary, identifying characters possessed by these populations that differentiate Kamloops trout from all other forms of rainbow trout? The answer to this question is affirmative if Kamloops trout are regarded as lake-adapted populations of the Columbia River redband trout, as I discussed in my article on redband trout in the autumn 1986 issue of *Trout*. Thus, Kamloops trout are part of the subspecies *Salmo gairdneri gairdneri* which also includes anadromous steelhead trout and resident redband trout native to the upper Columbia and Fraser Basins.

The vagueness and lack of a precise definition for Kamloops trout in relation to its position in an evolutionary and taxonomic context can be traced to work performed by a Canadian biologist, Charles Mottley, in the 1930s. At the time, the main criterion used to distinguish Kamloops trout from coastal rainbow trout (which I classify as the subspecies *S. g. irideus*) was the number of scales along the body. Kamloops trout were believed to have an average of about 20 more scales than the coastal rainbow. Mottley incubated Kamloops eggs at different temperatures and demonstrated that the fish hatched from these eggs had significantly different numbers of scales in relation to the temperatures of embryonic development. This work led to the unfortunate conclusion that character differences used to distinguish different forms of trout were mainly due to direct environmental influence and not heredity—nurture not nature was considered to be the main determinant of forms of trout.

The conclusion was unfortunate because it led to an unwarranted inductive leap that has long plagued fisheries management. If nurture not nature predominates in determining characters (including life history attributes such as feeding, growth, longevity, etc.), then any generic hatchery rainbow trout can duplicate all the attributes of a Kamloops trout if stocked in a "Kamloops" environment. This is a very wrong conclusion and it has taken many years for fisheries biologists and managers to begin to understand the dangers of a mistaken faith in nurture over nature in relation to forms of trout and salmonid fishes in general.

Haig-Brown is widely regarded as an author par excellence of angling literature. I highly admire his work because he was informed and accurate, without sham; his work has authenticity. His writings reflect outstanding judgment or, simply, common sense.

Regarding the status of the Kamloops trout, he wrote in *The Western Angler*: "As we have decided, the Kamloops is, strictly speaking, simply a subspecies of the steelhead. He is a rainbow trout which has certain slight structural differences from the originally-described members of the species, but none that may not be readily modified by change of environment. From the point of view of the scientist and naturalist, this is a thoroughly logical and desirable simplification, and the loophole left by the subspecific rating is all that the angler needs. An angler's view of his fish, though it should be at least related to that of the scientist, is not necessarily identical with it. Differences of habit, of habitat, of those qualities which go to make up what he considers a game fish—even superficial differences in appearance—naturally mean more to the angler than the slight structural differences that separate two closely related fish."

Although Haig-Brown's concept of the Kamloops trout subspecies somewhat differs from my current concept, the point he makes, that subtle differences in "habit and habitat" (life history and ecology) can be very important to anglers, is certainly valid—more so than he realized. The true significance of the notion that intraspecific life history differences, completely unrelated to formal taxonomic recognition as a species or subspecies, can be of extreme importance to fisheries management can be illustrated by using the Kamloops trout as an example.

A useful analogy to help understand the significance of intraspecific diversity in the rainbow trout species, and, also, of the roles of nature and nurture as determining influences on the ultimate product, is to consider wines made from grapes.

Virtually all wine is made from a single species of grape, *Vitus vinifera*. Differences in quality—color, taste, body, aroma—are due to intraspecific differences or varieties in the species *Vitus vinifera* interacting with differences in soils and climate. Thus, the hereditary basis of different varieties of vines determining the basic color, flavor, size, and shape of the grape are not influenced by soils and climate; but subtle flavor differences are environmentally induced by soils and climate, resulting in different vintages from the same vines in different years. Similarly,

in rainbow trout, there is a strong hereditary component governing life history and behavior attributes such as anadromy, nonanadromy, age at maturity, and maximum life span, but each year-class (or "vintage") of a single population may exhibit different growth rates and mortality rates in relation to climate and food supply.

A "taxonomy" of wines used for precise classification includes the variety of grape, the region where it is grown, and a particular subregion or estate.

To a wine connoisseur, the wine contained in a bottle from a prized estate has a much greater significance and value than the vin ordinaire in a gallon jug of "country red" or "mountain burgundy," although all of these wines represent intraspecific diversity in *Vitus vinifera* interacting with environmental differences.

For the intelligent use of intraspecific diversity in fisheries management, we must attain a degree of understanding of the subject com-

GERRARD KAMLOOPS TROUT
Oncorhynchus mykiss gairdneri

parable to that of a wine connoisseur. For example, consider a goal to produce a new world-record rainbow trout.

The Kamloops trout known to possess the hereditary attributes to attain an extremely large size can be identified as a small "estate" in a particular "region" of intraspecific diversity—namely, the Gerrard strain of Kamloops of Kootenay Lake, British Columbia (upper Columbia River Basin). A "generic Kamloops" won't do; only the Gerrard strain of Kootenay Lake is known to have the evolutionary specializations resulting in older age at maturity, long life span, and capacity for rapid and sustained growth necessary to produce a rainbow trout of more than 40 pounds. Virtually all Kamloops trout of the Gerrard strain in Kootenay Lake spawn for the first time when they are five-, six-, or seven-years-old (most generic rainbow trout have died of old age by age five). The average size of spawners is about 10 pounds and the general maximum age and size is 10 years and about 25 pounds in Kootenay Lake. When stocked in other waters with a superabundance of food, the Gerrard Kamloops can reach 50 pounds or more.

The two most obvious examples demonstrating the growth potential of the Gerrard Kamloops are Jewel Lake, British Columbia and Lake Pend Oreille, Idaho. Jewel Lake, in the Columbia Basin, is just north of the British Columbia–Washington State border. It was barren of trout until stocked with Gerrard Kamloops in 1924. Several stories of fish in excess of 50 pounds originated from Jewel Lake. The most authentic report is of a fish weighing 52 pounds 8 ounces caught in 1932. A photograph of this fish can be seen in *The Fisherman's Encyclopedia* (Stackpole, 1950). If this 50-pound-plus fish caught in 1932 originated from the 1924 stocking of Jewel Lake, then it would have been eight-years-old. Gerrard Kamloops stocked in Lake Pend Oreille in 1942 were exposed to a superabundance of kokanee salmon—their preferred food. In 1946, a four-year-old Kamloops was caught weighing 32 pounds, and in 1947, a five-year-old fish was taken at 37 pounds. The 37-pounder was 40½ inches in length and had a girth of 28 inches. A typical Gerrard Kamloops in Kootenay Lake would weigh about 25

pounds at about 40 inches in length and would be nine- or ten-years-old. An occasional fish can grow much larger. In Steve Raymond's book, *Kamloops*, he states that a 52-pound fish from Kootenay Lake was taken during spawning operations in 1930.

A most interesting aspect of the Kamloops trout of Kootenay Lake, which illustrates the importance of recognizing the specificity between races of trout analogous to estate-bottled wine, is that there are three or more races of Kamloops trout native to Kootenay Lake. One race is associated with the west arm of the lake, another with the south arm; the Gerrard race is associated with the north arm, but may range into other areas for feeding. Although a definitive study is yet to be made on the Kamloops trout diversity of Kootenay Lake, it appears that the other races, which do not spawn in the Lardeau River, can be classified as *vin ordinaire* rainbow trout. They apparently spawn when they are three or four years of age at about two to four pounds and their maximum size is about 10 pounds. No significant structural or quantitative genetic differences are known between the small, ordinary Kamloops and the giant Gerrard Kamloops in Kootenay. The truly significant difference concerns their life histories; each evolved to fill different trout niches in a large lake—these differences are genetically (hereditarily) based.

The Gerrard strain originally spawned in the Lardeau River and in the Duncan River, a tributary to the Lardeau (north end of lake). The giant Gerrard Kamloops was never highly abundant, but its numbers declined after a dam blocked spawning in the Duncan River. In recent years spawning runs have ranged from about 350 to about 950 fish, but only about 1,500 square yards of optimum spawning grounds are available in the Lardeau near Gerrard. In 1980, an estimated 1,200 trout caught in Kootenay Lake weighed more than 10 pounds, and about 700 of these weighed more than 15 pounds. Considering that Kootenay Lake is 65 miles long and covers 100,000 surface acres, the chances of an angler encountering one of these trophies is obviously slim.

The possible reality of producing 50-pound rainbow trout relates to finding opportune waters such as Jewel Lake and Pend Oreille that could be stocked with the Gerrard Kamloops. Lake Pend Oreille still produces a few trout of more than 20 pounds, but the glory days of the 1940s are not likely to be repeated. The Gerrard Kamloops has hybridized with ordinary rainbow trout stocked in tributaries, thus diluting their purity, and the abundance of kokanee has drastically declined. I suspect that Gerrard Kamloops could have produced specimens exceeding 50 pounds if they had been stocked in Lake Michigan during the boom in alewife abundance and before the lake was overstocked with Chinook and coho salmon.

The Gerrard Kamloops trout is a highly specialized fish for special types of environments; it is not the trout for all seasons or for all waters. Like rare estate wine, it is a fish for special occasions. Effective use of intraspecific diversity—such as the Gerrard Kamloops—in fisheries management, requires that fisheries managers acquire a knowledge and sophisticated understanding of the subject at least comparable to that of wine connoisseurs. They must at least be able to discriminate between estate-bottled and vin ordinaire, and appreciate the difference.

AUTHOR'S NOTE

My rather inclusive subspecies *Oncorhynchus mykiss gairdneri* for the native forms of rainbow trout east of the Cascade Mountains in the Columbia and upper Fraser River basins would horrify those that adhere to a taxonomy based on a strict interpretation of the finest evolutionary branching points. My classification of the subspecies *gairdneri* is based on the earliest invasion of a rainbow trout ancestor into the Columbia basin in the preglacial and early glacial periods, and, an early postglacial connection of the upper Fraser River to the Upper Columbia. After thousands of generations under natural selection to fill different ecological niches, three distinct types of life histories evolved. Especially in the upper Fraser basin, in large lakes with native populations of kokanee salmon, the redband trout coevolved a predator-prey relationship and attains a large size; potentially, the largest size of any form of rainbow trout. These are the Kamloops trout. The name comes from the Kamloops region of British Columbia, which, in turn, is based on a Shuswap

Native American term meaning a meeting of the waters. The North and South Thompson rivers meet at Kamloops Lake.

Another divergence specialized for an anadromous life history. These are the steelhead populations of the subspecies. The third life history form is made up of resident populations inhabiting a vast area northwards from northern Nevada to western Montana into British Columbia.

In this column, I emphasized the significance of recognizing the great range of diversity found in the subspecies *gairdneri*, regardless of the taxonomic system used to classify this diversity. I again make an analogy with wine and the wine grape, *Vitus vinifera*. The intraspecific diversity found in *Vitus vinifera* has a long history of recognition, appreciation, and management to preserve this diversity. It can serve as a useful model for proper management and preservation of the intraspecific diversity inherent in *O. mykiss*.

MEXICAN GOLDEN TROUT

SPRING 1988

TROUT HAVE LONG BEEN KNOWN TO OCCUR in Mexico, but the diversity and complexity of Mexican native trout have become apparent only in recent times. Several distinct forms of native trout are known from the Sierra Madre Occidental of the mainland, in high elevation tributaries to the Gulf of California (also known as the Sea of Cortez), and in one stream of the San Pedro Matir Mountains of northern Baja California. The most distinctive of these forms was in 1964 described as a new species: the Mexican golden trout, *Salmo chrysogaster.*

The Mexican golden trout and all Mexican trout, along with the Gila and Apache trout, have their closest relationships to the rainbow trout line of evolution rather than to the cutthroat trout line. They represent varying degrees of evolutionary divergences from a primitive ancestor of the rainbow. The Baja Peninsula and warm southern ocean temperatures have protected the Gulf of California from large-scale invasions of "modern" forms of rainbow trout, creating a refuge area for the persistence of ancient forms.

The first record of Mexican trout published in a scientific journal was by the famous paleontologist E. D. Cope in 1886. Cope's short note, entitled "The Most Southern Salmon," concerned two specimens of trout sent to him by Professor Lupton from "the southern part of the State of Chihuahua near the boundaries of Durango and Sinaloa." Cope believed the specimens to be cutthroat trout. He wrote, "The specimens are young and have teeth on the basihyal bones, as in *Salmo purpuratus*, which they otherwise resemble." (*S. purpuratus* is a name that was incorrectly used for cutthroat trout, *S. clarki*.)

This first record of trout in Mexico also introduces the first mystery and confusion concerning Mexican trout. The precise collection locality with identification of the river basin was not included with the specimens sent by Professor Lupton to Cope. The correct identity of these first specimens probably will never be known, because they were never seen again and have never been found in any museum collection. Cope's mention of "basihyal" teeth can be assumed to mean basibranchial teeth, the tiny teeth that occur between the gill arches in cutthroat trout (absent in rainbow trout). Examination of hundreds of Mexican trout specimens collected from numerous localities since 1886 has failed to find a single specimen with basibranchial teeth. If Cope was correct, and his specimens were a form of cutthroat trout, then this first record of Mexican trout represents a form of trout that has not been found since 1886.

This dubious record of cutthroat trout in Mexico has long persisted in the literature. The 1984 edition of Ernest Schwiebert's *Trout*, for example, gives the distribution of cutthroat trout "…from the mountains of northern Mexico to the Alpine tributaries of Alaskan rivers."

Most of the early records of the occurrence of trout after 1886 were made by E.W. Nelson, a naturalist with the U.S. Biological Survey who served as chief of this bureau from 1916 to 1927. (In 1940 the Biological Survey of the Department of Agriculture and the Bureau of Fisheries of the Department of Commerce were combined into a new agency, the Fish and Wildlife Service in the Department of Interior.) Nelson made natural history observations and collections on the Mexican mainland in 1898 and in Baja in 1905, traveling on horseback.

In 1898 Nelson attempted to find the trout described by Cope in 1886. He found trout in streams draining the slopes of Mount Mohinora, a few miles south of Guadalupe y Calvo in southern Chihauhua. There are three rivers tributary to the Gulf of California whose headwaters drain the slopes of Mount Mohinora; all are presently known to contain only the Mexican golden trout. The headwaters of the Rio Fuerte drain the northern and northeastern slopes of Mount Mohinora. The Rio Culiacan drains the southeastern slope, and the Rio Sinaloa drains the southern and western slopes. It can be assumed that Nelson collected Mexican golden trout in 1898, probably from the headwaters of the Rio Sinaloa. Unfortunately, the specimens were not described, and evidently they were not preserved in any museum collection.

Also in 1898, Nelson reported trout in a stream tributary to the Rio del Presidio near El Salto, Durango, about 70 miles west of Durango City. There has been debate concerning the origin of the Rio del Presidio trout—native or introduced. I believe the Rio del Presidio trout are native, because their distinctive characteristics cannot be explained by any known form of rainbow trout propagated in hatcheries. If they are native, the headwaters of the Rio del Presidio, just north and just south of 24° N latitude (virtually on the Tropic of Cancer and south of the southernmost tip of Florida) represents the most southern natural distribution of any species of the family Salmonidae. A subspecies of the Far Eastern masu salmon (*Oncorhynchus masou*) is native to the headwaters of a mountain stream on the island of Taiwan just north of 24° N latitude. The southernmost natural distribution of brown trout, *Salmo trutta*, occurs in the Atlas Mountains of North Africa at about 34° N–36° N latitude and in the Orontes River of Lebanon at about 34° N.

All of these distributions reflect a colder climate and colder ocean temperatures during glacial periods, which allowed salmonid fishes to extend their ranges much farther southward than has been naturally possible during the past several thousand years. These salmonid relics have persisted to the present in the most southern areas only where mountain rivers maintain cool temperatures.

Fossils of trout and salmon have been found in the Lake Chapala basin about 250 miles south of the headwaters of the Rio del Presidio. One of the fossils has been described as a new (but extinct) species, *Salmo australis*, by Ted Cavender (Ohio State University) and Robert Miller (University of Michigan), who have described many salmonid fish fossils.

The skull of *S. australis* indicates a trout of about three feet in length. Lake Chapala once connected to the Rio Lerma, which flows into the Pacific Ocean as the Rio Grand de Santiago about 100 miles south of the mouth of the Rio del Presidio (which enters the ocean about 10 miles south of Mazatlan).

Thus, it is likely that during the four major glacial epochs of the Pleistocene—beginning almost two million years ago with the onset of the first epoch and terminating only about 10,000 years ago—there were periods when trout and salmon occurred in Mexican rivers at least as far south as the Rio Grande de Santiago.

The effects of introduction of hatchery trout on the distribution and purity of the native trout of Mexico cannot be ignored.

In 1888, 33,000 McCloud River rainbow trout were sent by the U.S. Fish Commission to Señor Chazari of the Mexican Fish Commission. At that time, a hatchery was constructed on the upper Rio Lerma.

None of the Mexican trout I have examined, however, are identical to the McCloud rainbow.

During Nelson's Baja expedition of 1905, he preserved specimens of the Rio Santo Domingo trout. In 1908, B.W. Evermann described the Santo Domingo trout as a new species, *Salmo nelsoni*. The Baja rainbow has the most recent origin and the least differentiation from the modern coastal rainbow trout of all the Mexican trout. There is no valid basis to recognize the Baja trout as a distinct species. The ocean temperatures off northern Baja are still sufficiently cold to maintain Pacific salmon and steelhead trout. With a trend for a cooler and wetter climate allowing perennial flow in the Rio Santo Domingo to reach the Pacific Ocean, a steelhead run would likely become established. The present isolation of the Rio Santo Domingo trout has been a matter of only a few thousand years, not sufficient time for significant differentiation to take place. Taxonomically, there is little justification to recognize *nelsoni* as a subspecies of *S. gairdneri*. But the name has been officially endowed upon the Santo Domingo trout, and has well served to emphasize the fact that the Santo Domingo rainbow is the only trout native to Baja California. As such, Mexican fisheries biologists have undertaken studies and transplant operations to ensure the perpetuation of their native "*nelsoni*," a small segment of the biodiversity of the rainbow trout species and of the biological heritage of Mexico.

After Evermann's 1908 paper on Baja trout, little more was learned of Mexican trout until Paul Needham, then employed by the U.S. Bureau of Fisheries, led expeditions to the Rio Santo Domingo in 1936, 1937, and 1938. Needham visited Mexico with the objective of bringing live fish back to start a hatchery brood stock. The idea in back of the expedition was that the Rio Santo Domingo rainbow might offer advantages over available hatchery rainbow trout by a tolerance of higher temperatures and a lesser migratory propensity after stocking. Need-

MEXICAN GOLDEN TROUT
Oncorhynchus chrysogaster

ham was successful in bringing the Santo Domingo trout back alive, but all perished in fish hatcheries before they were spawned.

In 1952, Needham led an expedition to the Rio Truchas (tributary to the Rio San Lorenzo) on the Mexican mainland, also to bring back live fish for a hatchery brood stock—again, all fish died before spawning. This was followed by trips by Needham and University of California students in 1955 and 1956, during which trout were collected and preserved from numerous localities from several different river basins tributary to the Gulf of California. The collections and examination of the specimens culminated in a 1959 University of California Publications in *Zoology* (Volume 67, Number 1), titled "Rainbow Trout in Mexico and California," authored by Needham and Richard Gard. This publication might be considered as somewhat of a collectors' item by collectors of angling literature, because it contains a color plate of the Mexican golden trout painted by Tommy Brayshaw, whose artwork graced some of Haig-Brown's books.

The basic distinctions of the Mexican golden trout are well depicted in Brayshaw's painting—the sparse spotting pattern along the dorsal surface, the light golden body color intensifying to orange on the ventral region, the coloration and markings on fins.

In Needham and Gard's 1959 publication, none of the Mexican trout populations they compared was described as new species or subspecies; all were considered as "forms" of rainbow trout, *Salmo gairdneri*. Comparable data on characters such as the number of scales, vertebrae, fin rays, pyloric caeca (appendages on intestine) were not available on rainbow trout from throughout their range.

In 1957, I began my studies on Western trout with Needham, and we collected rainbow and cutthroat trout from California to Alaska. When the examination of these specimens was completed and their characters compared with characters of Mexican trout, distinctions were apparent; the Mexican golden trout was formally described as a new species.

Besides the distinctive appearance of the Mexican golden trout, they were found to have the lowest number of vertebrae and pyloric caeca of any form of rainbow or cutthroat trout. The typical number of vertebrae in Mexican golden trout is 57 and 58, whereas most rainbow trout have 62–64 (cutthroat typically have 60–63). The other Western trout with the lowest vertebrae numbers of 58–60 include the California golden trout and the Gila and Apache trout, which also exhibit yellow-golden colors, similar fin markings, and a yellow or orange "cutthroat" mark. Most likely, these are shared primitive characters reflecting traits of an ancient ancestral transition toward the evolution of rainbow trout after the rainbow and cutthroat trout lines of evolution split from a common ancestor.

Most surprising was the number of vertebrae found in the trout in the headwaters of the Rio del Presidio, typically 64 and 65—counts otherwise found only in the redband rainbow trout of the middle Columbia River Basin. The number of pyloric caeca, scale counts, and spotting pattern of the Presidio trout also indicate relationships to Columbia Basin redband trout and emphasize the diversity of ancestral origins and long isolation of the trout associated with the Gulf of California.

To summarize what is presently known of this diversity, the trout native to individual river basins can be considered, from south to north.

As mentioned, the trout of the Rio del Presidio, the southernmost natural distribution of Salmonidae, are characterized by a high vertebral number suggesting relationships to a northern form of redband rainbow trout. Of all native trout populations of mainland Mexico, the Rio del Presidio was likely the one most recently established in geological time—perhaps during the last glacial period.

The trout native to the next drainage north of the Rio del Presidio, the Rio San Lorenzo, is known only from one tributary, the Rio Truchas (or Trout River). The Rio Truchas trout are peculiar; they appear almost intermediately between the Mexican golden trout in the drainages to the north and the del Presidio trout to the south. (For example, they typically have 60–62 vertebrae.) Perhaps the golden trout was the original trout of the San Lorenzo drainage and a later invasion of the same ancestor which invaded the Rio del Presidio resulted in hybridization, but this is pure speculation. The next three rivers to the north of the Rio San Lorenzo, the Rio Culiacan, the Rio Sinaloa, and the Rio Fuerte all contain the Mexican golden trout in their high elevation headwater areas.

The two remaining rivers north of the Rio Fuerte which contain native trout are the Rio Mayo and Rio Yaqui. The Yaqui and Mayo trout are similar to each other, indicating a recent common ancestor. This trout shows some external similarities to the Mexican golden trout with its light golden color and tints of orange or red, but of lesser intensity. The Yaqui and Mayo trout have smaller and more profuse spots than does the Mexican golden trout. They have a general resemblance to the Gila trout of New Mexico. Observation on chromosome numbers, however, are puzzling, Gila and Apache trout have 56 chromosomes. (Most redband and rainbow trout have 58, but some California and Oregon coastal rainbow trout have 60 or 64 chromosomes.) The Rio Mayo trout has 64 chromosomes, the Mexican golden trout has 60. Based on the sum of the other divergent characters, it appears that the 64 chromosomes of the Mayo—and probably Yaqui—trout and the 60 chromosomes of the Mexican golden trout were evolved independently of the 60 and 64 chromosome population of some coastal rainbow trout. That is, the chromosome numbers do not reflect recent of common ancestry of all Western North American trout with 60 and 64 chromosomes.

On geographical grounds, it could be assumed that cutthroat trout were once native to Mexico. Immediately east of the Continental Divide, the drainages east of the headwaters of the Rio Yaqui, Rio Feurte, Rio Sinaloa, and Rio Culiacan were once part of the Rio Grande Basin. During glacial times when cutthroat trout occurred much further south in the Rio Grande and the Rio Casas Grandes and Rio Conchos had large volumes of colder waters connecting to the Rio Grande, cutthroat would be expected to inhabit these Mexican drainages. No trout has been documented in the Rio Conchos drainage, and a trout found in a small section of the Rio Casas Grandes drainage appears identical to the Yaqui trout—which occurs only a few miles to the west in the headwaters of the Yaqui—and was not possibly transported from the Yaqui drainage by man.

For adventurous anglers contemplating a trip to catch any of the native Mexican trout, I would suggest reading Robert H. Smith's book, *Native Trout of North America* (Frank Amato Publcations, 1984). Smith made expeditions to Baja and the mainland in search of Mexican trout. He describes the difficulties of travel and of finding and catching these rare trout. His book includes color photographs of the Mexican golden, the Rio Yaqui, the Rio San Lorenzo, and the Rio del Presidio trout. To reach the more remote and roadless areas of the Sierra Madre Occidental and to fish waters not yet surveyed for trout, one would have to emulate E.W. Nelson and go by pack trip with a knowledgeable guide.

Let me know what you find.

The trout native to high elevation streams of the Sierra Madre Occidental on the Mexican mainland represent several primitive evolutionary lines related to the rainbow trout species, *Oncorhynchus mykiss*. Their ancestors invaded these streams from the Gulf of California at different times during past glacial epochs. During warmer interglacial periods they found refuge and persisted in the high elevation streams.

The Mexican golden trout is the only segment of this diversity that has been formally named. Considering all of the diversity associated with the evolution of rainbow trout, the Mexican golden is the most morphologically divergent. Because of its extreme differentiation, it is now considered a distinct species *Oncorhynchus chrysogaster*. The Mexican golden trout occurs in the headwaters of the Rio Feurte, Rio Culiacan, and Rio Sinaloa. All of these headwaters drain from Mount Mohinora, the highest peak of the Sierra Madre Occidental at 10,984 feet. The other headwaters from Mount Mohinora drain eastward to the Rio Conchos of the Rio Grande basin.

RIO GRANDE CUTTHROAT

⟶

SUMMER 1988

THE RIO GRANDE CUTTHROAT TROUT has the distinction of being the first trout encountered by European man in the New World.

In 1541, Francisco de Coronado's army encountered only a series of disappointments in their fruitless search for mythical cities of gold in present-day New Mexico, but they did find abundant trout in the headwaters of the Pecos River, south of the present city of Santa Fe. I suspect that, in their failure to fulfill their greedy dreams of material wealth, they did not much appreciate the elegant beauty of this fish. This lack of appreciation for the Rio Grande trout also characterized white man's civilization that followed Coronado in the Rio Grande Basin. The rush to develop and pollute water for agriculture and industry, and the introductions of nonnative fishes in the Rio Grande Basin, exterminated the Rio Grande cutthroat from all but a relatively few small headwater streams.

Another distinction of the Rio Grande cutthroat is that it has the southernmost distribution of any form of cutthroat trout. The known southernmost natural distribution occurred in headwater streams on Sierra Blanca in southcentral New Mexico. I believe that Rio Grande cutthroat trout are native to the headwaters of tributaries in The Black Range of The Gila National Forest. These tributaries join the Rio Grande in the vicinity of Truth or Consequences, New Mexico, slightly south of the known distribution on Sierra Blanca. Thorough surveys of these streams have not yet been made to document the occurrence of native trout.

The formal discovery and naming of the Rio Grande cutthroat trout began in 1853 when Pacific Railroad Survey personnel stopped at Fort Massachusetts in the San Luis Valley of Colorado. A trout was caught in Ute Creek, preserved, and sent to the Philadelphia Academy of Natural Sciences. In 1856 this specimen was described as a new species, "*Salar virginalis*."

Although *virginalis* was described as a full species, and in the wrong genus, according to the rules of taxonomy, the name is valid for currently denoting the Rio Grande trout as a subspecies of cutthroat trout: *Salmo clarki virginalis*. The meaning of the name implies "like a virgin." Perhaps thoughts of purity and grace were stimulated by the form of the original specimen. In any event, there are relatively few virgin populations remaining of *virginalis*; they promiscuously hybridize with rainbow trout.

Several years ago, I first attempted to delineate the original distribution of Rio Grande cutthroat trout, and to diagnose characteristics which distinguished them from other subspecies of the species. I was stymied by a paucity of museum specimens and by a lack of detailed information in the literature. In 1958, two populations of apparently pure cutthroat trout were found on the Trinchera Ranch (now Forbes Trinchera Ranch) in the San Luis Valley. Specimens from these populations provided the beginnings for a diagnosis of *Salmo clarki virginalis*. Over the years, several more pure or almost pure populations of Rio Grande cutthroat were found, and sufficient comparative data were obtained to characterize *virginalis*. But questions still remain concerning its original distribution and ancestral origin.

I found that the trout native to the Pecos River drainage division of the Rio Grande Basin have larger spots and more scales than the typical Rio Grande cutthroat. The Pecos trout superficially more closely resembles the greenback cutthroat trout (*S. c. stomias*) of Colorado. This suggested that perhaps the Pecos native trout was derived from greenback trout from the Arkansas River basin via the headwaters of the Canadian River drainage. (The headwater tributaries of the Canadian River are contiguous with headwater tributaries of both the Rio Grande and Pecos drainages in the Sangre de Cristo Mountains.)

No documented records, such as museum specimens collected by the Pacific R.R. Survey, exist for trout in the Canadian River drainage. Convincing evidence that cutthroat trout did originally occur in the headwaters of the Canadian River can be found in old issues of *Forest and Stream* magazine. In an 1876 issue, a reader from Chicago asked if "brook trout" occur in "northwest Texas." (Texas at that time included part of present New Mexico.) The answer was that trout occur in "the

RIO GRANDE CUTTHROAT TROUT
Oncorhynchus clarki virginalis

headwaters of the Canadian River," but no basis for an answer was given. An 1877 issue contained an article on Rio Grande trout by "Apache," who wrote that excellent fishing for Rio Grande trout could be found in the headwaters of the Vermejo River. The Vermejo River is the northernmost headwaters of the Canadian River. It is also of interest that "Apache" evidently fished some of the time (when he wasn't using live grasshoppers) with floating flies.

In recent years a few populations of pure or nearly pure cutthroat trout have been found in uppermost headwater tributaries of the Canadian River, populations which I assume represent the native trout of the Canadian drainage. After careful comparison of these specimens, I found them to be identical to the typical Rio Grande form of *virginalis*, not to the Pecos form. Thus, I rejected the theory of origin of Pecos cutthroat trout from a greenback trout ancestor via the Canadian River.

In my column on Mexican golden trout, in the spring 1988 issue of *Trout*, I mentioned that early reports of cutthroat trout in Mexico have never been verified, although during the colder climate of the last glacier period, it might be expected that Rio Grande cutthroat trout moved southward into Texas and up major Rio Grande tributaries such as the Rio Casas Grande and the Rio Conchos into their headwaters in the Sierra Madre Occidental of Mexico.

I searched old issues of *Forest and Stream* for evidence of southern distribution of Rio Grande cutthroat.

J.W. Daniel wrote in an 1878 issue of his fishing experiences while serving as Assistant Surgeon with the Second Texas Rifles during the Civil War. Daniel thought he recalled catching trout in San Felipe Springs and in the Devil's River (tributaries to Rio Grande) in Texas. He had a more distinct recollection of catching trout in the Limpia River, a tributary to the Pecos River, while stationed at Fort Davis, Texas. It must be recognized that Mr. Daniel had no experience in fish identification and that both the Rio Grande and Pecos drainages contain a large native chub that was often called "trout" by early explorers. I believe Mr. Daniel was correct, however, in his recollection of catching

trout in the Rio Bonito, draining Sierra Blanca in southcentral New Mexico, while he was stationed at Fort Stanton.

The Rio Bonito cutthroat trout still persists from an early introduction in the headwaters of Indian Creek on the western side of Sierra Blanca on the Mescalero Apache Indian Reservation. I examined specimens of the Indian Creek trout and found them to be typical of the Pecos form of Rio Grande cutthroat, as would be expected if they were introduced from the Rio Bonito.

A letter to *Forest and Stream* by N. A. Taylor, also in 1878, recounted secondhand stories of trout in the Limpia River, Texas. The only self-reproducing trout population presently known in Texas occurs in McKittrick Creek on Guadalupe Mountain, but it is of introduced rainbow trout. It is doubtful that the southernmost distribution of Rio Grande cutthroat will ever be known with any certainty.

Another mystery concerns the ancestral origin of the present Rio Grande cutthroat.

All taxonomic comparisons made by comparative morphology and protein electrophoresis agree that the Rio Grande cutthroat, *S. c. virginalis*, the Colorado River cutthroat, *S. c. pleuriticus*, and the greenback cutthroat, *S. c. stomias*, are very closely related to each other and to the Yellowstone cutthroat trout. Isolation of these subspecies in separate drainage basins probably occurred during the last glacial period, perhaps about 20,000 years or so ago.

Admittedly, estimating the time of origin when the ancestor of the Rio Grande cutthroat trout first gained access to the Rio Grande Basin is largely speculation. Much is yet to be learned on the matter. For example, a 1985 publication on fossils of the San Luis Valley, Colorado, describes a fossil "cutthroat trout" that lived in the Rio Grande Basin more than 700,000 years ago.

If the present Rio Grande cutthroat is a direct descendent of this fossil trout—and if it was isolated from the Colorado River and greenback cutthroat subspecies for more than 700,000 years—it should show evidence of considerably greater evolutionary divergence than it does. I assume that the trout that occurred in the Rio Grande 700,000 years ago became extinct and that the present Rio Grande cutthroat had its origin in relatively recent geological time from a transfer from the Colorado River Basin.

Fossil cutthroat trout have also been found in the Estancia desert basin, which lies between the Rio Grande and Pecos drainages, southeast of Albuquerque (Route 66 crosses the northern part of the Estancia basin about 50 miles east of Albuquerque). During glacial periods, a large lake occurred in the Estancia basin and cutthroat trout lived in this lake basin from about 130,000 years ago to about 10,000 years ago when the lake desiccated for the last time. I would speculate that the Estancia cutthroat trout were descendents of the mid Pleistocene cutthroat of the San Luis Valley rather than the ancestor of the present *S. c. virginalis*. The fossil Estancia basin cutthroat trout raises an interesting question of the possibility that a population of a primitive form of cutthroat trout may have persisted in a headwater stream of this basin, completely isolated from connections to either the Rio Grande or Pecos drainages. The possibility is remote but intriguing.

Fortunately, for the Rio Grande cutthroat and other interior subspecies of cutthroat trout, there has been a resurgence of interest to protect and restore native trout. Both Colorado and New Mexico have active programs for protection and for establishing new populations by reintroductions. The American Fisheries Society will publish a volume on the management of inland cutthroat trout this year. Robert H. Smith's book, *Native Trout of North America* (Frank Amato Publications, 1984), which contains color photographs of both the Rio Grande and Pecos forms of *S. c. virginalis* (unfortunately, the color reproductions do not do justice to these beautiful trout), and Patrick Trotter's book, *Cutthroat, Native Trout of the West* (University of Colorado Press, 1987), are examples of semipopular literature that promote the wonders and beauty of native trout.

I would like to see Colorado and New Mexico establish more public fishing waters where anglers can have an opportunity to catch-and-release this rare trout in its native habitat. Some streams where environmental conditions may favor the Rio Grande cutthroat over nonnative trout (for example, brown trout) might have regulations promoting the removal of the nonnative trout while protecting the native cutthroat with a catch-and-release policy, similar to the greenback cutthroat fishery in Hidden Valley of Rocky Mountain National Park.

The problem of angler exploitation of cutthroat, especially when cutthroat occur together with a nonnative trout, is illustrated by a population of Rio Grande cutthroat trout of the Rio Chiquito near Taos, New Mexico. In 1965–1966, when a major section of the Rio Chiquito was on private land and closed to fishing, electrofishing sampling of the stream found 420 Rio Grande cutthroat and 37 brown trout. In 1967, the U.S. Forest Service incorporated the Rio Chiquito into Forest Service lands by a land exchange, and it was opened to public fishing. When the stream was sampled again in 1969, 137 brown trout and only 37 cutthroat trout were found.

A few years ago I served as an adviser to the Acoma Indian Pueblo in New Mexico in relation to legal action seeking damages from water pollution. The Acoma case, multiplied a thousand times, makes clear what happened to interior forms of cutthroat trout and many other species during the past 100 years.

Historical records of Spaniards in the eighteenth century and of U.S. Army observers in the mid-nineteenth century agree that the Acoma people practiced intensive, irrigated agriculture, but the river that ran through their land was sparkling pure and abounded with Rio Grande cutthroat trout. Later, upstream impoundments, diversions, and groundwater pumping reduced the flow in the Rio San Jose through the Acoma Pueblo to one third of its virgin flow; a considerable proportion of the new flow regime consisted of poorly treated sewage effluent.

By the 1960s, even the nonnative brown trout and rainbow trout could no longer maintain populations in the Rio San Jose. The Pueblo maintained a fee fishery for hatchery rainbow trout and channel catfish in an irrigation reservoir until water quality problems terminated the reservoir fishery. Finally, the Pueblo took legal action, demanding their right to a sufficient supply of clean water and damages for past abuse.

I advised that, if flows and water quality could be restored in the Rio San Jose, the native Rio Grande cutthroat trout should be restored in its waters. The Rio Grande cutthroat is part of the natural heritage of the people of the Pueblo—although I doubt any living member is old enough to recall when Rio Grande cutthroat lived in the Rio San Jose. Besides the spiritual values involved for restoring the native trout, I believe real economic benefits could result. My rationale for economic benefits concerns the fact that some economists classify anglers into different groups, according to their willingness to pay for fishing opportunities. I believe there is a group of anglers who is willing to pay considerably more for a memorable experience to catch (and release) a rare and beautiful native trout than other angler groups are willing to pay to catch and keep generic hatchery rainbow trout or channel catfish.

Last year the lawsuit was settled out of court just before a trial was scheduled. The Pueblo people received a considerable settlement for past abuse of their waters. I hope that, when the waters of the Rio San Jose again run clear and cold through the Acoma Pueblo, my recommendation for restoration of their native cutthroat trout is not forgotten.

AUTHOR'S NOTE

This column mentions that the Rio Grande cutthroat has the southernmost distribution of cutthroat trout. How far south? Did they occur in Texas and in the Rio Conchos of Mexico? These questions are yet unanswered. Based on the cold climate during the last glacial period, it would be expected that cutthroat trout extended their range in the Rio Grande southward into Texas to its confluence with the Rio Conchos. If the ancestral cutthroat did reach the Rio Conchos, did it persist in some of the many headwaters that are found between 6,000 and 9,000 feet elevation, similar to the trout native to west side of Sierra Madre Occidental?

Joe Tomelleri, trout illustrator *par excellence*, has a particular passion to discover new information on Mexican trout. He is determined to find the answer to an old mystery: Are cutthroat trout native to Mexico in the Rio Conchos? In 1886, E. D. Cope published a short note on "the most southern salmon" in the *American Naturalist*. Cope received two small trout specimens from Professor Lupton collected at an elevation of 7,000 to 8,000 feet. The locality was given as southern Chihuahua near the boundaries of Sinaloa and Durango. Cope identified the specimens as cutthroat trout, called *Salmo purpuratus* at the time. These specimens were never seen again and their true identity remains unverified. Joe set out to learn the routes of travel of Professor Lupton, a mining engineer who traversed a vast area of Mexico. Previous literature had surmised that Lupton got his trout specimens from the vicinity of Mount Mohinora, likely from the headwaters of the Rio Sinaloa, which has the Mexican golden trout. Joe has documented that Lupton traveled throughout the headwaters of the Rio Conchos.

This raised hopes that the trout specimens sent to Cope were cutthroat. My summer 2006 column tells of the discovery of a native trout in the Rio Conchos basin. This was exciting news, yet disappointing because the newly discovered trout is not a cutthroat. It resembles the Rio Yaqui trout and most likely originated from a headwater stream transfer from the Yaqui basin.

In April 2007, Joe Tomelleri joined a joint Mexican-American expedition to investigate a remote area of the Rio Conchos basin. They found a new trout native to the Conchos basin. Photographs of the new trout show that it is not a cutthroat trout, but it differs from the Conchos trout discussed in my summer 2006 column, "Ghost Trout of the Rio Conchos". It appears most similar to the Mexican golden trout. If this identification is correct, its origin would be from a headwater stream transfer from the Rio Feurte into the Conchos basin.

LANDLOCKED SALMON

———◆———

FALL 1988

THE LORE, HISTORY, AND CONTROVERSIES associated with landlocked salmon can be as fascinating as the fish itself. For about 100 years or more after Atlantic salmon, *Salmo salar*, was discovered to have lake populations which spent their whole lives in freshwater, the angling and scientific literature reflected contemporary speculation and opinion on the origins of such populations.

Why didn't they migrate to the ocean? Is the lake salmon the same species as the Atlantic salmon?

The main points of the controversy over classification of landlocked salmon were highlighted in the debate between Albert Günther, ichthyologist at the British Museum, and Francis Day, author of the 1887 book, *British and Irish Salmonidae*. On matters of fishes, Günther and Day rarely agreed. Day was correct in considering landlocked salmon as freshwater populations of *Salmo salar*. Günther's response was to name the salmon of Lake Vänern, Sweden, as a new species. By Günther's definition, then, the landlocked salmon was not *S. salar*.

Many different species names were given to landlocked salmon, but the first name officially published in the literature was *Salmo sebago* in 1854. It should be recognized, however, that Henry Herbert (a.k.a. Frank Forester) used the name *Salmo sebago* in his 1849 book, *Fish and Fishing*, but without a formal description; thus, Herbert's 1849 name lacks validity as a taxonomic name. The landlocked salmon of the Lake Saint John region, Quebec, (drainages to Gulf of Saint Lawrence) was named *Salmo ouananiche* in 1894 and was popularized in the 1896 book by E. T. D. Chambers, *The Ouananiche and Its Canadian Environment*. Landlocked salmon in Canada are still typically referred to as *ouananiche*.

The answer to the question of the classification of landlocked salmon relates to the origins of the populations. Do all populations in North America and Europe have a common origin from one common landlocked or freshwater ancestor? If so, they would qualify to be distinguished as a species separate from *S. salar*. The evidence, however, is overwhelming that all populations of landlocked salmon independently originated from many different populations of sea-run or anadromous *S. salar*—in relatively recent geologic times.

There are some convergent evolutionary characteristics that might distinguish most populations of landlocked salmon from anadromous Atlantic salmon, such as relative body proportions and degree of smoltification (it is good evolutionary strategy not to waste energy in preparation for ocean life if it isn't necessary). But the "most correct" contemporary classification of landlocked salmon throughout their entire distribution in North America and Europe is *Salmo salar*, albeit a form of *salar* with very different life history characteristics.

The original distribution of landlocked salmon occurs in areas that were inundated by the maximum rise of sea level during the last postglacial period of about 10,000 years ago, or in lakes near the border of the maximum sea level. One population in the River Namsen, Norway, lives its whole life in a river above a waterfall.

In Maine, landlocked salmon were originally found in a few lakes of four river basins: Saint Croix (Grand Lakes), Union (Green Lake), Penobscot (Sebec Lake), and Presumpscot River (Sebago Lake). By 1981, as a result of stocking, 297 Maine lakes contained landlocked salmon. Salmon also were native to Lake Champlain, New York–Vermont, and Lake Ontario, but these native populations are long extinct. The salmon native to Lake Ontario probably attained the largest size of all landlocked salmon. The greatest natural density of landlocked salmon distribution occurs in Eastern Canada. They are native to innumerable lakes of Quebec, Newfoundland, and Labrador.

In Europe, landlocked salmon were originally found in only a relatively few lakes: four in Norway, one each in Sweden and Finland, and six in the Northwest Soviet Union (Arctic Ocean Basin). Older literature may cite records of landlocked salmon existing in streams on the Adriatic coast of Yugoslavia. This is in error. The Yugoslavian trout, *Salmothymus obtusirostris*, is a very different species.

Why are landlocked salmon so much less prevalent in Europe compared to North America? The reasons may relate to relationships of European lakes to postglacial changes in ocean level and temperature and the fish species composition in the lakes. Most lakes to which landlocked salmon are native—and where the salmon attain a relatively large size—also have native populations of smelt to serve as food. Lake Ontario, however, was an exception to this rule. Smelt are not native to Lake Ontario, and its now extinct salmon reached a large size probably by feeding on species of whitefish and ciscos.

In evolutionary terms, the origins of the many populations of landlocked salmon can be attributed to a period when ancestors of the present populations who did not migrate to the ocean experienced a higher survival rate than those that did migrate. That is, in a particular body of water during some past time, nonmigrating individuals left more offspring than did anadromous salmon. Overtime, this behavior difference became firmly determined by heredity.

Once the existence of landlocked salmon became known, the minds of many anglers were captivated by this beautiful and mysterious fish. An 1832 issue of the *American Turf Register* and *Sporting Magazine* contains a story on fishing for salmon in Sebago Lake in 1830. J.V. C. Smith's 1833 book *Natural History of the Fishes of Massachusetts* mentions Sebago Lake and angling for its "primitive trout." (Smith determined they could not be salmon.)

Smith cannot be recognized as an authority, however. He began a trend in American angling literature whereby a bare thread of fact was woven into a whole cloth of fabrication. Smith's style was followed by Frank Forester and a series of successors. Early angling literature must be carefully evaluated in an attempt to sort fact from fabrication. Smith may have essentially lifted his account of angling in Sebago Lake from the earlier *Turf Register* story, but he did mention that the size and numbers of the salmon—or primitive trout, as he called them—had degenerated in Sebago Lake in recent years (even in the oldest literature, fishing was always better and the fish larger in "the old days"). Smith also mentioned that fishing for Sebago salmon consisted of trolling live or dead bait and that fishing with the artificial fly was seldom used, although "…it does not follow that the practice of fly fishing would not be attended with the same success which attends the act in England and Scotland."

Over the years of compiling historical records of early American fishes and fishing, one name stands out in regard to knowledge and authenticity of information on landlocked salmon.

Augustus C. Hamlin was a medical doctor from a distinguished

Maine family. His uncle, Hannibal Hamlin, was the first Republican Governor of Maine and Vice President of the United States during Lincoln's first term in office (Hannibal was also an ardent salmon fisher). Unfortunately, Hamlin wrote only a few papers between 1862 and 1903 of which I am aware. Evidently, he had a passion to learn about salmonid fishes. While studying in Europe, Hamlin became familiar with the works of European ichthyologists and visited museums to examine specimens of various species of trout and salmon.

Augustus Hamlin began angling for landlocked salmon in Maine in the 1840s. His early trips were to the Grand Lake area where he employed the services of an Indian guide, Peol Toma, who explained that the landlocked and anadromous salmon are the same fish (species) but that the landlocked form "forgot to go to sea." As might be expected from his background, Hamlin was a fly fisher. I was surprised, however, to learn that Toma also fished with flies he tied himself from

brightly colored bird feathers and practiced his fly-fishing skills with great success.

Of interest to most anglers is the size attained by landlocked salmon and lakes noted for producing particularly large fish. As mentioned, caution must be used when abstracting such information from the literature. The most comprehensive data on life history, management, and angling for landlocked salmon are found in two bulletins published in 1970 and 1985 by the Maine Department of Inland Fisheries. What may be surprising from the Maine data is the small average size of salmon in Maine lakes.

The typical maximum age of Maine landlocked salmon is six or seven years when the typical average maximum lengths and weights of 18–21 inches and 2½–3½ pounds are reached. Maine salmon lakes are not productive; the best lakes produce a catch of less than 1 pound per acre annually, and, on average, it takes about 20 hours of angling to

LAKE FORM ATLANTIC SALMON
Salmo salar

catch one salmon. These cold statistics have little relevance to the angler whose eternal optimism is buoyed by the occasional story or photo of the rare trophy-sized fish. The statistical averages do not reveal that, in the same lake, growth rates and maximum size of salmon may vary considerably from year to year, mainly in relation to smelt abundance.

Maximum size attained by salmon is influenced both by nature and nurture. That is, there are both genetic-hereditary and environmental (such as food abundance) components which determine maximum size a fish might attain.

The genetic component concerns maximum life span and age at first spawning. The older the age at first spawning, the greater the lifespan and the greater the potential to express maximum growth. The nongenetic or environmental influence can be demonstrated when salmon are introduced into new waters and growth and maximum size are compared between parental and introduced populations.

In 1903, the Argentina Department of Agriculture decided to begin trout and salmon propagation, and a hatchery was constructed at Lake Nahuel Huapi, a national park area near the Chilean border which contains numerous lakes and rivers ideal for trout and salmon. In January 1904, the first shipment of eggs of several species from the United States was made. In the shipment were 215,000 eggs from landlocked salmon obtained from West Grand Lake, Maine. In Lake Nahuel Huapi and downstream Lake Traful, the introduced salmon found an abundance of small forage fish and freshwater crabs that had evolved without large predators such as trout and salmon. Evidently, these forage species lacked innate predator-avoidance behavior and provided an abundant, readily available food supply to the introduced salmon.

A report of an American fisheries advisor who went to Nahuel Huapi in 1937 to supervise reconstruction of the hatchery noted that the average size of salmon seined in the Traful River for spawn-taking that year was 14 pounds. The largest salmon reported netted from the Traful River was claimed to be 36.4 pounds. The report mentioned that the largest rod and reel caught Traful salmon was caught on a spoon by Guy Dawson, owner of the Traful Hotel; it weighed 27.6 pounds. (Leander McCormick's 1937 book, *Fishing Round the World*, contains a photo of Guy Dawson and a "25-pound" salmon, evidently this same fish.)

Obviously, West Grand Lake salmon, when introduced into a new environment in Argentina, greatly exceeded the growth rate and maximum size characteristic of the parental population in its native waters. It is also interesting to note that the officially recognized world record angler-caught brown trout of 35 pounds, 15 ounces was caught from Lake Nahuel Huapi in 1952. Brown trout were introduced into Argentina soon after the salmon, from both the United States and Germany. Lake Nahuel Huapi obviously provided an extremely nurturing environment for trout and salmon.

The change in size of salmon in Sebago Lake is of interest in regard to possible explanations—nature, nurture, or both.

Sebago Lake was famed for its large salmon. The official world record rod and reel caught landlocked salmon for many years was a fish weighing 22½ pounds caught on August 1, 1907, from Sebago Lake. (The International Game Fish Association no longer separates landlocked from anadromous *Salmo salar* for recordkeeping.) On that same day, W. C. Kendall caught a 16-pound salmon from the lake. Kendall's 1935 book on New England salmon provides a wealth of historical information and provides some basis for comparison of former and present growth rates in various salmon populations. Kendall cites a record of a Sebago salmon taken during a hatchery egg-taking operation in the early 1900s which was reputed to be 39 inches in length and 35½ pounds in weight. Kendall also published records of the largest fish netted by the hatchery crew each year from 1916 through 1930. The maximum size showed a steady decline from 18 pounds (1916, 1917, 1918) to 8 pounds (1928, 1929, 1930).

Age and growth data of the 1950s and '60s show Lake Sebago salmon to be quite typical of landlocked salmon in other Maine lakes, attaining a typical maximum age of six or seven years with an average size of 18–21 inches and 2½–3½ pounds at these ages.

What happened to the growth of the salmon of Sebago Lake, once so famous for their large maximum size?

Considering the "nature" or genetic aspect, a possible explanation is that the original genotype of the Sebago Lake salmon which influenced life history characteristics such as age at maturity, maximum lifespan, and growth potential no longer exists. It may have been "homogenized" with other races by the fisheries management program. Landlocked salmon propagation began in Maine with the taking of eggs in 1867 from Grand Lake Stream. The Grand Lake salmon was a dominant source in early years, but other populations such as Sebago Lake were used to varying degrees over the years in hatchery propagation. Hatchery salmon from various sources were most probably indiscriminately mixed for stocking in the many salmon lakes of Maine. I doubt that any thought was given to maintaining "pure lines" of Grand Lake or Sebago Lake races.

Data from 1963–1974 for Sebago Lake revealed that the angler catch of salmon derived from natural reproduction ranged from 4 percent to 28 percent of the total catch, while the catch of stocked hatchery fish varied from 72 percent to 96 percent. With such catch statistics, and considering the unknown genealogy of the hatchery fish, it might be assumed that the original race of salmon native to Sebago Lake has been homogenized out of existence.

On the other hand, "nature" or environmental factors causing reduced growth should be recognized. As mentioned, Grand Lake salmon stocked in lakes in Argentina with unlimited food attained weights greater than the largest reported weight for Sebago salmon. Perhaps introduced fish species or environmental changes negatively affected the smelt population of Sebago Lake after the early 1900s.

In any event, a moral can be drawn to the effect that populations with special attributes such as the former large size of Sebago Lake salmon should be protected by fisheries management practices, not tampered with and possibly destroyed. I must admit, however, that, in relation to the history of fish culture and fish management, such well meaning advice is comparable to recommending that the barn door be locked after the horse is gone and the barn has burned down.

Examples of lakes which historically contained exceptionally large (20 pounds or larger) salmon are relatively few. The largest landlocked salmon reported in the literature are from Lake Ontario (to 45 pounds); Lake Champlain; Lake Vänern, Sweden; and Lake Ladoga, U.S.S.R. (35 pounds). Of these populations exhibiting superstar size, only the Lake Vänern and Lake Ladoga salmon still exist. It must be recognized, however, that the above-mentioned lakes had or have more than one population native to each lake and that fish of one particular population attain a size greater than the fish in the other populations living in the same lake. For example, the population spawning in the Gullspång River contains the largest salmon of Lake Vänern (age at first maturity typically six years, and average weight of males in spawning run is 19 pounds), and the Svir River population contains the largest Ladoga salmon.

Lake Vänern was also a great repository of genetic diversity of brown trout, some known to attain great age (at least 16 and 17 years) and size (40–45 pounds). Most of the distinct populations of brown trout of Lake Vänern became extinct when hydroelectric dams blocked their spawning tributaries. One population of large brown trout from Lake Vänern still spawns in the Gullspång River with the salmon. The Gullspång brown trout first spawns at six to eight years of age and the average size of fish in the spawning run is about 16½ pounds.

In 1975, the Gullspång race of Lake Vänern salmon was stocked in Lake Michigan. In 1981, landlocked Atlantic salmon of 32 and 34 pounds were caught in Lake Michigan. It is not known how many Atlantic salmon were taken in Lake Michigan and other Great Lakes because of confusion of identification between brown trout, *S. trutta*, and salmon, *S. salar*.

Three characters are commonly used to differentiate between *salar* and *trutta*: tail slightly forked in *salar* versus square in *trutta*; adipose fin without markings in *salar* versus spotted and/or fringed with lighter color in *trutta*; and teeth on shaft of vomer bone weakly developed in *salar* and well developed in *trutta*. The confusion in correct identification of large specimens of *salar* and *trutta* can be seen in the Russian literature relating to the "salmon" of the Caspian and Black Seas. For many years their classification alternately changed between *salar* and *trutta*. It was not until examination of chromosomes conclusively determined that Caspian and Black Sea "salmon" are, in reality, brown trout (56–58 chromosomes in *salar*, 80 chromosomes in *trutta*).

In 1987, a New York record brown trout of 29 pounds, 15 ounces was caught in Lake Ontario. A furor erupted in the media concerning the correct identification of the fish. Some claimed it to be an Atlantic salmon. I would agree with the evidence of identification of the New York State Department of Conservation that the New York record brown trout was correctly identified.

The other extreme of growth is illustrated by dwarf salmon in many small lakes and ponds of Canada, particularly in acidic waters of Newfoundland characterized by low productivity and the absence of forage fish. Under such conditions, populations of salmon may reproduce at 6 inches or less and attain a maximum size of only 8 or 9 inches.

Such extremes of growth of *S. salar* in very different environments demonstrate the adaptability of the species to cope with diverse environments. It should be kept in mind, however, that this diversity of life history types is not simply a matter of a homogenous species responding differently to different environments (the "nurture" aspect of nature and nurture), but rather each individual population has been selected for thousands of years to best survive in its particular environment. This evolution is reflected in life history characteristics such as migratory behavior, age at maturity, competition and predation relationships in large lake or marine environments, and invertebrate feeding in small lakes and ponds (the evolutionary or "nature" aspect). These evolutionary differences influencing the heredity of different populations of *S. salar* should be recognized and evaluated before a parental source of salmon is selected to introduce into new waters.

Outside of New York and New England, no state fisheries management programs have given serious consideration to establishing landlocked salmon fisheries. The only example in recent years of which I am aware is Hosmer Lake, Oregon.

Hosmer Lake covers about 160 surface acres in the Cascade Mountains about 40 miles west of Bend, Oregon. It lies at an elevation of 4,950 feet and is more of a flooded mountain meadow than a lake, with a maximum depth of only 11 feet. It appears to be very atypical for a landlocked salmon lake and it demonstrates the range of environments to which salmon can adapt if competing fish species are absent.

After Mud Lake was chemically treated to eliminate carp and chubs, it was renamed Hosmer Lake and stocked with Atlantic salmon in 1958. It was first opened to angling in 1961. For the next 25 years the success of the salmon stocking (there is no natural reproduction) and salmon angling experienced ups and downs. A major problem concerned the "nature" of the parental stock of salmon used to stock the lake-sea-run salmon from Quebec. The nature of the Quebec salmon caused them to smolt and most would leave the lake driven by their instinct to reach the ocean (the outlet of Hosmer Lake disappears into porous lava a short distance below the lake). Also, the young salmon exhibited a behavior pattern to remain near the lake surface where they became easy prey for ospreys.

In 1983, Oregon received 20,000 eggs of the Grand Lake stock of landlocked salmon from Maine. Yearling salmon raised from these eggs were stocked into Hosmer Lake in 1984, followed by annual stocking of "true landlocked" salmon since then. A report from Ted Fies, Oregon fisheries biologist at Bend (June 1988), verifies the significance of nature and nurture considerations in fisheries management.

Results from salmon stocking have much improved after the changeover from sea-run to landlocked salmon. The landlocked salmon do not smolt and attempt to migrate, they remain in deeper water and predator mortality is much less. The net result is that, from stockings of equal numbers of equal size, the landlocked race of salmon survive to maintain many more salmon in the lake than was possible with the fish of sea-run ancestry.

The Hosmer Lake salmon fishery is under flies-only, no-kill regulations. About 5,000 anglers fish the lake each year. A survey made in 1971 revealed that about 90 percent of these anglers were from out-of-state. The regional economic impact of this unique fishery for Atlantic landlocked salmon lake is enormously greater than if Hosmer Lake were to be managed for brook trout or hatchery rainbow trout.

Many Western reservoirs have much greater biological productivity than Maine lakes, and some of these waters contain forage fish such as smelt in much greater abundance than found in Maine. I believe there are opportunities to create new landlocked salmon fisheries throughout the country with greater salmon growth and production than is possible in their native state.

Fisheries managers, like automobile manufacturers, must understand the diverse preferences of anglers. A small percentage of drivers are willing to pay a premium for a prestigious car such as a Mercedes or Rolls Royce. And landlocked salmon can be viewed as the Rolls Royce of freshwater gamefish.

AUTHOR'S NOTE
Similar to brown trout, rainbow trout, and sockeye salmon, anadromous Atlantic salmon gave rise to "landlocked" populations during postglacial times mainly within the past 10,000 years. Compared to other salmonid species, the more glamorous reputation of Atlantic salmon created more debate and theorizing about why some populations go to sea and some do not. Because many populations of landlocked salmon are not physically isolated from the ocean, they are "landlocked" by choice, or more accurately by their heredity. Their life history omits migration to and from the ocean. This is a minor hereditary change that has been acquired many times independently. Each population of landlocked (or lake) salmon has evolved from anadromous *Salmo salar*, similar to sockeye and kokanee salmon.

The most rare life history type of Atlantic salmon is stream-resident. Stream-resident salmon spend their entire lives in streams without migration to lakes or to the ocean. Formerly, the only known stream-resident Atlantic salmon occurred above a falls in the River Namsen, Norway. In the 1990s, several stream-resident populations of dwarf Atlantic salmon were documented in some acidic streams of Labrador. These peculiar salmon attain maturity and spawn at 5–6 inches in length. Maximum size is in the range of 7–8 inches. Essentially, their life history does not go beyond the juvenile parr stage of the typical Atlantic salmon. If the entire spectrum of adult size in *S. salar* were to be duplicated in *Homo sapiens* the range of weights of human adults would be from 1 to 1,000 pounds.

Lakes Vänern and Vättern in Sweden are among the largest lakes in Europe. Both have native populations of brown trout. Lake salmon are native only to Vänern and arctic char only to Vättern. The evolutionary adaptations of a species to subdivide into distinct ecological races that are of great significance for fisheries management is exemplified by the brown trout and Atlantic salmon of Lake Vänern. The Klar River and the Gullspång River are the two major spawning tributaries. Both the trout and salmon spawning in the Gullspång River have an older age at maturity, a longer life span and attain a much larger maximum size compared to the races spawning in the Klar River. The column mentioned

32- and 34-pound Atlantic salmon caught in Lake Michigan from an introduction of the Gullspång salmon. In the 1990s Gullspång salmon were stocked into Lake Vättern. In subsequent years, several of these Gullspång salmon were caught weighing from 40 to 45 pounds. With an abundance of forage fish, Gullspång salmon have the hereditary potential to attain a great size.

WE'RE PUTTING THEM BACK ALIVE

FALL 1989

MORE THAN A CENTURY AGO, the Reverend Myron W. Reed— a "noble man and an excellent angler," in the words of David Starr Jordan and Barton W. Evermann in their classic *American Food & Game Fishes* (1902)—indulged in a bit of angling futurism. His, said Reed, would be the last generation of trout fishers. Not that trout would cease to exist. But, in the future, they would be "hatched by machinery and raised in ponds, and fattened on chopped liver, and grow flabby and lose their spots."

Fortunately, the good reverend's prediction was off the mark. He failed to take into account the adaptive and survival capabilities of wild trout.

Yet the historical significance of Reverend Reed's comments is the early and clear distinction made between wild and hatchery trout. The high value placed by observant anglers on stream-bred trout and their waters led to the founding of Trout Unlimited in 1959. The organization was a formal expression of frustration, even anger, at a state fishery agency's inordinate emphasis on the production of hatchery trout—to the detriment of wild trout. Early members of TU realized that managing quality trout streams by stocking them with catchable-sized hatchery fish was not natural resource management. (Such catchable trout

management is analogous to a corporation whose money managers decide to invest funds periodically that return only 50 to 75 cents on the dollar—with only a small proportion of the stockholders receiving most of the return. The irresponsible managers would be thrown out of office!)

An obvious management alternative to the vicious cycle of ever-increasing hatchery production of catchable trout is the recycling of wild trout—permitting the same fish to be caught again and again. TU was quick to embrace this alternative, boldly announcing in 1960 a philosophy for the contemporary angler: "Trout Unlimited believes that trout fishing isn't just fishing for trout. It's fishing for sport rather than for food, where the true enjoyment of the sport lies in the challenge, the lore and the battle of wits, not necessarily the full creel. It's the feeling of satisfaction that comes from limiting your kill instead of killing your limit..."

During the last 30 years, every important coldwater state has designated trout streams and lakes for catch-and-release only fishing. Actual results to the quality of angling have varied; so has the acceptance of special regulations among anglers. Overall, however, one of the impressive changes in trout management has been an increasing willingness of the angling public to watch the trout brought to hand swim away. In fact, some anglers have become so strident in favor of catch-and-release fishing that they will behave in no other way—even in circumstances where letting go of plentiful hatchery trout makes no real biological sense. Moreover, some of these zealots want all trout fishermen to follow their lead, and think poorly of those who don't. Because most licensed anglers prefer to keep at least some of the fish they catch, inevitable conflicts have developed. The outcomes of these often emotional battles have, unfortunately, sometimes been determined more by political arm-twisting than sound biology. Fraudulent implementation of special regulations is no better than fraudulent reasons for stocking. Worse, their future application to achieve biologically measurable results may be compromised. A major lesson of the last three decades is that special regulations definitely work—but only in the right places, for the right reasons.

SPECIAL REGULATIONS DEFINED

Let's take a critical look at our experience across America with specially-regulated trout fisheries. We may begin by agreeing on a simple definition of special regulations: those fishing regulations designed to recycle all or some of the angler's catch by specifying the release of all fish; or fish below, above or in-between stated lengths.

And what of the goal?

The goal of special regulations should be to maintain or improve the quality of a fishery expressed in catch rate and/or the proportion of larger fish in an angler's catch (for example, percent of catch 12 inches and larger, 14 inches and larger, etc.).

The significance of special regulations in wild trout management becomes apparent with some reflection on supply and demand. Ask this basic question: How many wild trout are available to be caught each year from all the trout swimming in the waters of your state (the supply), and how many of your fellow anglers are wading those waters for how many days trying to catch those trout (the demand)?

Take, for example, Colorado with an estimated 8,000 miles and 20,000 surface acres of trout streams. Western trout streams vary enormously in their carrying capacity—from a few pounds to more than 500 pounds per acre of biomass. The general average biomass or standing crop of trout is about 50 pounds per acre. Thus, a combined estimate of one million pounds of wild trout biomass can be reasonably made for all the trout streams in Colorado (20,000 acres with an average of 50 pounds per acre). To estimate how many of these million pounds of trout might be caught (and killed) by anglers each year, on a sustained yield basis, trout production must be considered. Production is the addition of new flesh, that is, the total growth during one year. For populations to be self-sustaining on a relatively stable basis, the biomass lost to total annual mortality (natural mortality plus angling mortality) must be replaced by annual production—entry and growth of new fish born into the population ("recruitment") and growth of older fish.

Consider that, even in heavily-fished waters, more annual trout production can be expected to be lost to natural mortality than to angling mortality. "With the typical constraints on production rates in streams, a best case scenario would predict that a wild population existing at 50 pounds per acre biomass could not provide more than 25 pounds per acre for angler removal each season and remain stable.

Thus, under optimal conditions, 20,000 surface acres of western trout streams may yield a total maximum catch (and kill) of 500,000 pounds of wild trout. If the average trout in the catch is about 9 inches, or three trout per pound, then 1.5 million trout are available to be removed under normal angling regulations.

Colorado currently sells about 800,000 angling licenses and projects sales of 900,000 by 1990. According to Colorado Division of Wildlife data, it is estimated that the average angler fishes 10 days per year (eight million angler days) and that 29 percent of all angling effort occurs on coldwater streams (2.3 million angler days). The goal is for the average angler to catch 2.8 fish per angler day, which would require Colorado trout streams to yield an annual catch of 6.44 million fish—about five million more trout than can be expected from maximum production of all wild trout populations in streams.

The stocking of catchable hatchery trout in put-and-take fisheries plays a role to bridge this enormous gap between the supply of stream trout and angler demand. But the fact is that current production of catchable trout in all Colorado hatcheries is slightly less than five million fish, and most of these are not stocked in streams.

From a cursory review demonstrating great discrepancy between supply and demand, it should become apparent why increased use of special regulations is necessary: to recycle trout in wild trout fisheries in order to maintain acceptable catch rates in heavily fished waters. It should be made clear, at this point, that special regulations are not synonymous with no-kill regulations. No-kill, where all fish must be released, is only one form of special regulation. With creative use of regulations tailored for specific conditions such as minimum, maximum, or slot size limits, a portion of the annual surplus production of a population can be removed by anglers while the rest is recycled.

WHY THE CONTROVERSY?

Now that the necessity of special regulations for the management of heavily fished wild trout streams has been demonstrated, the logical question is: Why aren't special regulations more widely used? Why is there still such controversy over their use? One reason, of course, is simply human nature. A dramatic change in attitudes and management practices does not occur suddenly. The great majority of anglers still wants to keep fish. A more significant reason is the severe constraint on the growth and survival dynamics of a trout population in most streams.

Very few streams have the optimum combination of habitat and food supply to allow continued growth and survival of a significant proportion of a population to attain an older age (age five to six or older) and a large size (more than 14 inches). In the typical environmentally-limited population, special regulations can effectively recycle the two- and three-year-old trout (approximately 8–12 inches). But no angling rule can modify Nature's: the elimination of older fish by natural mortality once their growth ceases due to an inadequate food supply.

Virtually all the failures of special regulations can be traced to our failure to understand the environmental limitations for growth and sustenance of a particular population. Many anglers have a naive faith that if only angling mortality could be eliminated or greatly reduced, then trout would continue to survive and grow almost indefinitely. We now clearly know that this is not so. Virtually every stream trout population can be characterized by a terminal size and terminal age—a size and age that very few fish in the population will exceed. This terminal size and age is determined by environmental conditions and cannot be changed by special regulations.

I shall return to examine the environmental factors determining terminal size and age but, first, a brief historical review of special regulations. This will help us to understand the origin of much of the present areas of controversy.

I have not performed in-depth historical research on the matter of special regulations to document all of the names and dates associated with the promotion of the concept of releasing fish. In such a situation there is a great temptation to follow a long tradition in the literature of reworking mythology. For example, most historical reviews of dry fly-fishing follow the format of the Biblical version of Genesis; it all began with A, who begat B, who begat C, etc. In recent years, however, the appearance of writers such as Paul Schullery, whose work reflects outstanding historical research, makes me resist the temptation for oversimplification and I simply admit that I am not an authority on the subject. I did, however, seek the help of angling literature scholars, James R. Adams and Donn M. Johnson.

AN AMERICAN PHENOMENON

The concept of releasing fish and the formalization of this concept into statements promoting catch-and-release fishing as a management option appears to be largely an American phenomenon.

J. C. Mottram, a keenly perceptive British author, in his books *Fly Fishing: Some New Arts and Mysteries* (Field Press, 1915) and *Thoughts on Angling* (H. Jenkins, 1953) made eloquent arguments that trout are too grand and noble to be considered as a mere food fish. He discussed the release of trout but did not elaborate his thoughts on the matter into a proposal that catch-and-release should be an integral part of the management of a trout fishery. (Many British private waters still dictate that any trout caught must be killed—to avoid the accumulation of so-called "wise old cannibals.")

In the nineteenth century it was common for angling writers to condemn fish hogs and poachers who were viewed as threats to the sport. The typical view of a nineteenth century fish hog, however, was someone who killed 100 or more trout per day, in contrast to the "sportsman" who killed only the legal limit of 20 or 25.

I suspect that the promotion of catch-and-release fishing was first associated with angling for anadromous Atlantic salmon. Perceptive anglers must have realized this was a limited resource. The average salmon is large; most anglers traveled long distances to salmon rivers. It would seem only a matter of common sense and fairness that anglers should not wantonly kill more salmon than they could eat or carry home in good condition. Although there were likely many early advocates for releasing salmon, I have not found any early documentation that this advocacy position was translated into law.

The first state special regulation trout fishery designed to recycle the catch, of which I am aware, was instituted in Pennsylvania in 1934. The Pennsylvania Fish Commission set aside a section of Spring Creek to create "Fisherman's Paradise" by highly restrictive regulations and the stocking of large hatchery brood fish.

For those who would seek a father figure, the most popular father of catch-and-release angling seems to be Lee Wulff. But there are antecedents in earlier literature.

F. G. Afalo, in his book, *Sunshine and Sport in Florida and the West Indies* (1907), made a plea that tarpon "should be released alive" rather than taken to a taxidermist. George Parker Holden's book, *Streamcraft* (1919), contains a quote of Harold Trowbridge Pulsifer from an issue of *Outdoor Magazine*. Pulsifer was a promoter of catch-and-release angling with barbless hooks. He wrote, "Do not be afraid to join the slowly growing fraternity of those anglers whose password is 'we put them back alive'."

Many years ago, Edward Ringwood Hewitt and his guests practiced catch-and-release angling on his private section of the Neversink River in the Catskills. Hewitt gave the following advice in his 1931 book, *Better Trout Streams*:

"Don't overfish a stream. If the numbers and size of trout caught are decreasing, don't take out so many, return them to the water; very few will ever die from the effects of having been caught. We must realize that every stream has only so much trout-growing ability, and if we overtax this, we reduce our stock and the average size as well. Treat a stream as you would any other productive agency; don't try to make it do more than it can do. Give it a chance and you will be surprised how quickly it will respond to improved conditions."

The Modern Angler, authored by John Alden Knight and published in 1936, included this passage:

"The angler has a definite advantage over the hunter from the standpoint of preserving good sport for himself. When a duck is dropped with a splash among the decoys or when your setter comes to you with a quail or a grouse in his mouth, that particular bird has served its purpose and its usefulness to the sport of hunting is ended. A dead bird has the air of finality about it—it is so completely and definitely dead as it lies limply in your hand. With the fisherman, however, the question of killing is nearly always optional. A fish, hooked with a fly and played to the net, is usually not materially hurt and may be returned to the water, slightly weary but otherwise as good as ever, to be caught again next year."

The first written statement I have found from Lee Wulff on the subject is in his 1939 *Handbook of Freshwater Fishing*. "Game fish are too valuable to be caught only once." Thus we now had an economic rationale for releasing our fish—to be recycled, thereby maintaining or increasing catch rates. Whereas, Mottram's release of trout was for his own spiritual well being, Wulff's was for better management.

A RALLYING CRY

Although John Alden Knight had already stated that a released trout could be caught again, Lee Wulff provided the angling world with a simple, memorable slogan for his philosophy. He also became far more active—and influential—than previous writers had been in promoting the benefits of releasing one's catch. Wulff's 50-year-old slogan has been repeated many times, in numerous modified versions, over the decades. It has become the rallying cry for devout no-kill anglers. Wulff's phrase is a gem; it condenses great truth and wisdom into a few words.

A problem, however, for basing fishery management policy on a one-line slogan concerns details: How many of the fish that are released will, in fact, be caught more than once? When—next week, next month, next year?

When such questions are critically evaluated on factual evidence, it becomes apparent that the "value" of released fish in relation to their contribution to the future fishery varies enormously. There are several reasons. Different species of trout display a wide range of vulnerability to angling (brown trout being most difficult to catch and catch again, cutthroat being most vulnerable). The amount of angling pressure on a particular water matters. Then, once again, there is Nature: the environmental limitations determining the terminal size and age of a wild trout population (how long a released fish can be expected to live).

Wulff also popularized a scientific rationale or biological basis for catch-and-release angling. If the biggest and best breeders are killed off and the runts are left to reproduce, he speculated, a population will become hereditarily stunted. In a 1973 article in *Sports Afield*, entitled "The Myths That Are Exhausting Our Angling Resources," Wulff vented his wrath on professional fisheries biologists for not understand-

ing basic laws of genetics. He wrote, "If we were to cut off the heads of everyone more than five feet tall for two generations, what kind of basketball teams do you think we would have?" and, "The one sure way to miniaturize a species is to kill off the best of the breeding stock and breed the runts." While these statements appear to be a matter of common sense truisms, in the light of biological reality, this is the same kind of "common sense" that once led people to assume the earth was flat.

There certainly is a genetic influence on growth and maximum size—in trout as well as in all living creatures. And it is theoretically possible to change heredity for slower growth. But it is highly improbable that angling has ever changed the genetic basis for growth in any population of wild trout. This is due to the fact that in resident stream populations, the largest, oldest fish have almost certainly spawned at least once and passed on any fast-growing heredity material to the next generation.

It is also a fact that larger females lay more eggs than smaller females, and larger trout are dominant over smaller trout. This means that, if we greatly oversimplify the genetics of growth on the basis of fast growth and slow growth genes in a population, then fast growth fish spawn many more fast growth genes than slow growth fish spawn slow growth genes. Larger females select the optimum spawning sites if in competition for space with smaller females; thus, a higher percentage of the eggs of the larger fish would be expected to hatch. Larger males have first crack at spawning with the larger females. If growth of wild trout were under such simple genetic control, a quantitative (but simplistically unreal) model which takes into account the size-fecundity relationship would demonstrate that wild trout populations are "fixed" for the fastest growth genes.

Actually, there are many, many factors of natural selection influencing the heredity of growth and survival of trout from birth to death. Even in heavily-fished waters, more trout in a population are lost to natural mortality than to angling mortality. The overwhelming majority of trout taken by predators is small (6 inches or less). Any trout remaining "small" greatly increases its mortality risk in comparison to growing larger and taking its chances of being killed by an angler. In any event, there is no real evidence that a wild trout population in any stream has ever experienced a genetic-based growth change due to angling. Where evidence of growth change (or change for an earlier age at spawning) related to exploitation does exist, it concerns species of Pacific salmon exposed to intensive size-selective commercial fisheries. Pacific salmon spawn only once, so all fish taken in a fishery are removed from a population before they spawn (and pass on their heredity to the next generation). In an intensive (approximately 75–80 percent or more of a spawning run harvested), size-selective fishery, the mesh size of gillnets filters out the larger salmon and allows smaller fish to pass on to spawn. Under such circumstances, a hereditary change for earlier age and small size at maturity might be expected.

Except for a few special situations, such as some steelhead fisheries exposed to commercial exploitation and the giant Gerrard Kamloops trout of Kootenay Lake, which typically spawns for the first time weighing about 10 pounds, I do not consider the genetic issue a valid basis for special regulations. The valid issue concerns the use of special regulations as a practical fishery management tool in bridging the gap between the potential supply of wild trout and the angler demand for wild trout.

DEATH BY WORMING

In relation to formal studies on the effects of special regulations, many studies in the 1930s and 1940s verified that, if a high survival rate is expected from released trout, artificial flies and lures are necessary. Mortality of trout caught on bait and released averages about 40 percent, whereas mortality of trout, caught on artificial flies and lures averages about five percent or less (but with no significant and consistent differences among hook type or lure type).

In 1942, Dwight Webster of Cornell University reported on an experiment conducted by the Cornell fly tiers club which made clear that trout caught and released could be caught again. A section of a stream was fenced to prevent upstream and downstream movement, and stocked with 200 hatchery rainbow trout. In two months of catch-and-release fishing, club members recorded a total catch of 601 trout; each trout, on average, was caught three times. By the 1950s, under the impetus of Lee Wulff and his followers, some states began to initiate some form of special regulations in scattered trout fisheries, but only in a token manner. Beginning in 1944, Michigan imposed highly restrictive regulations on a few waters, essentially making them catch-and-release. In 1952, Dr. Albert Hazzard, Director of the Institute for Fisheries Research in Michigan, attracted considerable attention to the subject with an article in *Sports Afield* magazine: "Better Fishing—and How." This was a front page story and included such attention-grabbing headlines as, "Do you want to catch from two to four or even more trout an hour and none of them under twelve inches?" This is one of the most startling proposals ever made! "All anglers had to do to achieve this anglers' paradise was to "secure passage of a law in your state making it illegal to have trout in possession at any time." Dr. Hazzard had a long and distinguished career in fisheries, and I suspect that most of his *Sports Afield* article reflected an editor's rewriting as a hype job.

The letters to the editor of *Sports Afield* following the publication of Hazzard's article were predictable but also informative by making clear the diversity of preferences of the angling public. There were letters of resounding endorsement from the Izaak Walton League and others. More typical was the letter from a fellow who felt cheated and wanted his money back. He believed the headlines on the cover were about how to catch more fish, not about putting them back. Other comments were: "If we can't have our sport and eat it, too, then the State Game Commission should not have our money" and, "If Dr. Hazzard doesn't like fresh trout, that's all right, but…"

After Hazzard's article appeared in *Sports Afield*, special regulations for trout fisheries (typically no-kill regulations) became popularly known as the "Hazzard Plan" or "fishing for fun." Although the Hazzard Plan was instituted on several waters in several states, the concept of special regulations as a management tool to recycle trout was not taken seriously by state fish and game agencies. In general, biologists and administrators looked on the subject as people management, rather than fish management—in the realm of sociology rather than biology. This was unfortunate, because studies were not made and good data were not obtained to understand the factors that influence the success of special regulations—where they work and why, and where they don't work and why.

The Sport Fishing Institute is an organization funded by fishing tackle manufacturers. A bulletin published by the Institute reports on current topics of fisheries management and, in general, reflects current opinion in the field of fisheries. In the 1960s, articles in the SFI bulletin did not reflect kindly on the "fishing for fun" trend. On almost all waters where it was tried, angler use declined, which had unfavorable implications for the fishing tackle industry. A 1964 issue of the bulletin first used the phrase "catch and release" as a preferred replacement for "fishing for fun." It was pointed out that all sport fishing is for fun if the fish are released or not. As an indication of progress made on special regulations, the Sport Fishing Institute now actively supports the intelligent use of special regulations, which are particularly important in heavily-fished lakes to maintain proper predatory/prey ratios between large-mouth bass and forage fishes.

During the past 20 years, besides a constant increase in the numbers of anglers, there has been a large increase in the proportion of anglers who prefer to fish in streams for wild trout. It was apparent to these avid anglers (the "purist," "elite" or "high skill" group of angler classification used by some economists) that special regulations must play a larger role in wild limit management programs. They made their demands loud and clear to state agencies. The generally low level of expertise of agency personnel to understand what special regulations could and could not accomplish caused a period of foundering until it was realized that the application of special regulations is the proper domain of fish management, and that they have a biological basis. In the meantime, agencies lost credibility in the eyes of many anglers demanding more specially regulated waters. This led to controversies, many of which still surround the issue.

VARYING VULNERABILITY

In my summary to the 1987 Symposium on Catch-and-Release Fishing, I attempted to focus on a few basic factors that must be understood if special regulations are to be an effective fisheries management tool, as well as to be more widely accepted and implemented.

The first consideration is the species of trout involved and its relative vulnerability to being caught, released and caught again. For a quantitative assessment, we might ask how many hours of angling per surface acre does it take, on average, to catch each trout (of catchable size) in a population once, twice, three times. In order of vulnerability to angler catch, the rankings are: brown trout (least vulnerable), rainbow trout, brook trout, cutthroat trout (most vulnerable). It may take from 200 to 2,000 hours of angling per acre per year to catch each brown trout twice (depending on expertise of anglers and difficulty of fishing in a particular stream). Cutthroat trout, at the opposite end of the spectrum, can be caught twice, on average, with only 10 to 20 hours of angling per acre.

In the 1970s the first clearcut indication that special regulations can work to greatly increase the catch rate by recycling the released fish and by greatly increasing the survival of older, larger fish, occurred in northern Idaho and in the Yellowstone River in Yellowstone National Park. Both examples involved cutthroat trout.

Even light fishing pressure in catch-and-kill fisheries can cause extremely high mortality in a cutthroat population. It was also fortunate that the cutthroat populations protected by special regulations existed in environments that allowed for an old terminal age (about seven years) and relatively large terminal size (about 18 inches). The significance of the terminal age can be understood when it is realized that any reduction in the total annual mortality rate is compounded dramatically. For example, if angling mortality is eliminated or greatly reduced in a population so that the total annual mortality (natural, plus angling) is reduced from 75 to 50 percent, note what happens to the age structure of the population. At a 75 percent annual mortality rate for every 1,000 age two trout, there would be 250 age three fish. If the annual mortality rate is reduced to 50 percent, there would be 500 age three trout per 1,000 age two fish. Continuing these comparisons on through ages four, five, six and seven, we see four, eight, 16, and 32 times more of the respective ages in populations with a 50 percent annual mortality compared to a population suffering a 75 percent annual mortality.

It should now be readily perceived why the susceptibility of a species to being caught and caught again—in combination with the age structure of a population in relation to percent survival to an older terminal age—is a major determinant of success or failure of special regulations.

The question of what environmental factors determine the terminal size and age in a trout population can now be addressed. This concept is important to understand, because special regulations cannot alter the terminal size and age. Once the terminal size and age of a population is known, the impact on any proposed special regulations can be assessed.

THEIR DAILY RATION
In most small-to-moderate-size trout streams, the overwhelming majority of invertebrate organisms are very tiny species, typically larvae of mayflies, caddisflies, and midges imitated by hook sizes of 18–20 or smaller—and most of these organisms fed on by trout are taken in the drift (the period when insect larvae detach from substrate and drift downstream). Consideration of the average particle size of the dominant food organisms in relation to trout growth energetics (energy expended in feeding and normal activity versus energy gained by food consumption), provides some insight into the limitations on growth

and maximum life span expected in a trout population. The amount of food consumed each day is known as the "daily ration." The daily ration, in turn, can be divided into maintenance ration (amount of food with energy content equivalent to energy expended by daily activity) and growth ration (food energy that goes into growth after maintenance requirements are fulfilled).

If a feeding area in a stream utilized by an individual trout provides one gram of drift organisms per day, this one gram of daily ration would provide both maintenance ration and growth ration for a small trout weighing one ounce (or 30 grams), and this trout would maintain positive growth. If a larger trout of 10 or 12 ounces received only one gram of food per day, maintenance rations would not be met and negative growth (weight loss) would be the result. Unlike humans, where dieting and negative growth can be a life-prolonging action, trout do not survive for long after negative growth begins. Natural mortality rate greatly accelerates.

In most streams with good natural reproduction and recruitment, great numbers of young, small trout abound, and they will consume most of the small particle food supply. It is true that larger trout are dominant over smaller trout and the larger fish will monopolize the best feeding areas. But at some point the larger trout cannot control sufficient space to consume an adequate daily ration to meet maintenance requirements; negative growth and death will soon follow. For the typical brown trout population under such circumstances the terminal age can be expected to be about four and the terminal size about 12 inches. Streams where the terminal size of trout are considerably greater are characterized by an alternate food supply of large organisms such as scuds, crayfish and forage fishes. When trout reach a size of about 12 inches, they can then begin to feed on larger organisms, avoid competition with smaller trout and maintain positive growth. As long as positive growth is maintained, the lifespan can be greatly extended.

Although terrestrial insects can make a major contribution to the trout's diet in many streams, terrestrial food is sporadic and unpredictable. It cannot be counted on to supply the trout's daily ration over long periods of time.

DEATH IN WINTER

Besides food supply, the amount and quality of overwintering habitat and severity of winter conditions can be a "bottleneck" in survival from one year to the next. Most natural mortality after a trout's first few weeks of life occurs in winter.

This was demonstrated in a study on a stream on Vancouver Island, British Columbia, where young-of-the-year coho salmon were fed supplementarily to increase the normal autumn biomass of the population by sevenfold. The following spring there was no significant increase in the population compared to the long-term average. The overwinter mortality rate increased approximately seven times over normal; that is, it was "density dependent."

If fish and wildlife agencies have the personnel with the biological expertise to understand the points discussed above, they can institute special regulations with credibility. They should know the environmental limitations for success: which streams allow the recycling of two- and three-year-old fish and which streams have the potential for maintaining positive growth and good survival to ages five, six, seven years or more. Because resident adult trout typically move only short distances, a whole stream does not have to be placed under special regulations. Sections of one or a few miles can have special regulations for wild trout management, and roadside sites heavily used by the average angler can be stocked with hatchery trout to reduce conflicts.

I believe the fundamentals and principles of trout biology are now sufficiently established to set the stage for increased application of successful special regulation fisheries. The most important attribute for a management agency is its credibility. If agency personnel do a credible job and anglers observe successes, then new programs such as special regulations should have public support.

There is still a people management problem that must be recog-nized. First is the problem of "discrimination" perceived by many anglers. Special regulations for trout require the prohibition of bait-fishing to ensure high survival of the released fish. In a Colorado survey, 11 percent of license buyers said they were solely or predominantly fly fishers, whereas more than 50 percent said they fished at least occasionally with flies and artificial lures. Thus, a regulation allowing any type of artificial lure has the potential for much broader support than fly-fishing only. This, however, raises another problem. Among the most ardent fly fisher no-kill purists, there are many with deep antipathy toward other methods of angling for trout, especially spin-fishing. Such purists will not believe that it could be possible that the survival rate of trout caught and released on a spinning lure (especially a treble hook lure) is similar to trout caught and released on a fly (especially a barbless fly).

BARBLESS DOESN'T MATTER

Gear restriction is still a major source of friction associated with special regulations. Many states prohibit all terminal tackle except single, barb-less hooks for special regulation fisheries. Therefore, a logical conclusion might be that the agency personnel in these states must know what they are doing; they must have solid evidence that barbed hooks and treble hooks kill more released trout than single barbless hooks. Actually, this would be a wrong conclusion. It is an example of lack of agency credibility. More likely, the decisions to enforce a single, barbless hook regulation were made by a commissioner or a director of the agency, acting on a "gut" feeling. If staff biologists were consulted on the matter, their advice was ignored or the biologists were not familiar with the evidence compiled over many years on hooking mortality.

In the proceedings of the 1977 Catch and Release Symposium, all hooking mortality studies were exhaustively reviewed and summarized by Richard Wydoski, who concluded that "use of barbless hooks does not significantly reduce mortality, and restrictions requiring the use of barbless hooks are not biologically justified." In 1984, the Washington State Game Department had another review made of hooking mortality studies, including work preformed after 1977. The Washington report concluded, "There is no valid technical basis for requiring single, barbless hooks."

What is still the most comprehensive, in-depth analysis of hooking mortality of wild trout in relation to hook type, degree of exhaustion (stress), water temperature, and sexual maturation was conducted by Leo Marnell in 1964 and 1965 at Yellowstone Lake as part of his Ph.D. research. (Dr. Marnell is now the aquatic biologist for Glacier National Park.) Many hundreds of Yellowstone cutthroat were caught on various hooks and lure types and held for 10 or 30 days to document mortality. With all factors constant except hook and lure type, 3 of 75 trout (4 percent) died after release on barbed flies, 2 of 60 (3.3 percent) died after being caught on barbless flies, 3 of 113 (2.7 percent) on barbed treble hooks (spoon lure) and 6 of 100 (6 percent) on barbless treble hooks. Statistical analysis of the data showed these differences to be nonsignificant; that is, this amount of variation in mortality caused by the different hook types is explainable by random chance. A highly significant difference in mortality did occur with trout caught on trolled live bait (worm) and released. Of 161 worm-caught fish, 78 (48 percent) died after release. Of these bait-caught trout, only 5 of 61 (8 percent) died if they did not swallow the bait, and 73 of 100 (73 percent) died after swallowing the bait.

In the stress test with fish caught on a treble hook lure, 4 of 100 died after landing as soon as possible, 6 of 100 died after five minutes of playing, and 5 of 100 died after 10 minutes of playing (fish were not allowed to rest during playing). Again, there was no significant difference among groups experiencing different levels of exhaustion. In regard to the cause of mortality of released trout, Marnell found that, of 33 deaths (of 652 trout caught and released on artificial files and lures), 30 were the result of hooks causing bleeding—typically, from rupture of gill filaments. Only 3 of the 33 deaths were unknown causes, which might suggest lethal stress.

For those who want to examine the details of Leo Marnell's research (without wading through his Ph.D. thesis), he and his associates published two papers in 1970, one in the *Transactions of the American Fisheries Society* (Volume 99, Number 4) and another in the *Progressive Fish Culturist* (Volume 32, Number 4).

A trend for increased mortality with higher water temperatures was apparent only in the bait-caught trout in Marnell's study. Yet the highest temperatures in Yellowstone Lake during the study were only from 58° to 62° F. The accumulated evidence to date indicates a significant increase in mortality can be expected when water temperatures exceed 60° F.

DEATH BY WARMING

The most recently published study demonstrating the relationship between mortality of released trout and temperature, concerns the Lahontan cutthroat fishery of Heenan Lake in California. The lake is managed with no-kill regulations. Trout were caught on Phoebe spinning lures with single barbless, barbed treble and barbless treble hooks during early June, mid-July and September. Released fish were held in live boxes in the lake for four days to determine mortality. In the June and September trials—with water temperatures ranging from 50° F to 60° F—4 of 282 (1.4 percent) and 1 of 82 (1.2 percent), respectively, of the released fish died. There was no significant difference among hook types. During the July trial, when surface water temperatures reaches 70° F, 82 of 169 (48.5 percent) trout expired after release. The highest mortality (55 percent) occurred with a single barbless hook.

A body of water such as Heenan Lake has special physical characteristics that differ from those of stream environments. About 15 feet below the surface in July, the temperature in the thermocline was only 57° F. During this period, I suspect, the trout live in the cooler layer with occasional forays into the warmer surface for feeding (if sufficient food is not available in the more comfortable thermocline zone). The holding of the caught-and-released trout in live boxes in the warmer surface water probably greatly increased mortality, compared with fish normally freed and allowed to seek deeper, cooler sanctuary. This experience does, however, confirm the assumption that a curve, depicting the mortality-temperature relationship of released trout, will show a sharp upward inflection between 60° F and 70° F.

In streams, I would expect the temperature-related mortality problem to be more or less self-regulating. Trout feeding is sharply reduced as temperatures rise from 60° F to 70° F Thus the quality of fishing, the number of anglers and the trout caught at higher temperatures is greatly reduced. In a recent conversation with Richard Vincent of the Montana Department of Fish, Wildlife and Parks, he told me of a study on the Madison River in which catch rates were related to changes in temperatures. As the water rose to 60° F and above, angler success showed an inverse relationship—the higher the temperature, the lower the catch rate.

Each stream or lake presents a special situation. If it is documented that excessive mortality occurs during a certain time of year, negating benefits of special regulations, then a seasonal closure of the fishery might be warranted.

There is a caveat. Higher mortality is not always bad. If the density of a trout population exceeds the limit of its growth rations, growth rates may significantly decline, and some additional thinning by angling mortality can be beneficial. This phenomenon was reported at the Wild Trout III symposium in 1984. Some New York State trout streams under no-kill regulations accumulated high densities of brown trout which exhibited reduced growth in comparison to the period under normal regulations. Age three trout declined from 12–14 inches to 10–11 inches after no-kill was enforced. A change in regulation allowed limited take, density was reduced and the growth rate improved.

I suspect that mortality due to stress or acidosis is strongly related to water temperature. The most recent research paper I have read on acidosis mortality concerned hatchery rainbow trout that were stressed by continual prodding until they turned belly-up. Blood samples taken at regular intervals revealed a sharp drop in the blood pH to acid levels. This study verified that, acidosis is not caused by lactic acid.

Roderick Haig-Brown, in his 1964 book, *Fisherman's Fall*, reported on research at the University of British Columbia which demonstrated that lactic acid levels in stressed fish do not reach lethal levels. Although not caused by lactic acid, some unknown acid does cause acidosis. In those trout that recovered, the blood soon returned to normal pH; in those that died, the blood remained acidic. My suspicion is that the blood pH recovery rate may be related to water temperature and/or the intensity of acidosis is greater when temperatures are higher.

There is still some interesting research to be conducted before all of the precise mechanisms causing mortality are understood. There is not, however, need for further research before special regulations are more widely implemented, unless data are needed on specific trout populations to understand what might be expected from special regulations and what type of regulations would be best suited to a particular fishery. There is no need for further research on hooking mortality. Enough studies have been done to allow for a prediction that 95 percent or more of trout caught and released on flies and artificial lures in streams will survive if the water temperature is less than 60° F. The type of hook—single, treble, barbed or barbless—is not a significant influence on mortality. Virtually all mortality that does occur is due to rupturing of blood vessels in the gills and mouth, not from stress.

ORDERING OUR PRIORITIES

My final comments on special regulations concern priorities.

It is understandable and quite predictable that many of the most sincere and dedicated trout fishers will embrace the concept of special regulations with great zeal and fervor (typically, no-kill regulations restricted to barbless flies only) and become narrowly focused on the issue to the exclusion of all other aspects of trout conservation. To put the matter in perspective, if 1,000 miles of our best trout streams are managed under special regulations and the regulations work at optimum success to recycle trout again and again, the numbers and pounds of additional trout caught each year would number in the hundreds of thousands. This indeed would be impressive, but would still be a minor gain in comparison to the numbers and pounds of trout and salmon that have been lost due to environmental degradation. Consider the problems of acid rain, logging practices, urbanization, road construction and pollution in the East; recognize that most western salmonid waters and their watersheds are on federal lands where thousands and thousands of miles of coldwater streams have been lost or continually threatened under multiple use management where dominant interest groups have historically called the shots. The protection and restoration of degraded streams and their fish populations hold the prospect of millions more pounds of wild trout that could be fished for and caught annually.

The zeal possessed by many dedicated purists is understandable. Their almost religious belief in fishing regulations to protect—and preferred tackle to catch—trout is a personal credo that will not be readily changed. Truly effective trout conservation, however, is a matter of ordering priorities.

Just as nineteenth century anglers zealously were on guard to protect trout populations from "fish hogs" while whole watersheds were being stripped of cover and destroyed by pollution, modern anglers often fritter away precious energies on controversies about allowable hook types while taxpayer-subsidized cattle herds continue to destroy thousands of miles of formerly excellent trout streams.

After a favorite trout stream is safe from destruction, its habitat restored, then we may divert our concerns to implementation of the best regulations to manage its fishery.

AUTHOR'S NOTE
I wrote this article explaining the factors that make special regulations, designed to recycle the catch, achieve success or failure. This subject was of great importance to Trout Unlimited in view of the pervasive ignorance at that time among anglers and agencies making the regulations. Trout Unlimited philosophy was originally based on influencing fisheries agencies to give priority to wild trout management over put-and-take stocking of hatchery trout. Recycling the catch by special regulations was basic to TU's philosophy as expressed in the slogan: "Limit your catch, don't kill your limit." During the first few years, TU received mostly negative reactions from agency people citing failures of special regulations fisheries to achieve their goals. Once it was understood that different species of trout have quite different susceptibilities to be caught-and-released and caught again, and that different populations in different environments exhibit large differences in growth rates and life spans, special regulations began to achieve success.

Success has also created problems. A hardcore group of fly fishers fervently lobby to impose no-kill regulations limited to barbless flies as the only regulation acceptable to them. I would recommend that before such anglers rant and rave at a commission hearing demanding their monolithic view be imposed as law, they should read my 1989 article and base their demands on sound evidence supporting their position; but, I realize that this would be comparable to the horse at the watering trough who won't drink because it's not thirsty.

Two points from this piece need some correction. I stated that special regulations are an American phenomenon. Sir Humphrey Davy in his book, *Salmonia*, published in 1828, mentions that a private fishery on the English River Colne required anglers to release all trout of less than two pounds so they could be caught again the next year. I stated that bait fishing must be prohibited with special regulations because it causes too high a mortality in caught-and-released trout. There are exceptions to this general rule. In streams in Pennsylvania and Connecticut where toxic pollution didn't appear to affect the trout but made them unfit for human consumption, no-kill regulations were instituted that did not prohibit bait. The trout populations greatly increased. It was obvious that bait-caught trout did not suffer the expected high mortalities. I believe this was due to bait anglers knowing they would not keep the trout and set the hook as soon as they felt a bite. The bait-caught trout were simply not hooked deeply.

The famous fishery for brown and rainbow trout in the North Platte River, Wyoming known as the Miracle Mile allowed a bag limit of two trout per day and no restrictions on bait. With these regulations, on average, each rainbow trout was caught-and-released almost eight times during a year and each brown trout 1.2 times. The success of these regulations, despite allowing bait, is explained by the fact that about 75 percent of the anglers are non-residents who mainly fish with flies and release all trout caught. Also, reservoirs above and below the Miracle Mile section have walleye and are stocked with hatchery rainbow trout. Anglers who want to take fish home for dinner concentrate their efforts in these reservoirs.

THE FAMILY TREE

SPRING 1990

OUR CONCEPT OF TIME IS COLORED BY EXPERIENCE. A human life span of 100 years is perceived of as one of extreme duration. To examine the evolutionary history and origin of the family Salmonidae, a time frame of 100 million years is suggested. The events and changes on earth during this enormous duration, acting to direct the course of evolution, are known only by bits and pieces. Any attempt to recreate a scenario of the evolutionary history of trout and salmon—from the origin of the family to living species—must include considerable speculation.

To place the family Salmonidae in a larger evolutionary context, we must go back about 500 million years to the origin of vertebrate animals.

The earliest vertebrates (animals with backbones—although the primitive "backbone" is a cartilaginous rod, or notochord, without bone) are grouped in the class Agnatha (jawless vertebrates). Agnathas had mouths but no skeletal elements forming jaws. They lacked paired fins—no pectoral or pelvic fins. They had only a single nostril. About 60–70 species of Agnatha still persist which we know as lampreys and hagfishes.

Evolution is often thought of as new groups of more advanced species replacing more primitive species which become extinct. In this light, it may seem strange that several extremely primitive species, retaining the same basic physiology and anatomy possessed by their ancestors of hundreds of millions of years ago, are still around. One species, the sea lamprey, is not only still around, but it devastated the modern fish fauna of the Great Lakes once it got above Niagara Falls and gained access to the upper lakes. It also has proved highly successful in persisting despite intensive efforts to eradicate it by traps, electrical wires, and chemical treatment of spawning streams. The sea lamprey might be considered as an "evil" species in relation to its impact on the Great Lakes, but it is certainly an evolutionary success story.

The primitive lamprey's success story might, at first, seem analogous to a Model-T Ford winning the Indianapolis 500, finishing ahead of all the most advanced vehicles. Actually it is more analogous to a Model-T, fitted with balloon tires, winning a race across a swamp. Its lightness would give the Model-T an advantage over modern cars in that particular environment. That is, it would fill the "swamp" niche better and win the race in that environment. Living species of lampreys and hagfishes occupy unique niches. They use their jawless mouths for a variety of feeding specializations in different species or different life history stages such as filter feeding, scavenging, and parasitism-feeding specializations for which no modern fish species competes.

An understanding of niche specialization explains the origin and persistence through time of trout and salmon and of all existing species—they do something better in a particular environment, under particular conditions, than other species (which also persist by doing something else better to avoid or reduce interspecific niche overlap).

During the period from about 500 to 400 million years ago, primitive fishes developed many anatomical advancements including jaws and paired fins. These advancements resulted in a proliferation of new "models" to fill new niches. By 400 million years ago, two main trends of jawed fishes became established—the cartilaginous fishes of the class Chrondrichthyes (sharks and rays), and bony fishes of the class Osteichthyes. The bony fishes subdivided into three subclasses—one for lungfishes, one for coelacanths, one for ray finned fishes (subclass Actinopterygii). During the late Paleozoic era to the middle of the Mesozoic, or from about 250 to 150 million years ago, the ray finned fishes evolved many further advancements leading to the origin of modern body fishes, or teleosts, which gained overwhelming dominance in the world of fishes.

There are about 750 living species of sharks and rays, six species of lung-fishes, and one living coelacanth. The more primitive Actinopterygii persist as about 30 species of sturgeons and paddlefish, about 11 species of African bichirs or reedfish (order Polypteriformes), five species of gar and one species of bowfin. In contrast, there are about 20,000 known species of teleostean fishes, with about 100 or more new species described each year. The teleosts dominate in numbers and biomass in virtually all freshwater and marine environments. Once a certain combination of evolutionary advancements in jaws, fins and skeletal structure was attained, teleosts proliferated with great evolutionary success.

During the early to mid Cretaceous period of the late Mesozoic era, from about 100 to 130 million years ago, several divergent lines of teleost evolution became established which have persisted to the present. These include groups we recognize as the orders Clupeiformes (herrings, shad, anchovies, sardines), Osteoglosiformes (bonytongues, including the mooneye and goldeye of North America), Elopiformes (tarpons and bonefishes), and the very successful superorder Ostariophysi which includes all the minnows, suckers, catfishes and characins. All of the above teleostean orders possess some specialized features which indicate they were not in the mainline of teleost evolution leading to the modern spiny-rayed fishes (such as perch and bass).

The order Salmoniformes includes a Southern Hemisphere group exemplified by the families Galaxiidae and Retropinnidae of Australia and New Zealand, a Northern Hemisphere group including Salmonidae and Osmeridae (smelts) plus several families of deep-sea fishes. The general, primitive features exhibited by various families of salmoniform fishes indicate that the mainline of teleost evolution went through the Salmoniformes (or via a common ancestral branch). Thus, the order Salmoniformes most probably had its origin well over 100 million years ago. This ancient evolutionary heritage can be readily observed in living species of salmon and trout. Primitive characteristics include the smooth (cycloid) scales, fins without spines, position of the pelvic fins under dorsal fin rather than under pectoral fins (as in perch and bass), upper jaw formed by maxillary bone (premaxillary in perch and bass), rays of caudal fin (tail) supported by three upturned vertebrae, vestige of spiral valve intestine, absence of oviducts, presence of abdominal pores, etc.

There is little doubt that the combination of these primitive traits denotes a very ancient origin for the family Salmonidae. Until the fossil record is better known, however, the timing of this origin is a matter of educated guessing. An origin of about 100 million years ago appears reasonable in relation to the great antiquity of the order Salmoniformes. It is probable that trout-like fishes of the family Salmonidae, not vastly different in appearance or in ecology from living species, inhabited coldwater streams when dinosaurs still roamed the earth. The origin of the family was likely the result of a polypoid event (doubling of chromosome numbers) in a common ancestral species. All three subfamilies, Coregoninae (whitefishes), Thymallinae (grayling), and Salmoninae (trout salmon, char), have about twice the amount of DNA in their chromosomes as do species in other families of the order Salmoniformes. Thus, it can be assumed that this polypoid event occurred in a common ancestor prior to the divergence into evolutionary lines we now recognize as subfamilies.

The earliest documented fossil definitely classified as Salmonidae was found in Eocene deposits of British Columbia (45–50 million years old) and named *Eosalmo driftwoodensis*. *Eosalmo* was a trout-like fish, apparently of the subfamily Salmoninae. If further research confirms subfamily classification, it would demonstrate that the three subfamilies had diverged from each other by at least 50 million years ago; this would lend credence to an estimate of about 100 million years since the origin of the family.

The question of habitat of the original ancestral salmonid fish— freshwater or marine—has been long debated but never fully resolved. The evidence that all living species reproduce in freshwater argues for a freshwater origin. The fact that many whitefish species and most species of salmon, trout and char have anadromous populations is evidence that the physiological adaptation for osmoregulation in the sea (ability to retain water and excrete salts) has been passed on from the earliest ancestor.

It is probable that, from the earliest ancestor to the present, salmonid fishes have always been coldwater species, restricted to the cold waters of the Northern Hemisphere. During the early periods of salmonid evolution (Eocene and earlier) the Northern Hemisphere was one great land mass (Laurasia = North America, Greenland, Europe and Asia) which became separated by continental drift and the intervening area filled in by the Atlantic and Arctic oceans. Such geological events are typically associated with evolutionary divergences. For example, with living species of trout and salmon we can trace a Pacific basis origin for Pacific salmons, rainbow and cutthroat trout, and an Atlantic basis origin for brown trout and Atlantic salmon.

During the history of the earth there have been many alternating periods of global warming and global cooling which would shift the distribution or salmonid fishes. During warming periods the distribution shifted from south to north and vice-versa during cooling periods. During the Eocene period, when *Eosalmo* inhabited waters of British Columbia, a series of large lakes (the Green River lakes) occurred in southwest Wyoming, northwest Colorado and northeast Utah. The fossil fishes of the Green River lakes have been well studied. The fish fauna inhabiting the Green River lakes of 40 to 50 million wars ago was typically warmwater fishes—species of gars, bowfins, paddlefish, suckers, ancestors of mooneye and goldeye, herrings and catfishes. But no salmonid fossils have been found. Evidently the climate was too warm for coldwater fishes in this region during that period.

The fossil record for Samonidae is spotty. There are two reasons. First, the preservation of an organism as a fossil is a rare, chance event and the finding of fossil is also largely a rare, chance event. The second reason concerns the number of people who study fossil fishes (paleoichthyologists) and who have a particular interest in salmonid fossils. Currently, most research on salmonid fossils is centered at two universities—the University of Michigan (Dr. Gerald Smith and associates) and Ohio State University (Dr. Ted Cavender).

In recent years, an increasing number of salmonid fossils have been discovered in the western United States, representing species which lived during the Miocene to early Pleistocene times or from about 20 million to about two million years ago. I must emphasize again that the fossil evidence is sketchy; an evolutionary scenario presented now is likely to change in the future as more fossils are found and studied. Attempting to envision how the family of Salmonidae was constructed during a distant time period from the evidence of a very few terminal branches (fossil specimens) is analogous to a blind person describing the morphology of an elephant from assessing a few parts of the animal—a rough approximation might be possible.

With this reservation in mind, the following approximation is given.

After *Eosalmo*, a gap of about 25 million years in the fossil record of Salmonidae occurs which obviously leaves a large blank area on the family tree. The early Miocene fossils suggest that a major branching in the subfamily Salmoninae had become well established with one branch leading to the present genera of *Brachymystax* (Siberian lenok), *Hucho* (European huchen and Siberian taimen), and *Salvelinus* (chars), and the other branch leading to the trouts and salmons of the genera Salmo and Oncorhynchus. Evidently, both ancestral char-like and huchen-like species occurred in western North America during the early to mid-Miocene period.

By the late Miocene, species we now classify in the genus *Oncorhynchus* were widely distributed in western North America. Three major groups have been distinguished. Besides the ancestors of the living species of Pacific salmon (Oncorhynchus in the strict sense as limited by former classification), there were two groups of trout-like species. Among northern fossils (Oregon and Idaho), a trout with a rod-like upper jaw bone predominates. This type of fossil trout was originally described as the genus *Rhabdofario*. In Nevada, late Miocene fossils of trout, evidently ancestral to rainbow and cutthroat trout, have been more commonly found. Some of these fossil species apparently were anadromous. Some lived in lakes and some lived in streams, similar to the present types of life histories.

Many of the ancient species were probably not vastly different from living species in size, appearance or ecology. Some fossils, however, represent rather bizarre evolutionary models highly divergent from the mainstream of evolution. The sabertooth salmon of Pliocene times reached lengths of six feet or more and possessed a large fang at the tip of its jaws. The great development of gillrakers in the saber-tooth salmon, however, indicate it fed by straining plankton, probably in the ocean.

Ancient southward distribution of trout during periods of global cooling are documented in the fossil record from the Lake Chapala basin of Mexico, about 250 miles south of present distribution of living species. In other parts of the world, populations of living species exist as glacial relicts. Because these relict populations do not exhibit significant divergence from more northern populations of their species, it is assumed that they attained their southern distribution in relatively recent times. Perhaps this occurred during the last glacial epoch (10,000 to 50,000 years ago when ocean temperature were cooler. Such examples include the masu salmon of Taiwan, the taimen of the Yangtze basin of central China and the brown trout of North Africa. For Europe and Asia, the fossil record of Salmonidae is virtually unknown and there are no paleoicthyologists studying Eurasian salmonid fossils.

Today about all that can be done to backtrack on the family tree, to assess the times and places of branching leading to all living genera and species, is to compare various types of characters denoting the different genera and how they change through evolutionary time. This is essentially how ichthyologists arrive at a system of classification that reflects evolutionary relationships. Admittedly, the evidence is often inconclusive and calls for professional judgment to arrive at a classification of all living species and their assignment to genera. Because of this uncertainty, disagreement exists among ichthyologists regarding which classification is "best"—which most accurately reflects evolutionary relationships and branchings of the family tree. With this warning of hazardous authenticity, I plan to present my classification of salmonine fishes (subfamily Salmoninae) in the upcoming summer issue of *Trout*.

AUTHOR'S NOTE

This column, placing the evolution of the family Salmonidae within the context of fish evolution, is similar to lecture notes I used when I taught ichthyology. An updating concerns the estimated number of species of modern bony fishes (given as 20,000 in 1990). Based on projecting the number of new species discovered each year, the current estimate is about 35,000. But there are problems with any estimate of the number of species due to lack of general agreement about the definition of species.

HOW MANY SPECIES?

SUMMER 1990

I CONCLUDED MY LAST COLUMN in the spring issue of *Trout* with an announcement that I would present my classifications of the species of trout, salmon and char of the world in this issue. This was somewhat of a rash statement on my part but, before I had second thoughts on the matter and could retract the announcement, the spring issue went to press.

My uneasiness in producing a classification concerns the uncertainties and ambiguities of classification—resulting in individual interpretations and controversy. Disagreement among fisheries experts regarding the classification of salmonid fishes is analogous to disagreements among experts giving opposing testimony during a trial on the sanity of a defendant, or among experts testifying on the true significance of cholesterol or the nutritive value of oat bran in relation to human health. In all of these situations, essentially the same data, evidence, and information is used to arrive at different and opposing conclusions—the experts disagree because of personal bias which results in different emphasis and interpretations. A personal bias may be the result of many reasons. A psychiatrist, testifying as an expert witness in court, using the same evidence, but with different emphasis and interpretation, could make a case for sanity or a case for insanity based on who was paying for the testimony.

If scientists lead or are part of a research program, they can also be expected to have a bias of self-interest to defend and promote their program as superior to contending programs. Thus, the diverse types of evidence used to classify organisms—morphological, biochemical, molecular, etc. result in different types of research programs with biases reflecting different emphases. Different interpretations of the same evidence is possible because there is no set of rules or generally agreed upon definitions of categories of classification such as genera, species or subspecies. One ichthyologist may recognize two or three separate species, while another would classify these same fish as two or three subspecies of one species.

What does a non-specialist do in such a situation? Typically, an "appeal to authority" is used. A committee of ornithologists might come up with a consensus of opinion on the number of species and genera of birds classified in a family. This is published as an "official" classification endorsed by a society. The classification is by decree; it may not be an accurate reflection of evolutionary reality but it is an official list which can be cited as the authority—yet subject to change.

As mentioned in the spring issue, there is still no official list of species of salmonid fishes of the world. The American Fisheries Society has a list of North American fish species. I have some disagreement with this list concerning species versus subspecies classification of some of the trouts listed. But I have not elevated my disagreement to controversy status.

Before I present my interpretation of how many species of trout, salmon and char exist in the world, a brief review of concepts and definitions of a species would be helpful.

Historically, species have been defined as a group of organisms that reproduce their own kind. That is, species identity is maintained through time. In modern times, the biological species concept has developed which emphasizes the degree of reproductive isolation of a species. If a species is to maintain its identity (reproduce its own kind) it should not hybridize with other closely related species; if it did to any extent, it would lose its identity. A problem with the use of the reproductive isolation criterion for species recognition is that a whole spectrum of degrees of such isolation may occur between and within species, essentially unrelated to the magnitude of evolutionary divergence. For example, I would agree with the official American Fisheries Society's list that rainbow trout and cutthroat trout are two separate species. This is based on the fact that along the Pacific Coast, from northern California to southern Alaska, rainbow and cutthroat trout maintain their separate identities. The limited hybridization that does occur is insufficient to break down species identity to a significant degree. From a biological point of view, they are two separate species occupying two different niches when they coexist.

In inland waters where cutthroat trout are native but rainbow trout did not naturally occur, the two species did not evolve together. Niche differentiation is thus less distinct, resulting in a lack of reproductive isolation. In this case, the introduction and establishment of rainbows almost invariably has led to massive hybridization and loss of identity of native cutthroat populations. The subtleties and complexities of factors determining reproductive isolation—or lack thereof—can be observed within one subspecies of inland cutthroat trout: the west slope cutthroat, *Oncorhynchus clarki lewisi*.

In sections of the John Day River drainage of Oregon, and of the Salmon and Clearwater drainages of Idaho, the westslope cutthroat is native; it coevolved with native rainbow trout. In these waters the two species maintain distinct niches and avoid hybridization. In the Saint Joe drainage of Idaho and the Clark Fork drainage of Montana, westslope cutthroat trout are native and rainbow trout originally were absent (coevolution did not occur). Here, reproductive isolation is absent and the two species cannot maintain their separate identities after rainbows become established.

Another extreme of reproductive isolation between closely related populations of one species can be observed with rainbow trout. A single river might contain summer-run steelhead, winter-run steelhead and resident, non-anadromous rainbow trout—all coexisting with reproductive isolation from one another. In this case, separate species recognition is not given because different races of steelhead and rainbow trout are the result of multiple, independent origins within the species in relatively recent geological time.

With an admonition concerning the uncertainty involved in compiling a list of species, I will invoke my "authority" and proceed to examine the branches identified as genera in that part of the family tree identified as the subfamily Salmoninae in the spring issue of *Trout*.

The first major divergence examined is the char genus *Salvelinus*. The number of species which should be recognized in this genus is, by far, the most controversial aspect of the classification of salmonid fishes. For many years, controversy has raged in the international literature on char classification. I have contributed my share to this controversy and, looking back, I admit I have often been less than charitable in expressing my disagreements with opposing viewpoints.

An observation can be noted on the lack of consistency correlating common names of species with their scientific classification. In North

America, for example, we recognize lake trout, brook trout and bull trout in the genus *Salvelinus*, rainbow trout and cutthroat trout in the genus *Oncorhynchus*, and brown trout in the genus *Salmo*.

No matter if we call them trout or char, the species of the genus *Salvelinus* can be clustered into three main evolutionary lines within the genus. Two of these lines lead to single species: lake trout and brook trout, native only to North America. Trying to unravel the cluster of species associated with the third evolutionary line which includes Arctic char, Dolly Varden and bull trout is enormously difficult and complex. Besides the three above mentioned species, a fourth "good" species, the Far Eastern char, *Salvelinus leucomaenis*, occurs in Asia (*S. leucomaenis*, is a good species because there is no disagreement on its recognition—only its relationships to other species). I would recognize the stone char, also in Kamchatka, named *S. albus*, as a good species. In my classification, I group the stone char with *S. confluentus*, as species sharing a close evolutionary relationship (more closely related to each other than to other species of char). Only an educated guess can be made on how many "good" species are included among the char currently lumped as Arctic char, *S. alpinus* in Europe, Asia and North America.

In recent times, three new species of char have been described from the Soviet Far East. Two of these new species occur in only one lake on the Chukokst Peninsula (across the Bering Strait from Alaska) and are highly divergent from any known species. How many new species remain to be discovered when the remote char lakes across Siberia are investigated? Until then, I would make a rough estimate that the genus *Salvelinus* contains about 15 species of char, among which is the third largest species of the family Salmonidae, the lake trout, *S. namaycush*, with a maximum recorded weight of 102 pounds. Other species of char that can attain a large size include Arctic char and bull trout which have been recorded at about 30-plus pounds.

Also associated with the genus *Salvelinus* in my classification are the genera *Brachymystax* and *Hucho* (species of all three generally lack teeth on the shaft of the vomer bone in roof of mouth and have a highly specialized type of lateral line scale). The genus *Brachymystax* is generally considered to contain a single species, the lenok, *B. lenok*. The lenok is a trout-like fish occurring in river basins across Siberia from the Ob River eastward and south to the Amur River drainage and mountainous sections of the Yellow, Lo, and Han river drainages of China (the lenok of China was described as a separate subspecies from other lenok). It has long been known, however, that two forms of lenok occur: a sharp-snouted lenok and a blunt-snouted lenok. Both forms occur in the Amur River basin. It is likely that the fish called lenok actually represents two distinct species.

Lenok are not known to go to sea. They feed mainly on invertebrates and readily take flies and lures. Their maximum size is about 15–16 pounds.

For anglers, the genus *Hucho* is of interest, because it contains the Siberian taimen, probably attaining the largest size of any salmonid fish. I classify the huchen (*Hucho hucho*) of the Danube River of Europe and the Siberian taimen as two subspecies of one species—*H. hucho hucho* and *H. hucho taimen*. They are very similar to each other, but the taimen appears to attain a greater maximum size than the huchen (perhaps about 150 pounds versus 110 pounds). Exactly how large a size taimen may attain is unknown. They occur in remote areas with little sport fishing and no official record keeping. The taimen is not an important commercial fish so few detailed studies on size and growth can be found in the Russian literature. The largest size I have found documented in the literature (based on specimens weighed and measured) is 123 pounds (which is less than the 126-pound commercially caught Chinook salmon) but the hearsay evidence of much larger fish is enticing.

In the realm of science fiction hearsay, a few years ago, one of the supermarket tabloids had a headline story of a 35-foot-long, 2,000-pound "trout" in a lake of Sinkiang Province, China, which fed on horses and goats. Although I consider such fish stories in the same category of tabloid veracity as the 80-year-old woman who gave birth to a two-headed baby, the name of the lake was given (Hanas Lake).

I consulted a Chinese book on the wildlife of Sinkiang Province, and found that taimen do indeed occur in Hanas—where they "attain a size of up to 10 kilogram (22 pounds) and more." How much more? I doubt 2,000 pounds more. More substantative hearsay in the Russian literature includes an 1871 report mentioning that in the Yenisei, Pyasina and Khatanga (rivers of Siberia draining to the Arctic Ocean), "taimen may reach 80 kilogram (175 pounds) and more."

A 1929 publication recounted testimony of local people on the Uda River (a tributary to the Okhotsk Sea north of the Amur River) that taimen may reach six pud (a "pud" is an old Russian weight equal to 16.4 kilograms or 36 pounds). There do indeed appear to be large taimen in the Uda River.

In 1989, Larry Shoenborn, producer of the *Fishing the West* television program, visited the Far East to do some angling for exotic fishes. He sent me a photograph of a taimen caught in the Uda River which he estimated to be about 80 pounds—evidently the trophy was cut up and consumed before an official weight could be recorded. Obviously the taimen of Siberia and the Soviet Far East offer a great opportunity to anglers seeking trophy and world record size fish. Be forewarned, however, that there is no transportation network that can easily bring you to a prime taimen river. Accommodations and services typically associated with tourism are nonexistent.

As more foreign anglers fish for taimen, we can expect to learn more about their maximum size. Most sport fishing for taimen is with large spoons and plugs. A size 4/0 muddler minnow, though, might really turn them on, or perhaps a horsehair streamer would do the trick on the Hanas Lake monster. Anglers who enjoy tarpon on a fly rod might find the taimen an exciting new challenge.

The distribution of taimen is quite similar to that of the lenok, except the taimen occurs farther to the west—to the Pechora River.

A second, quite different species of *Hucho*, *H. perryi*, occurs in Hokkaido and Sakhalin islands of the Far East. In contrast to the Danube huchen and the Siberian taimen, which are strictly freshwater fish, *H. perryi* spends part of its life at sea.

A fish named *Hucho bleekeri* is known from a small segment of the Yangtze River basin. Virtually nothing is known of *bleekeri*. I suspect it represents a subspecies of *H. hucho* or *H. perryi*.

Moving from the char, lenok and taimen, to the "pure" trout and salmon branches of the family tree, the genera *Oncorhynchus* and *Salmo* can be assessed to determine how many species they contain. As discussed in the winter issue of *Trout*, the genus *Oncorhynchus* has been expanded to include species of western trout formerly classified in the genus *Salmo*. I recognize six species of Pacific salmon in North America and Asia. The masu or cherry salmon, *O. masou*, is restricted to the Far East; the other five species occur in both North America and Asia. The western North American trouts can be divided into two major evolutionary groupings classified as rainbow trout, *O. mykiss*, and cutthroat trout, *O. clarki*. The American Fisheries Society officially recognizes four additional species: California golden trout, *O. aguabonita*; Apache trout, *O. apache*; Gila trout, *O. gilae*; and Mexican golden trout, *O. chysogaster*. A problem for classifying these four kinds of trout as species or subspecies concerns reproductive isolation, or lack thereof. None of them can maintain its identity when occurring with either rainbow or cutthroat trout. Their original distribution isolated them from contact with other trout, and they lack behavioral or ecological distinctions which could provide reproductive isolation.

My classification is a compromise. I would recognize Gila trout and Apache trout as two subspecies of one species, *O. gilae gilae* and *O. gilae apache*. Species recognition is based on the distinctive chromosomes shared by both Gila and Apache trout, but the extremely close genetic relationships between them argues that they should be classified as two subspecies of one species rather than separate species. The Mexican golden trout is quite different from other trout in several characteristics. I would retain separate species classification for *chrysogaster*, at least until more is known about its evolutionary history. I would classify the California golden trout as a subspecies of rainbow trout, *O. mykiss aguabonita*, based on its close genetic relationship to rainbow trout and lack of reproductive isolation.

In the genus *Salmo*, the Atlantic salmon, *S. salar*, and the brown trout, *S. trutta*, are two well-known species. A well marked, but lesser known, species is the marbled trout, *S. marmoratus*, of tributary rivers to the northern Adriatic Sea. The marbled trout is a large predator, attaining weights to about 50 pounds. It has only light colored, marbled markings on its body, similar to char of the genus *Salvelinus*. The genetic relationship of *S. marmoratus*, however, is close to *S. trutta*, and the two species are known to hybridize when they occur together. Two additional species are commonly recognized in the genus *Salmo*: *S. letnica* of Lake Ohrid, Yugoslavia, and *S. ischchan* of Lake Sevan, U.S.S.R., represent ancient invasions of an *S. trutta* ancestor into these lakes and subsequent specializations and differentiation.

There are a few odds and ends of species on the family tree whose connecting points remain largely unknown.

In 1968 I described a new species of trout from Turkey in the genus *Salmo*. This species is known only from three specimens. These specimens are highly divergent from *S. trutta* and I created a new subgenus (*Platysalmo*) to emphasize the uncertain relationships of the species *platycephalus*. Until additional specimens become available, this Turkish species remains in an uncertain position on the family tree. *S. platycephalus* is the only trout on the world's list of endangered species.

In a few rivers on the Adriatic coast of Yugoslavia, at least one— probably two—species of trout classified in the genus *Salmothymus* occurs. As the genus name implies, this fish was originally believed to be intermediate between trout (*Salmo*) and grayling (*Thymallus*). Undoubtedly, *Salmothymus* belongs in the subfamily Salmoninae, probably close to the genus *Salmo*. They attain a maximum size of only a few pounds, but are loads of fun on a dry fly.

The most distinctive species of "trout" apparently far removed from any other living species, is *Acantholingua orhidanus*, existing as a single population in Lake Ohrid, Yugoslavia. This species has a smelt-like appearance and possesses the most primitive dentition pattern of any salmonid fish. All of its near-relatives are long extinct and its position on the family tree is uncertain.

Now that anglers have at least a provisional list of the known, the good and dubious species of trout, salmon and char of the world, perhaps a phenomenon comparable to the bird watcher's bird list might develop. World travelers who enjoy exploring remote regions might vie with one another to see who can list the greatest number of species fairly captured by angling.

As a final word on conservation, I would point out that controversy over precise classification, and recognition of a particular form of trout as a species or a subspecies, should not be allowed to interfere with conservation programs to preserve the biological diversity within species. The truly significant diversity in life histories and ecological adaptations are not associated with formal classification.

The winter-run Chinook salmon of the Sacramento River, for example, is the only race of this species that spawns in the spring. Because of a highly modified winter flow regime in the Sacramento River, this significant form of diversity within the Chinook salmon species faces extinction. It has been proposed for protection under the Endangered Species Act. The Endangered Species Act defines a "species" to include subspecies and even unique populations (such as the winter-run Chinook population). An effective endangered species conservation program must protect the diversity within a species.

The "world record" size fish of each species of trout, salmon and char typically are associated with a single race or population. The world's largest Chinook salmon is a race which spawns in the Kenai River, a moderate sized Alaskan river. The largest rainbow trout is the summer-run steelhead of the Skeena River drainage, British Columbia, and the Gerrard population of Kamloops trout, spawning in a single tributary of Kootenay Lake.

The world's largest cutthroat trout was the original population native to Pyramid Lake, Nevada (cutthroat trout of the same subspecies introduced into Pyramid Lake do not attain half the maximum size of the original population). The world's largest brown trout is the population of winter-run fish in the Kura River from the Caspian Sea. These examples of significant biological diversity should be preserved no matter how they are classified.

AUTHOR'S NOTE

How many species of trout, and salmon, and char depends on the classification system and the philosophy or ideology on which it is based. A popular current trend follows the phylogenetic species concept. This system recognizes the smallest differences that can be found down to the population level as distinct species. If applied to the great variation found in trout and char, the number of species would be beyond comprehension, and, in practice, meaningless. Such a classification would collapse under its own weight. The classification I use is eclectic, borrowing from different species concepts. I try to make my classification practical and understandable for non-taxonomists.

AMERICA'S CHANGING FISH FAUNA

⌃

SPRING 1991

THE NOVEMBER–DECEMBER 1989 ISSUE of *Fisheries*, the magazine of the American Fisheries Society, contained articles on "Fishes of North America—Endangered, Threatened or of Special Concern" and "Extinctions of North American Fishes During the Past Century." These articles represent an effort by the American Fisheries Society to reverse the trend of extinction.

During the past 100 years, 27 species and 13 subspecies of North American fishes have been declared extinct. The AFS Endangered Species Committee prepared a list of 364 species and subspecies that they consider as endangered, threatened or of special concern to call attention to the plight of rare and declining fishes. Of these 364 species and subspecies, 22 occur in Canada, 254 in the United States and 123 in Mexico. The majority of the fishes listed are native to the West and Southwest in arid and semiarid regions of the Colorado River Basin and the Great Basin, a group of western drainages with no outlet to the sea.

The factors causing extinction and declines in abundance and distribution leading toward extinction are discussed in the articles. The major factors are environmental changes occurring from water development (dams, river regulation, flow depletion), livestock grazing, logging, etc., as well as the establishment of nonnative fishes. These impacts on native fishes are particularly severe in water-short regions with a limited diversity of native fishes. For example, a recent checklist of the fishes of Nevada recorded 108 species, 63 (58 percent) of which are nonnative species and 45 (42 percent) are native. It is not surprising that more species and subspecies (43) of Nevada fishes occur on the AFS list of fishes endangered, threatened or of special concern (in addition to eight extinct species and subspecies) than those of any other state.

Although several species and subspecies of Great Lakes cisco became extinct from a combination of overfishing and predation by sea lamprey (a nonnative species above Niagara Falls), overfishing is only a minor factor causing extinction or threats of extinction, overall.

The negative impact of nonnative species, particularly in combination with environmental changes, in reducing or eliminating native species can be understood in the context of evolutionary theory.

When different species evolve together in an ecosystem, they must coevolve and coadapt if the various species are to persist through time. They must evolve life history strategies whereby competition for food and space is reduced among the species, and predator-prey relationships must evolve so that predatory species do not cause extinction of prey species. Each species fills its own unique niche and coevolution-coadaptation results in reducing the amount of niche overlap among species, allowing coexistence. When nonnative species are introduced into a coevolved ecosystem, a new species with a new niche is superimposed on the niches of the native species.

The outcome of this niche superimposition can vary greatly. It may be neutral if the new species exploits a resource unused by any of the native species—a rare event. Or it may be beneficial, in our interpretation, if an introduced species exploits a previous unused resource (for example zoo-plankton in a lake) and provides a new source of food for native predator species thereby increasing growth and abundance of the predators—also a rare event. More probable is a negative impact of introduced species by broad niche overlap with native species or by predation by nonnative species on native species lacking adequate predator avoidance behavior.

One species (the silver trout, *Salvelinus agassizi*, of Dublin Pond and Christine Lake, New Hampshire) and two subspecies of cutthroat trout (yellowfin cutthroat of Twin Lakes, Colorado, and Alvord Basin cutthroat trout, Nevada-Oregon) are listed extinct as pure populations by the AFS. All three extinctions were caused by nonnative species introductions leading to hybridization and replacement. The western trouts listed by the AFS as endangered, threatened or of special concern include three species: Mexican golden trout, Gila trout and Apache trout. (As discussed in the summer 1990 issue of *Trout*, I regard the latter two as subspecies of one species.) Also listed were eight subspecies of cutthroat trout (Lahonton, Paiute, Humboldt, Whitehorse, Bonneville (all Great Basin subspecies) (p. 137) , Colorado River, Rio Grande, greenback) and 10 subspecies of rainbow or redband trout (Little Kern, Kern River, six forms of interior redband trout, Baja [Rio Santo Domingo], Rio Yaqui). The decline in most of these species and subspecies is attributed to introduction of nonnative species of trout and environmental changes. The aurora trout, a subspecies of brook trout native to three small lakes in Ontario, is now extinct in all of its native waters as a result of acid rain. The aurora trout persists in a hatchery and as introduced populations.

The Montana grayling, a subspecies of the Arctic grayling, is listed as a subspecies of special concern. The Montana grayling coevolved and historically coexisted with the native subspecies of cutthroat trout (*lewisi*) in the upper Missouri River Basin, Montana. When the niches of nonnative brook trout, rainbow trout and brown trout were superimposed, both the grayling and cutthroat trout suffered catastrophic declines.

Surprisingly, the extinction of the Michigan grayling is not mentioned in the *Fisheries* articles. This is probably due to the dubious taxonomic status of the Michigan grayling as a subspecies of the Arctic grayling. This omission of the Michigan grayling raises a most important issue in regard to efforts to preserve biological diversity. Some of the most significant life history diversities among salmonid fishes are not associated with species or subspecies as a whole, but with populations within a species or within a subspecies (intraspecific or intrasubspecific diversity) that are not taxonomically recognized. For example, the vastly different migratory behavior and life history differences between steelhead and resident rainbow trout, or among the different runs (summer, fall, winter) of steelhead are indeed a real manifestation of intraspecific diversity, but are not recognized as different subspecies.

The wording of the federal Endangered Species Act recognizes that a program to preserve biological diversity, to be truly effective, must include types of diversity that are not taxonomically recognized. Thus, the definition of a "species" in the Endangered Species Act includes not only subspecies but populations within a species or subspecies.

Last year, the California–Nevada Chapter of the American Fisheries Society, along with a coalition of environmental organizations, forced the National Marine Fisheries Service and the U.S. Bureau of Reclamation to recognize the winter run of Chinook salmon in the Sacramento River as an endangered species under the Endangered Species Act.

Since then, the Shoshone-Bannock tribes of Idaho and environmental organizations have petitioned the National Marine Fisheries Service to list Snake River races of Chinook and sockeye salmon and Columbia River coho salmon as endangered species. This petition will certainly cause a ruckus among federal and state agencies and those concerned with water development in the Columbia River Basin. I also expect it will generate statements and testimony concerning classification and evolution (such as what is a sockeye and what is a kokanee) that will reflect a wealth of ignorance.

The proposed listing of certain races of Columbia Basin Chinook, sockeye and coho salmon is certain to generate intense controversy, considering what is at stake. I hope, however, that this controversy will stimulate a more holistic understanding of the historical factors that have caused the great loss of intraspecific diversity of these species (and of races of steelhead) in the Columbia Basin.

The overwhelming majority of "upriver" (east of the Cascade range) Chinook salmon and steelhead now consists of hatchery fish; viable wild populations now exist at only a small fraction of their original abundance and much of the original diversity of life history types has been lost. Native races of upriver coho salmon are extinct and races of sockeye salmon native to the entire Snake River drainage are probably extinct as pure populations. For the Columbia River Basin, as a whole, 96 percent of the original surface area of sockeye spawning and nursery lakes have been lost as a result of dams blocking access.

In 1931 the U.S. Army Corps of Engineers unveiled their ambitious plans to control and develop the waters of the Columbia River Basin for flood control, electric power generation, irrigated agriculture and navigation (Lewiston, Idaho is now a "seaport"). Construction on the largest mainstem dam, Grand Coulee, was started in the mid 1930s (completed 1941) and this wiped out all runs of salmon and steelhead that had historically spawned in 1,000 miles of the river and its tributaries above Grand Coulee. Bonneville dam, the first dam on the Columbia east of the Cascades was completed in 1938 (all fish migrating past Bonneville dam are considered as upriver fish).

Bonneville dam and subsequent dams between it and Grand Coulee and dams on the Snake River were constructed with fish ladders to allow passage of salmon and steelhead. For a fish to get from the ocean to the Okanogan or Methow rivers (the present uppermost spawning tributaries on the Columbia River), a series of nine dams and reservoirs must be traversed—and downstream passage of young through the turbines or over the spillways of each dam and migration through reservoirs full of predators. To make it to the Salmon or Clearwater rivers of Idaho, salmon and steelhead must traverse eight dams (four on the Columbia River and four on the Snake River). It is not difficult to understand why the upriver runs of salmon have experienced such great declines.

Besides the negative influence of dams, historical abundance of salmon and steelhead has also been affected by land and water use practices resulting in loss and degradation of habitat. The Yakima River drainage of Washington was once one of the most productive segments in the Columbia Basin for Chinook, sockeye and coho salmon and steelhead reproduction. Irrigated farmlands converted the Yakima valley into a highly productive agricultural region, but water use is so intensive that, in most years, only about 25 to 30 percent of the virgin flow in the Yakima River reaches the Columbia. Coho and sockeye are gone from the Yakima, Chinook and steelhead spawners occur at a tiny fraction of historical abundance (the spring race of Chinooks occur at about one to three percent of their historical abundance) and reproduce in only a small part of their original spawning range.

The intraspecific diversity of salmon species and steelhead in the Columbia Basin was designed by natural selection to maximize abundance of each species by perfecting life history adaptations for each local region of the basin. How much has been lost in regard to numbers and biomass of annual salmon and steelhead runs in the Columbia Basin is not definitely known.

The Columbia Basin covers about 260,000 square miles in the Pacific Northwest, extending inland to portions of northern Nevada, northern Utah, to the continental divide in Yellowstone Park, Wyoming and northward through Idaho, western Montana and a large part of

British Columbia. About 90 percent of the basin's area lies east of the Cascade Mountains and, historically, most of the Chinook and steelhead abundance was from these upriver runs that were affected by dams.

Based on commercial catch records and calculations of the amount of pristine spawning and nursery habitat, best estimates of virgin abundance of annual salmon and steelhead spawning runs range 6–8 million to 10–12 million fish (about 60 percent Chinook) with total biomass ranging from about 80 million to 160 million pounds. Because annual abundance would fluctuate, it is likely that low abundance years would have runs of 6–7 million fish and high abundance years would have 10–12 million.

The Columbia River was, by far, the world's greatest producer of Chinook salmon. The largest commercial catch of 43 million pounds for Columbia Chinook was recorded in 1883 (plus unknown catch by Indians and white inhabitants along the river). The largest commercial catch of coho salmon was about 6 million pounds in 1895; the maximum catch of sockeye was about 4.5 million pounds in 1898; and the maximum catch of steelhead was about 5 million pounds in 1892.

In recent years, total runs of all salmon and steel head into the Columbia River have averaged about 2.5 million fish (about 20 million pounds), but most of the current abundance is based on hatchery fish and most occurs "downriver" (west of Cascades). The overwhelming majority of upriver runs of Chinook and steel head are dependent on the stocking of massive numbers of hatchery fish. With modern techniques of hatchery rearing and barge transportation of smolts through dams, upriver steel head runs have responded well to hatchery enhancement. The results of stocking hundreds of millions of upriver hatchery Chinook smolts in recent years has been dismal. Although remnants of spring, summer and fall runs have been maintained and increased, the costs have been enormous. Probably due to hatchery exposure to bacterial kidney disease (BKD), survival of hatchery Chinook from smolt to adult has been abysmally poor. On average, only one or two adults return for every 1,000 smolts stocked. Costs to produce some of the returning adults range from $100 to more than $400 per fish.

Although the native fish species of the Columbia River Basin receive virtually no mention in the American Fisheries Society's list of fishes extinct, endangered, threatened or of special concern, environmental changes in the basin have caused the extinction of a considerable amount of intraspecific diversity and a great reduction in abundance of salmon and steel head.

If nothing more is accomplished by the proposal to have certain races of salmon listed as endangered species than to focus attention on the factors that have caused the loss of intraspecific diversity and the recognition of the values associated with maintaining the remnant diversity of wild stocks, then the efforts will not be in vain. The popular slogan of those promoting dam building in the 1950s was "We can have fish and power too." They weren't entirely wrong, but the slogan requires clarification: "We can have fish, but they will be mainly of generic hatchery stocks, at greatly reduced abundance and very expensive."

The extinction of species and subspecies and the replacement of native fishes by nonnative species had its origins in the nineteenth century when a materialistic and utilitarian view of nature drove government policies. Natural resources were valued solely as commodities. Nature was thought of as consisting of valuable or beneficial species, pest, vermin, predator, or "trash" species, and all other species were categorized as worthless. The U.S. Fish Commission was established in 1871. Its mission was to propagate and distribute valuable species (generally nonnative species in relation to where they were stocked) to replace native, worthless species. The "success" of this mission was enhanced by government policies that assigned the highest values associated with water to power generation and irrigation to promote industry and agriculture. Land management focused "best use" on livestock grazing, timber production, mining, and other commodities. Changing perceptions, paradigms and laws during the last half-century have helped to preserve what's left of America's biological heritage. Extinction and species replacement, however, are irreversible changes caused by the accumulative forces created by the goal of economic development at any cost (that was referred to as for "the common good").

FROM HATCHERIES TO HABITAT?
LOOK AGAIN.

⟶

FALL 1991

TROUT UNLIMITED WAS FOUNDED IN 1959 specifical-ly to address the issue of wild trout versus hatchery-raised catchable trout—and to the emphasis given to each in a state's trout management program. Since then considerable progress has been made toward in-creasing emphasis on wild trout management by special regulations and better understanding of habitat. All this was summarized by Ray White in his excellent feature article, "We're Going Wild: A 30-Year Transition from Hatcheries to Habitat," in the summer 1989 issue of *Trout.* Yet greater progress is needed.

I served as the summarizer for the Wild Trout IV symposium in 1989, where I pointed out that this transition from emphasis on hatch-ery trout to emphasis on wild trout during the past 30 years has not been proceeding as rapidly as most anglers believe it has. I cited presenta-tions given at the first wild trout symposium in 1974. The tenor was one of euphoria, celebrating a new age of fisheries management—I then cited figures comparing total production of catchable-sized trout in all state and federal hatcheries from 1958 to 1983. During this 25-year period, catchable trout production increased in the United States from 50.2 million to 78 million fish. The cold facts reveal that, during this period of transition from hatcheries to habitat, catchable trout produc-tion increased by 55 percent.

I provided data in my summary to show that, in many states, the continuing emphasis on catchable trout results in inequities in relation to cost-benefits to the majority of anglers. A relatively small proportion of licensed anglers is heavily subsidized by all other anglers in large-scale catchable programs.

The battle for more rapid implementation of shifting emphasis from catchable trout to wild trout will not be won by emotion or rhetoric. Changes for the better will come about by compiling, analyzing, and documenting evidence from diverse sources—making a case much as a skillful attorney prepares for trial. Gain an in-depth understanding of all of the evidence favoring your point of view and all of the evidence supporting the opposing viewpoint.

I will review some of the evidence that relates to the issue of wild trout versus catchable trout and will attempt to present an unbiased interpretation—while admitting that I am handicapped by a strong bias for wild, natural trout, especially in wild, natural environments.

Some important fundamentals that relate to the wild trout/catchable trout issue concern the missions, mandates, and goals of government agencies involved with fisheries management, economics of fisheries management, and economic values associated with angling.

Probably all state conservation agencies have a legislative mandate that directs the agency to preserve, protect, and enhance the natural resources of the state. A public fisheries program based on catchable trout is not natural resource management; it does not preserve, protect, or enhance natural resources; it is at variance with the agency's mandate. Many agencies have recognized the internal contradiction inherent in their catchable trout programs. (Typically nonnative rainbow trout are stocked.) The agency's fisheries management plans or policy statements may have a footnote or a parenthetical disclaimer to the effect that the stocking of catchable trout is necessary in certain areas to maintain recreational fishing. The implication is that the catchable program is de-emphasized, a minor part of the state's overall fisheries program.

A basic question concerns the distinction between major and minor: If 10 percent to 20 percent of all funds derived from angling license sales are devoted to raising and stocking catchable trout, would this be considered minor? What about 30 percent to 40 percent or more? A critical examination should also be made of the accuracy and veracity of how costs are computed. How does the percentage of license fees devoted to catchable trout production compare to the percentage of total angler days expended in the state that are dependent of catchable stocking?

Concerning economic valuations of wild trout versus catchable trout fisheries, I will not attempt a weak imitation of Roderick Haig-Brown to extol the more intangible aesthetic values associated with wild trout, but a value differential becomes apparent by playing a game of "what if." Consider the changes in impact, meaning and symbolism in Ernest Hemingway's story, "Big Two Hearted River," if Hemingway had Nick Adams drive to a stocking site, toss out his bait, and haul in a fish transported from a hatchery a few hours before.

With more tangible economic analyses, the value of an angler-day is always higher for a wild trout fishery than for a catchable trout fishery. The differential varies from slight to enormous depending on the quality of the fishery, demand in relation to supply, and the method of economic valuation.

In relation to the economics of a fisheries program, an in-depth, critical economic evaluation of the true costs of producing fish in hatcheries has yet to be done, to my knowledge. Historically, state and federal hatchery costs have been computed by cost accounting methods, not by economic evaluation as done by economists. Thus, in many instances, the cost to produce the fish does not include capital construction costs. For example, if $10 million is invested to construct a large hatchery which produces one million pounds of catchable trout per year, with good interest rates, a private investor may pay off the debt in 20 years for $20 million. During that 20 years, each pound of trout produced would have an additional cost of two dollars just to retire the debt, but this cost can be hidden in computing fish costs in government hatcheries. Construction and many other costs (land acquisition and taxes) borne by the private sector are not calculated in computing fish production costs by many state and federal hatcheries. Until a true economic evaluation is made of fish production costs, all that can be said is that the true economic cost to produce a catchable trout in a state or federal hatchery is considerably more than the official figure arrived at by selective cost accounting.

To this point, it may seem like an open and shut case for reducing catchable trout programs—diverting funds to more morally and economically defensible fisheries programs. It's not that simple. Changes for the better will come about slowly and only after all aspects of a state's fisheries program are critically analyzed and the findings effectively communicated to the public (including legislators and commissioners). Some fundamental factors that favor continual expansion of catchable trout stocking must be clearly understood before effective counter arguments can be developed.

The first concerns public perception of fish hatcheries and the role played by the stocking of hatchery fish to maintain public fishing.

For more than 100 years, the public, political, and business perception of fish hatcheries and fish stocking has been enthusiastically favorable. In 1872, Congress appropriated $15,000 to fund the United States Fish Commission to investigate the causes of decline in our fisheries and to come up with a solution to reverse this decline. The obvious solution was to build many hatcheries and propagate and stock millions and billions of baby fish of many species and scatter them about like Johnny Appleseed.

The unbridled optimism of fish culturists in their belief that they would make our waters teem with fishes is epitomized in an address made by Robert Barnwell Roosevelt at the annual meeting of the American Fish Culturist Association in 1876. Roosevelt recounted the great deterioration of our fisheries but concluded that "there is no need to fear scarcity of fish food either in the ocean or in our great lakes—we have only to take advantage of these opportunities" (to build more hatcheries and stock increasing numbers of fishes). Roosevelt continued:

> "This is the national centennial; fish culture has existed only a few years; what will be its condition at its centennial the most enthusiastic can hardly conceive…A new science was being born into the world…but the clear light is visible at last…There need be no fear for the future, and in much less than a hundred years, the waters of America will teem with food for the poor and hungry, which all may come and take."

Roosevelt's prophecy came true, but with an ironic King Midas–like twist. The following year, 1877, the U.S. Fish Commission began the propagation of carp, imported from Europe, and soon dispersed them all over the country. In much less than 100 years, the carp became the dominant species in freshwaters of America—that is, there are more pounds, tons and megatons of carp than of any other single species—but even the poor and hungry don't want to come and take them.

During the 1940s and '50s, the rearing and stocking of catchable trout for instant put-and-take fisheries increased at a rapid rate. Objections were raised on moral, aesthetic, economic and biological grounds, but no real organized opposition to catchable trout came about until Trout Unlimited was established. During the past 30 years, however, the catchable trout tidal surge that began in the 1940s has not been checked to a significant degree. The annual production figures for state and federal hatcheries continue to rise.

The tide cannot be easily turned because the public, in general, still maintains a favorable perception of fish hatcheries. Hatcheries and stocking are typically the only tangible part of fisheries management of which the public is aware. Angler surveys consistently show endorsement of catchable trout stocking. The most common response when the average angler is asked how the state fisheries agency can make his fishing better is, "to stock more and bigger fish." This is due to the makeup of the angling public.

Anglers can be commonly grouped into categories for economic analysis. The largest group are the "casual" (or occasional) anglers who fish incidentally as a secondary aspect of an outdoor recreational experience such as family picnics or camping trips, and the "skilled" (generally experienced) angler whose primary outdoor experience is focused on fishing and who have a typical goal to "catch a limit." The overwhelming majority of the anglers grouped as casual or skilled have no real preference for wild trout over catchable hatchery trout—to most of them, a trout is a trout, is a trout. The smallest group (about 10–15 percent of all anglers in states where trout fishing is dominant but where warmwater fishing is available) is the "purist" (or expert) angler group who are concerned with tackle and techniques and have a distinct preference for wild trout. Almost all angler opposition to catchable trout comes from the purist group. When a state agency transforms a stream or a section of a stream from a catchable trout fishery to a wild trout fishery with special regulations, which prohibit bait, there is often a backlash of outrage from the main body of anglers who believes that wild trout management with special regulations is simply a ploy by elitist fly fishers deny them fish that are rightfully theirs—frequently they have the backing of politicians and local business people.

If anyone believes that a rapid turning of the catchable trout tide will be a reality soon, the experiences of the Idaho Department of Fish and Game in recent years is instructive.

The ratio of miles of wild trout streams or surface acres of salmonid waters per licensed angler in Idaho is about the most favorable of any state. That is, Idaho has the least need for catchable trout stocking to meet angler demand. Idaho, however, stocks more catchable trout per licensed angler than does Pennsylvania—by popular demand. When the Idaho Department of Fish and Game declared certain sections of the Henry's Fork of the Snake and Wood River drainage to be wild trout waters with special regulations, the changes were met with fierce opposition from organized anglers, resulting in legal challenges and threats of legislative injunction.

Because of the abundance of high quality wild trout waters, it is predictable that catchable trout fisheries in Idaho are wasteful to an extreme degree. A study was conducted in 1976, 1977 and 1980 on five sections of the Henry's Fork stocked with catchable trout. A total of 105,000 catchables was stocked in these sections during these years. The catchable trout averaged 11 inches in length and slightly more than a half pound in weight. The return of these catchables to anglers in the various sections ranged from 3 percent to 46 percent of the numbers stocked. In total, 18,743 (18 percent) of the 105,000 fish stocked were caught by anglers. Of about 60,000 pounds of catchables stocked, no more than 10,000 pounds were harvested by anglers. Even in the section where catchable trout made their greatest contribution to the fishery, 56 percent of all trout caught were wild rainbows. Despite such statistics, many anglers and business people vehemently protested against replacing catchable stocking with wild trout management and special regulations; they believed the Fish and Game Department had caved in to a small group of fly fishing elitists.

An important finding on the Henry's Fork was that in the special regulation, wild trout section in the Box Canyon, more than half of the anglers were non-residents (from other states). These are the anglers who produce the greatest angler-day value, especially in relation to money spent in the local region—these are the anglers that chambers of commerce want to attract. They won't come to Idaho to fish for stocked trout.

It should be obvious that the catchable tide cannot be stemmed by an "us versus them" approach based on morality, ethics or poetry. There are many more of them than there are of us.

"Us" or any grouping is far from a unified entity. In any event, we must convince "them," whoever they may be, that better fisheries management is in their own best interest. We must examine options that will provide as many or more catchable trout to those anglers who want them, distribute them in a more equitable manner, while creating more wild trout waters. In the Henry's Fork area, for example, if there are waters such as gravel excavation ponds where catchables can be dumped, a return of 75 percent of the stocked fish could be expected. (Angler profiles show that most anglers in the casual and generalist groups do not place much emphasis on aesthetic considerations of their fishing sites.) With a 75 percent return, the same number of fish would be caught by stocking 25,000 catchables as were caught in the Henry's Fork from stocking 105,000. Could the money saved be put to better use?

Several studies have agreed that with catchable trout stocked in streams, 50 percent of all the catchables caught are caught by a small proportion (6–8 percent) of the anglers fishing that stream (the catchable trout specialist). In ponds or small lakes (typically less than 100 acres surface area) with good access, not only is the percent return typically higher than with catchables stocked in streams, the catch is better distributed among all anglers and extends over a longer period of time.

The key to stemming the catchable trout tide is not to cease or even reduce production, but to hold the line and develop strategies to make more effective use of hatchery fish. For example, a hypothetical state agency presently takes in about $10 million annually in license sales and spends $3–4 million on catchable trout; if the expenditures for catchable trout production remains stable over the next 10 years, while license sales rise to $15 million, an additional $5 million would be available for better fisheries management, including greater emphasis on wild trout, warm water species, and studies on how to use hatchery trout more effectively to increase returns to the angler. This sounds good, but the success or failure for additional funding to result in better fishing depends on the talent and enthusiasm of agency biologists. In agencies that have long devoted a large proportion of their total fisheries budget to operating hatcheries and stocking great numbers of catchable trout, and where the administrative hierarchy is dominated by hatchery people, management and research has suffered. Such an agency may be staffed by management and research biologists who have no feasible alternatives for spending additional funds to provide more fish for more anglers except by stocking more catchable trout.

In my summary for the Wild Trout IV symposium I suggested some ideas how money could be well-spent in fisheries programs. A program that should yield a greater cost-benefit ratio concerns strain evaluation of hatchery trout stocked at a small size in lakes and reservoirs for what is known as put-grow-take fisheries. Where natural selection factors such as competition and predation are prevalent, the genetics of the stocked fish can be extremely important for survival and growth. There are tremendous opportunities to increase the effectiveness of put-grow-take fisheries.

A recent paper in the *North American Journal of Fisheries Management* reported on salmon and trout stocked into Lake Michigan by the Wisconsin Department of Natural Resources. From 1968 through 1980, 4,354,471 yearling rainbow trout were stocked. The angler catch one and two years later equalled a 9.8 percent return of the stocked fish (considering that after one or two years of growth in Lake Michigan, the rainbows caught should be large and the weight of caught fish probably exceeded the weight of fish stocked). From 1981 through 1984,

1,832,487 yearling rainbows were stocked but only 5.1 percent were subsequently caught by anglers. For every million yearling rainbows stocked, the difference between a 5.1 percent return and a 9.8 percent return is 47,000 fish (and probably well over 100,000 pounds). The difference in percent return was the result of the strain of rainbow raised in Wisconsin hatcheries. During the 1981–1984 period, the highly domesticated Shasta strain was used, probably because they are cheaper to rear. In the 1980s, could it be that Wisconsin fish culturists were unaware of evidence accumulated over many years that there is a strong inverse correlation between degree of domestication (cheapness to raise) and survival-return to angler in put-grow-take fisheries, especially in lakes with an abundance of competitors and predators?

Wisconsin has some excellent trout biologists; were they asked for advice?

How good is communication among management, research and hatcheries?

Fish culturists may be doing an outstanding job, based on job performance ratings for cost effective fish production, but the fate of the fish after leaving the hatchery is not part of their job. Wisconsin stocked more than five million brown trout yearlings, which returned to the fishery at a 12.2 percent rate. Skamania strain steelhead rainbows stocked in Lake Michigan by Indiana returned at a 12.8 percent rate. When one considers the multitude of strains represented by diversity within trout species, the potential to greatly increase the effectiveness of put-grow-take fisheries appears almost unlimited.

This same issue of the *North American Journal of Fisheries Management* contained a report comparing three strains of cutthroat trout stocked in two Montana ponds. Over a two-year period, the total return to angler of the three strains were 11, 28 and 52 percent of the fish stocked—quite significant differences and fisheries management implications resulting from very slight intraspecific genetic differences.

What is your state agency doing on the matter of improving the returns of hatchery fish? Probably all would agree that it would be a good idea to devote the time of one or more biologists to study the issue, but that funds are not available to staff such a position. Why not? Any state with a large-scale catchable program, no matter how efficient the return to the angler is assumed to be, will have pockets of wasteful stocking as bad or worse than what occurred in the Henry's Fork. Elimination or large reduction of wasteful stocking should result in savings to fund several professional positions.

The progress made in fish culture techniques, engineering, improved diets, disease control, and overall skill levels and efficiency during the past 30 years, far exceed advances made in fisheries management and research (which have been inhibited by funds diverted to fish culture). In relative dollar terms, hatcheries can produce a pound of trout for much less cost than they could 30 years ago. And better use is made of catchable trout in relation to percent return and reduced conflicts with wild trout management in streams. Much improvement is yet possible, however, in increased effectiveness of hatchery fish utilization to provide more fish for more anglers.

Before any new major hatchery construction for continued expansion of a state's catchable program is approved, I would urge critical scrutiny.

AUTHOR'S NOTE

Trout Unlimited's crusade for agencies to give priority to wild trout over hatchery trout in fisheries management programs is not simply wild versus hatchery issue, but more correctly a wild versus put-and-take stocking of catchable trout. No doubt, in many lakes and reservoirs there is insufficient natural reproduction and trout fisheries are maintained by stocking fingerling or subcatchable trout. This type of stocking holds the highest potential for the most cost-effective use of hatcheries. When 90 percent or more of the total hatchery production is made up of catchable trout, waste occurs and more effective options are inhibited. This column is one of many I've written on this topic including numerous papers in proceedings of conferences and symposia. My position is that if fisheries programs were managed as a business enterprise to minimize waste and maximize "profits," it would be perfectly clear that wild trout fisheries have much greater economic value at all levels from local to national than do put-and-take fisheries.

In my publications I've made the following points:

· Less than 10 percent of the anglers fishing for catchable trout catch more than 50 percent of all catchables caught. A great inequality and unreasonable subsidy to a small group, especially if 30 percent or more of the total fisheries budget is devoted to raising catchable trout. This becomes especially apparent when analyses of data revealed that in California, only six to seven percent of the total number of angler days of recreation can be attributed to stocking catchable trout. In Colorado, a maximum of 12–13 percent of all angler days can be associated with catchable trout stocking. This inequality of investment to return would bankrupt a business.

· A statistical study of data from California and Colorado found no relationship between the number of catchable trout stocked and sales of fishing licenses.

· In 1995 I coauthored a paper with natural resource economists that concluded that the true costs of producing catchable trout are at least twice the cost claimed by the agencies. And, anglers fishing for catchable trout were not willing to pay the costs of providing their catch.

All of these points argue for needed reform in fisheries programs and to put catchable trout programs in their proper perspective. It's a classic example where entrenched establishments do not readily accept change.

GRAYLING

———◦———

SUMMER 1992

WHEN I ATTENDED THE WESTERN DIVISION of the American Fisheries Society meeting in Bozeman, Montana in July 1991, bags, caps, and t-shirts emblazoned with grayling were seen everywhere. I was pleased to note a new—and long overdue—example of stewardship by a state fish and game agency to fulfill a mandate to protect and preserve native species. The Montana Department of Fish, Wildlife and Parks hosted the meeting. The symbol and honored fish of the meeting was the Montana grayling.

Native populations of grayling—in contrast to hatchery grayling stocked in numerous lakes—have been rapidly declining in Montana. Let us hope that the resurgence of interest and dedication to preserve the remnant diversity of Montana grayling has not come too late, as was the case with the Michigan grayling.

At the meeting in Bozeman, I decided I must write an article on grayling which recognized a worthy conservation program by a state agency for a native fish which, on a purely economic level, cannot compare with the nonnative brown and rainbow trouts in relation to selling fishing licenses. The Montana program illustrates an important concept of conservation biology: The preservation of biodiversity should not be based solely on the preservation of formally described species and subspecies, but on the preservation of unique types of *diversity within a species*—commonly known as Significant Evolutionary Units—without regard to formal taxonomy.

The Montana program aims to preserve both lacustrine (lake adapted) and fluvial (river adapted) forms of native grayling. Special emphasis is on saving native fluvial populations which have almost disappeared from their native range.

An article on grayling also provides opportunity to present some information accumulated during and since my graduate studies but never heretofore published. My classification of the family Salmonidae includes three subfamilies: the trouts, salmons, and chars (Salmoninae), the whitefishes (Coregoninae) and the grayling (Thymallinae). Most of my research publications have been on salmonine fishes, a few on coregonine fishes, with graylings given only an occasional passing reference. It is not that I have deliberately slighted grayling, only that the evolutionary diversity and unknowns that stir controversy and stimulate research reside in the Salmoninae and Coregoninae. Each of these subfamilies contain about 25 to 30 species, the classification and most correct evolutionary relationships of which has long generated heated controversies in the international literature. If one reads some of what I have written over the years attacking people who have disagreed with my opinions on salmonine and coregonine classification, it would be difficult to believe that we are all friends sharing common interests. It's somewhat like a sporting event where friends compete; everyone wants to be the winner and beat the competition.

Compared to the Salmoninae and Coregoninae there is little diversity among graylings. Only three or four species are generally recognized, all classified in the genus *Thymallus*. For many years, there has been little controversy in regards to grayling classification. There are, however, many unknowns concerning the evolution and distribution of graylings and some old mistakes and influences of ancient folklore are still incorporated into modern texts.

An interesting question for speculation concerns why there is such limited species diversity in the subfamily Thymallinae. The evolutionary divergences that resulted in the separation of the family Salmonidae into three major groups (subfamilies) probably occurred more than 50 million years ago, yet the divergence leading to the two widely distributed and closely related species, the European grayling, *T. thymallus*, and the Arctic grayling, *T. arcticus*, probably occurred within the past million years. A third commonly recognized species, *T. nigrescens* is restricted to Lake Kosogol, Mongolia, in the very headwaters of the Yenesei River basin. The Kosogol grayling is a highly specialized lake form derived from the Arctic grayling, perhaps within the last 100,000 years. It could just as well be recognized as a subspecies of *T. arcticus*.

ARCTIC GRAYLING
Thymallus arcticus

The fourth commonly recognized species, *T. brevirostris*, is found in internal basins of western Mongolia—similar to our western Great Basin where drainages are isolated from rivers draining to the ocean. From an evolutionary point of view, *brevirostris* is the most divergent, ungrayling-like species.

Evidently, with an abundance of small forage fishes and with no other salmonid predator, the ancestral grayling that gained access to the present Mongolian basins evolved as a specialized predator. It has well-developed teeth instead of the vestigial teeth characteristic of the European and Arctic graylings. Its jaw is much longer and its dorsal fin smaller than in other grayling. It has a more trout-like appearance. There is no evidence, however, that *brevirostris* attains a size larger than other grayling species. Despite rather fast growth in the first two or three years, the maximum size of grayling in most regions of Europe, Asia and North America, is only about two or three pounds. The official world record grayling (an Arctic grayling) is 5 pounds 15 ounces for a fish caught in Canada in 1967.

Attention should be called to the possibility that another, even more divergent, species of grayling occurs in Mongolia. In 1897, Mr. St. George Littledale returned to England with a fish specimen from "the south side of the Altai Mountains." The specimen was presented to the British Museum and the ichthyologist George Boulenger was so impressed with the specimen that he described a new genus and species, *Phylogephyra altaica*. The genus name denotes a "bridge." Boulenger believed that the new species represented an evolutionary line intermediate between salmonine and thymallinine fishes ("bridging the gap" between the subfamilies). Later, the famous Russian ichthyologist Leo Berg, assumed that the specimen on which *P. altaica* was described came from the internal Mongolian basins and was, in reality, *T. brevirostris*. Because *brevirostris* is the older name, Berg made *altaica* a synonym of *brevirostris*. That is, in Berg's opinion, both names refer to the same species, for which *brevirostris* is the valid name. Berg, however, did not examine the British museum specimen of *P. altaica* to compare with specimens *T. brevirostris*.

About 30 years ago I examined the specimen of *P. altaica* at the British Museum and I also examined many specimens of *T. brevirostris* at the Zoological Institute of the Soviet Academy of Sciences. The British Museum specimen had probably been preserved in salt for transportation from Mongolia to London. It is in poor condition, but I noted several characters which led me to believe that *altaica* and *brevirostris*, although of common ancestry, probably represent two distinct species. The teeth are even more strongly developed in the specimen of *altaica* than in *brevirostris*, especially the teeth on the tongue and the pharyngeal teeth (teeth associated with the gill arches). The British Museum specimen has 12 pelvic fin rays; *brevirostris* specimens have predominantly 10, sometimes 11 pelvic rays. I expect that greatly renewed interest in grayling taxonomy would result if someone could find the source population on the "south side of the Altai Mountains" from which Mr. Littledale obtained his specimen in 1897.

The Altai Mountains of south central Siberia and western Mongolia are drained to the Arctic Ocean by the Ob and Yenesei river basins. The Altai Mountains form a rim isolating the internal basins of western Mongolia and the southern slopes of the southern most extremes of the range drain toward the great Gobi Desert region. The fishes of these south slope drainages are largely unknown.

Until now, I have not mentioned *P. altaica* since I briefly discussed the matter in my graduate school thesis in 1964. I assume that once a thesis is written it is read rarely, if at all; I thought that I was the only one in the world believing the case was not closed on *P. altaica*. Thus, I was pleasantly surprised and impressed to note in a 1989 article in a bulletin of the British Museum on Mongolian fishes that the author had not only seen my thesis but also examined Mr. Littledale's 1897 museum specimen. This author also agreed with my conclusion that the case for *altaica* being the same species as *brevirostris* should be reopened.

A "rehearing" is necessary, but the necessary evidence to resolve the matter, grayling specimens from Altai Mountain streams draining to the southern deserts, is lacking. Evidently, no one has documented the occurrence of a grayling-like fish in this region since Mr. Littledale's visit almost 100 years ago.

There are still some questions on European and Arctic grayling that require clarification. For example, did grayling once occur in Ontario, are they native or introduced into England, and is there another species of "brightly speckled" grayling in Adriatic rivers of Yugoslavia?

In 1848 a French book on fishes described a new species of grayling, *ontariensis*, based on a specimen believed to be from Lake Ontario. Although Lewis and Clark found grayling in the Beaverhead River, Montana, in 1805 and referred to it as a new species of "white trout," the occurrence of grayling in the lower 48 states remain undocumented until the Michigan grayling was named *T. tricolor* in 1865 and the Montana grayling named *T. montanus* in 1873. The Montana grayling had a range in the upper Missouri drainage similar to that of the native cutthroat trout, but it was not so ubiquitously distributed in all tributary systems. Thus, it was generally unknown to most anglers.

James A. Henshall, besides writing a famous book on bass, also was superintendent of the federal fish hatchery at Bozeman, Montana. In the 1905–1906 biennial report of the Montana State Game and Fish Warden, Henshall pointed out that he was the first person to recognize that the "white trout" described by Lewis and Clark was, in reality, the Montana grayling. He also pointed out how little was known about Montana grayling—many believed it to be a hybrid between a cutthroat trout and a mountain whitefish. Until the Michigan grayling was described, the Ontario grayling was assumed to be an error, a mix-up of specimens and labels at the Paris Museum (which most likely was the case). When it became known that grayling did occur in Montana and Michigan, the matter of the mysterious Ontario grayling was brought up in *Forest and Stream* magazine. Predictably, this resulted in what

might be called the Loch Ness monster syndrome—if a mythical or mysterious organism is once reported, it will be reported again and again. Letters came in with reports of grayling, not only in Ontario, but also in Quebec, Maine and Vermont, and all of these "grayling" localities are listed by Charles Hallock (then editor of *Forest and Stream*) in his 1877 *Sportsman's Gazetteer*.

Because no specimens of Ontario grayling ever appeared, it can be assumed that it never existed. If grayling did occur in Lake Ontario tributaries they should have been about identical to Michigan (and Montana) grayling and the name *ontariensis*, as the oldest name, would be the subspecies name if subspecies are recognized for grayling native to the lower 48 states. Because the original description of *ontariensis* is considered invalid (a *nomen dubium*), the next oldest name, *tricolor*, would be used.

The beauty of grayling, especially its very large, brightly spotted dorsal fin, has stimulated a rich folklore since ancient times. Some of these folk tales were repeated by Izaak Walton—such as the French myth that the bright spots on grayling were the result of eating gold and their odor was derived from eating water thyme. It had been generally known in Walton's time that carp were not native to Great Britain but were transported from the European mainland to stock in monastery ponds. This gave rise to tales that other fish species such as char and grayling, with only limited distribution in the British Isles, were also introduced from the mainland by monks. Thus, in Ernest Schwiebert's book *Trout*, one can read, "and history tells us the grayling was originally introduced into the British Isles when the first French monks established their monasteries after the Battle of Hastings." Actually, folklore—not history—is responsible for this mistake.

The grayling is, indeed, native to Great Britain, but only in the area where the Rhine River flowed to the Atlantic across England. This was during the last glacial epoch when ocean levels were much lower and Great Britain and the English Channel were part of the continental landmass. From this area, the grayling was not able to penetrate far to the north or south; thus the grayling are not native to Scotland or Ireland, but they are native to England.

The mention by Schwiebert of a brightly speckled grayling in Adriatic tributaries of Yugoslavia, south of the range of the European grayling, is probably based on confusion with the species *Salmo* (or *Salmothymus*) *obtusirostris*. This species whose head and jaws resemble a grayling, is actually most closely related to brown trout (the genus name *Salmothymus* denotes the assumed intermediacy between *Salmo* and *Thymallus*). In 1923 David Starr Jordan published a book on fish classification and incorrectly placed *Salmothymus* in his family Thymallidae. Such errors often linger in literature for some time.

The European grayling does extend southward to the Adriatic, but only in the Po and Soca rivers in the northernmost section of the Adriatic basin. From there the grayling extend northward through Europe, in the Danube, Rhine and Rhone river basins, but grayling are not native to the Iberian Peninsula (Spain and Portugal). Grayling cannot tolerate seawater. Their distribution pattern is explained only by connections between freshwater basins. The European grayling is native to most of Scandinavia and ranges eastward in Arctic Ocean drainages to the Kara River. From the Pechora River to the Kara River, the ranges of the European grayling and Arctic grayling overlap. The fact that they occur in the same rivers together and maintain their integrity by avoiding hybridization is a sound basis for the validity of the species *T. thymallus* and *T. arcticus*. Otherwise, the two species are quite similar in appearance and life histories—reproduction, growth rate, feeding, habitat, etc. They obviously are two closely-related species. The Arctic grayling occurs in all major river basins draining to the Arctic Ocean from the Pechora, eastward. Arctic grayling are distributed southward in Asia to the Amur and Yalu river basins. It can be assumed that Arctic grayling extended its range into North America across the Bering Straits during times when ocean levels were lower and the Bering Land Bridge formed a direct connection between Asia and North America.

Prior to the last glacial epoch, about 50,000 years ago, the upper Missouri River in Montana drained to southern Hudson Bay. During an unknown time, when the upper Missouri was a Hudson Bay tributary (such a drainage pattern may have been in place for hundreds of thousands of years), fishes of northern origins such as the grayling and goldeye (*Hiodon alosoides*) became established in the upper Missouri via southward migrations among Hudson Bay tributaries. During the last glaciation, ice sheets converged to cover all of Canada, southern Alaska and the present Great Lakes. Glacial refugia existed in the Yukon basin and upper Missouri (which was deflected southward from Hudson Bay to the Mississippi basin) where Arctic grayling persisted as two isolated groups. As the glaciers retreated, a series of large lakes and connecting waters formed along the glacial fronts. During this time (around 10,000 years ago) grayling from Montana migrated to the Great Lakes region where they persisted in Michigan in one river in the Upper Peninsula (Otter River, a Lake Superior tributary) and several rivers of the Lower Peninsula (tributaries to both Lake Michigan and Lake Huron) until becoming extinct in the twentieth century.

Elk Lake in the upper Missouri drainage of Montana is the only lake in Montana which has a native population of lake trout (*Salvelinus namaycush*). Evidently, while grayling were moving from west to east along glacial fronts, the lake trout was moving from east to west. Both species found very limited suitable environments in their reciprocal range extensions during postglacial times—the lake trout persisting in one lake in Montana and the grayling occurring in some Michigan rivers, until man-induced environmental changes (siltation and warming of previous cold streams from logging) and introductions of nonnative brown and rainbow trout. The brook trout, although native to Michigan and the Great Lakes basin, for reasons unknown, did not originally occur in most Michigan grayling rivers. Apparently, brook trout and grayling naturally occurred together only in the Otter and Jordan rivers. In all other grayling rivers, the brook trout is a nonnative species. The last known native grayling in Michigan occurred in the Otter River until about the mid 1930s. John Lowe, a teacher of biology at Northern State Teacher's College, Marquette, Michigan, made many fish collections and recorded voluminous notes on Upper Peninsula fishes. During the early 1900s, Lowe recorded grayling and brook trout as the dominant species in the Otter River. His notes of 1925 mention turbid waters, much siltation and the rainbow trout as the dominant species. In about 10 years, the last Michigan grayling was gone.

I would say "gone forever"—except for a taxonomic technicality.

From the points brought out, all the evidence indicates that the grayling in Montana and Michigan became separated only about 10,000 years ago—insufficient time to develop subspecific differentiation. Thus, if the Montana grayling is recognized as a subspecies, distinct from the Arctic grayling of northwest Canada and Alaska (which could be recognized as *T. arcticus signifer*, then its subspecific name should be *T. arcticus tricolor*. After the last glaciation, grayling from the Yukon refuge extended their range southward and eastward only to tributaries of northwestern Hudson Bay and to the Skeena River, on the Pacific Coast. Grayling are not native to the Fraser or Columbia river basins. A considerable gap in geographical distance and geological time separates

Montana grayling from Arctic grayling, indicating that *tricolor* might be a "good" subspecies. The subspecies *tricolor* could be "brought back" to Michigan from Montana, but the Significant Evolutionary Unit represented by the native Michigan grayling is gone forever. Many attempts to restore grayling to Michigan waters have all failed.

A status report on Montana grayling, with emphasis on preservation of the fluvial form was prepared by Cal Kaya of Montana State University. The information in this report could be useful for restoring at least a token population of grayling in Michigan. Although the grayling cannot, in all honesty, be regarded as a great fighting fish, and fish of 12 to 14 inches are considered large, they take flies with more reckless abandon than even cutthroat trout. And their unusual beauty makes them a very special fish. When fishing in Montana, no matter how great the angling is for nonnative rainbow and brown trout, my angling experience is not fulfilled without at least a day fishing for native cutthroat and grayling.

Finally, I can't help but mention that the current work of the Montana Department of Fish, Wildlife and Parks in preserving the diversity of the native grayling illustrates the good conservation work a state agency can accomplish when it is no longer burdened with raising catchable trout for put-and-take artificial fisheries.

AUTHOR'S NOTE

The mysterious grayling specimen from Mongolia donated to the British Museum by St. George Littedale is mentioned in this column—my summer 2005 column provides the answer to the general locality where Littedale and his party caught grayling in 1897 during a sheep hunting expedition.

It had been commonly believed that grayling, in general, have a maximum life span of about 7–10 years with an extreme of 12–13 years. A paper published in 2006 on Alaskan grayling found a maximum life span of 29 years!

APACHE TROUT

$\blacktriangle$

WINTER 1993

MY FIRST EXPOSURE to what later proved to be Apache trout caused considerable consternation. This occurred in the late 1950s while conducting graduate research on the native trouts of the Great Basin (mainly the cutthroat trout native to the Lahontan and Bonneville basins of Nevada and Utah). I had borrowed all of the preserved specimens available in museums to examine in order to characterize the subspecies described from the Lahontan and Bonneville basins. These diagnoses would allow me to recognize these subspecies if they still existed. Both the Lahontan subspecies *henshawi* and the Bonneville subspecies *utah* were generally regarded to be extinct as pure populations at the time. The problem was: If these subspecies still existed, how could they be verified?

No valid diagnosis of the subspecies had ever been made.

My study was progressing nicely as I compiled the diagnostic traits of the two subspecies when I received three specimens from the U.S. National Museum labeled. "Panguitch Lake, Utah" (a lake in Bonneville basin). These specimens were collected in 1873 and were entirely distinct from any form of cutthroat trout known to me. The specimens were only about 5–8 inches in length but their deep bodies, long fins, spotting patterns, and other internal characters such as the number of vertebrae were very different from any other trout with which I was familiar. I pondered the question in my M.S. thesis: How could a trout so distinctively different from the Bonneville cutthroat have existed in the Bonneville basin and not been previously recognized?

I became aware that mix-ups of specimens and locality records of fish collections made by geological surveys and railroad surveys in the nineteenth century were a common occurrence. A bit of further investigation revealed that these three specimens (U.S. National Museum number 15,999) were actually collected from the White Mountains of Arizona (from the White River) and described by the zoologists E.D. Cope and H.C. Yarrow in 1875 as a variety of the Colorado River cutthroat trout—"*Salmo pleuriticus*." Cope and Yarrow most likely considered the peculiar trout they encountered in the White Mountains of Arizona as a variety of the Colorado River cutthroat trout because all of the rivers there drain to the Colorado River. They were not aware that the natural distribution of cutthroat trout in the Colorado basin did not extend to the Grand Canyon—the San Juan River of Utah, Colorado, and New Mexico is the southern limit of *pleuriticus*.

The early settlers in that region drained by the headwaters of the Little Colorado and Salt rivers of eastern Arizona were familiar with the Apache trout, which they commonly called "yellowbelly" trout in reference to its coloration. Until the 1950s, however, little was known of the Apache trout except that it had become very rare. It has been estimated that the original distribution of Apache trout consisted of about 600 miles of streams, mainly at elevations between 6,000 and 9,000 feet. Before reintroductions, pure populations of Apache trout existed in about 30 miles of a few small headwater streams.

In 1950, R. R. Miller of the University of Michigan described the Gila trout of the upper Gila River basin of New Mexico as a new species, *Salmo* (now *Oncorhynchus*) *gilae*. In this 1950 publication, Miller mentioned the native trout of the White Mountains of Arizona which he regarded as a form of the Gila trout. Subsequent studies comparing Gila trout and Apache trout found several distinctions between them and, in 1972, Miller formally described the Apache trout as a new species, *Salmo* (now *Oncorhynchus*) *apache*.

The Apache trout is distinguished by its deep body, long fins, and light yellow coloration on the ventral part of the body. The sides of the body typically have yellowish-brownish-olive colors with purplish tints. The dorsal, anal, and pelvic fins have pronounced cream to yellow-orange tips. Black pigment on the iris of the eye anterior and posterior to the pupil gives a mask-like appearance to the eye. The spotting pattern of Apache trout with relatively large, rounded spots sparsely distributed over the sides of the body is similar to that of some interior subspecies of cutthroat trout. Apache trout also have a pale yellowish "cutthroat" mark.

Looks, however, can be misleading.

The Gila and Apache trout are most closely related to each other and, in turn, both are more closely related to rainbow trout than to cutthroat trout. The cutthroat-like characters of Apache trout are primitive traits retained from an ancient common ancestor to both rainbow and cutthroat trout. In recent years modern techniques of genetic analysis have been used to demonstrate degrees of relationships. On a scale of 1 to 10, with 1 being most close genetic relationships and 10 the most

distant, the relationship between Gila and Apache trout would be in the range of 1–2; between both Gila and Apache trout grouped together on one hand, and rainbow trout on the other, the relationship measure would be about 3–4—between Gila and Apache and cutthroat trout, about 9–10. Because of the close relationship between the Gila and Apache trout, I classify them as two subspecies of a single species, *Oncorhynchus gilae gilae* and *O. g. apache*.

The origins of Gila and Apache trout, in my assessment of the evolution of western trouts of North America, can be traced to a common ancestor which moved from the Gulf of California into the Gila River basin, probably during a cold glacial period of the mid-Pleistocene (perhaps around a million years ago). Subsequently, the ancestral form became separated and differentiated into two groups, one in the northern part of the basin (Salt River segment of Gila basin = Apache trout) and one in the upper main Gila basin (Gila trout). Warmer and drier climatic periods produced the present landscapes with cactus, sagebrush, and mesquite at lower elevations, progressing through pinyon-juniper stands to the alpine conifer forest at the highest elevations. The trout that radiated from the Gulf of California include the Mexican golden trout and other rainbow-like trout of mountain tributaries to the Gulf, besides the Gila and Apache trout. During warmer climatic periods, these trout persisted in isolated islands of high elevation refugia along with other southerly distributed pockets of cold-adapted alpine flora and fauna—an assemblage of glacial relicts.

Because of their relatively close relationship to rainbow trout—and because neither Gila trout nor Apache trout can coexist with rainbow trout without hybridizing and loss of identity—a logical argument could be made that both Gila and Apache trout should be classified as subspecies of rainbow trout. The Gila and Apache trout do have a unique complement of chromosomes (their karyotype). Both species have fewer chromosomes than any form of rainbow or cutthroat trout (56 versus 58–68) and their chromosomes have a higher number of "arms" (106 versus 104—they have relatively more V-shaped than

I-shaped chromosomes). The unique karyotype could be used to argue that the Gila and Apache trout should be recognized as a separate species (with two subspecies). There are no universally accepted rules or definitions to determine the question, what is a species? In cases such as the "most correct" classification of Gila and Apache trout, the official decision is typically made by committee consensus—not necessarily "right," but "official."

No matter how Gila and Apache trout are classified, both are rare and worth saving. But they require active intervention to preserve the remnant populations from extinction. Although some of the decline can be attributed to degradation of habitat, the major cause leading to placement of both Gila and Apache trout on the endangered species list (and protection under the Endangered Species Act) has been the stocking of nonnative brown, brook, and rainbow trout. Brown trout

and brook trout replace the native trout by competitive interactions. Rainbow trout hybridize with Gila and Apache trout, and the offspring are fertile so that no reproductive barriers exist which can prevent the native trout from being modified or "absorbed" into introduced populations of rainbow trout.

The life history and "niche" characteristics of Gila and Apache trout broadly overlap those of other trout species so that coexistence by partitioning of resources doesn't work very well, especially in relatively small streams with limited habitat diversity. Like rainbow and cutthroat trout, the Apache trout is a spring spawner. Spawning is initiated by rising water temperatures (spawning begins at about 45° F) and declining flows. In different years and at different elevations spawning may occur from April into June. In small, cold headwater streams, Apache trout may be only 5–6 inches at three years of

APACHE TROUT
Oncorhynchus gilae apache

age, when first spawning typically occurs. They feed opportunistically, mainly on aquatic and terrestrial insects (as would other trout species in the same habitat). Apache trout readily take artificial flies (too readily for their own good if brown trout are present). In a stream on the Fort Apache Indian Reservation, electrofishing revealed that brown trout greatly outnumbered the Apache trout, but Apache trout were overwhelmingly dominant in the catch of fly fishers in this same stream.

The story of saving the Apache trout from the brink of extinction and subsequent restoration efforts is interesting and instructive. In the 1940s, long before the Apache trout was officially recognized as a distinct entity, before it was officially described and named, the White Mountain Apache tribe realized that the native yellow belly trout which once inhabited most of the waters on the reservation, had become very rare. As a first step to prevent extinction, a few headwater streams that still contained Apache trout were closed to angling by the tribe.

In 1964, a management plan was developed to restore the native trout on the reservation by chemical treatments of some streams to eliminate nonnative trout and restore Apache trout. Lakes were constructed where Apache trout could be stocked and attractive sport fisheries could be established. In 1975 an Apache trout recovery team was established, consisting of representatives of state and federal agencies and tribal members. Also in 1975 the status of the Apache trout under the Endangered Species Act was changed from endangered to threatened. This was an important change because a threatened status allows for regulated angling. Apache trout stocked in Christmas Tree Lake and Hurricane Lake grew to five pounds or more, and these lakes were opened to a limited entry fishery (limited to 20 anglers per day per lake) for an additional fee and special regulations (flies and lures only, two

trout bag limit, 14-inch minimum size). A world record Apache trout of 5 pounds, 3 ounces was caught in 1991; I expect new world records to be forthcoming.

The Apache trout recovery team began reintroductions and restoration projects on U.S. Forest Service lands. Steady progress has been made toward the establishment of 30 self-sustaining populations and eventual removal from the endangered species list. The most ambitious restoration program is being carried out by the U.S. Fish and Wildlife Service at the Alchesay-Williams Creek national fish hatchery. A brood stock of Apache trout has been established with a goal of annually producing about a half million Apache trout, about half of them of catchable size. The hatchery reared Apache trout will replace rainbow trout for stocking in waters of the Apache reservation which support intensive angling.

My column in the summer 1985 issue of *Trout* was about Gila trout. I'll conclude this one with a brief resume of what has happened to Gila trout since then.

Restoration efforts were progressing nicely, according to the recovery plan, and the status of the Gila trout was proposed to be changed from endangered to threatened in 1989. In the summer of 1989, however, a series of catastrophic natural events occurred in the upper Gila River basin—an extended drought and forest fires followed by floods devastated the populations of Gila trout in their small sanctuary streams. This setback delayed the change in status and led to a new restoration strategy that could better cope with catastrophes. When we revisit the Gila and Apache trout at some future time, I hope to be able to report good news on all fronts to the effect that these rare aquatic gems are flourishing and secure in their native, wild sanctuaries.

The summer 1985 column on Gila trout mentions the origins of both the Gila and Apache trout from a common ancestor that moved into the Gila River basin from the Gulf of California during an earlier glacial period of the Pleistocene. The ancestor giving rise to Apache trout became established in the Salt River division of the Gila basin. During warmer, interglacial periods, Apache trout were limited to about 600 miles of headwaters of the White and Black river drainages mainly at elevations from 6,000 to 9,000 feet. By about 50 years ago, nonnative brook, brown, and rainbow trout had replaced Apache trout throughout most of their range. Pure populations occurred in only about 30 miles of tiny headwater creeks. Most of the former and present distribution of Apache trout is on the Fort Apache Reservation of the White River Apache tribe. Long before the Apache trout was formally described in 1972 as *Salmo apache* (now *Oncorhynchus gilae apache*), and it received protection under the 1973 Endangered Species Act, the tribe initiated is own program for its own native trout. The protective attitude of the tribe is of cultural interest because the ancestral nomadic Apaches did not eat fish. A hatchery program stocks Apache trout in waters on the reservations for tourist anglers. If anglers desire to catch an Apache trout, they should visit the Fort Apache Reservation. Besides restoration of Apache trout on the reservation, restoration has also occurred on National Forest Lands in the White Mountains of Arizona.

THE CHARRS
OF NEW ENGLAND

>

FALL 1993

"NO HIGHER PRAISE CAN BE GIVEN, to a salmonoid than to say it is a charr" was the opinion of David Starr Jordan, America's most influential authority on fishes of the late nineteenth and early twentieth century. Note that Jordan and I write charr rather than char. This controversy over proper spelling will never be settled except by decree. It is certainly an inconsequential matter that would attract little attention except for the fish in question. Charr have historically generated an aura of mystery, interest, and controversy much out of proportion to their economic importance. I personally prefer charr over char because of its linguistic roots and unambiguity of meaning. The name probably is of Celtic language origin; in Gaelic, *ceara* means a blood red color. Other fishery terms of Celtic origin (via the Scotch) are redd (the nest of a salmonid fish) and parr (a juvenile Atlantic salmon). Note that if the second "d" or "r" is removed, pronunciation doesn't change, but the precision of meaning is lost. A char-broil restaurant doesn't serve broiled charr and if you char meat you make it black, not red.

When is a trout a charr? The most concise definition of charr (or char, the "preferred" dictionary spelling) is a fish of the genus *Salvelinus*. In the American Fisheries Society's "Common and scientific names of fishes from the United States and Canada," five species of the genus *Salvelinus* are listed; their common names are: Arctic char (spelling by AFS decree), bull trout, brook trout, Dolly Varden, and lake trout. There is only one "official" charr (or char) among the five North American species of *Salvelinus* according to the American Fisheries Society. This current usage reflects the fact that the first English-speaking settlers of North America were probably unaware of a fish called "charre" (in seventeenth century England). They were familiar with the brown trout, a species ubiquitously distributed in the British Isles and Europe, so the charr they encountered in North America became "trout," a precedent still followed. Izaak Walton never saw a charr but he knew of this elegant, rare fish because some fisherman at Lake Winderrnere learned to catch and sell them. By baiting a small hook with a bait such as a maggot and sinking it to the bottom of the lake, many charr could be caught in Lake Windermere and neighboring lakes. These were pickled and sealed in a pot to be sold at high prices to a select clientele. In English history, charre, charr, or char have considerable esteem as a rare, beautiful and mysterious fish.

There is considerable variation in charr from lake to lake in Britain and northern Europe. This led to the naming of many species (15 species were named for the charr of England and Ireland alone). In modern times, the Arctic charr, *Salvelinus alpinus*, is considered to include the charrs of Europe, Iceland, Greenland, Siberia, and North America (except for Dolly Varden, brook trout, bull trout, and lake trout in North America and Dolly Varden and other species of charr from the Chukotsk Peninsula southward in the Far East). There is such great variation in size, coloration, life history, and genetics of *S. alpinus* throughout the Holarctic region, that it is often referred to as the *S. alpinus* species complex (which means no one knows how many species and subspecies actually exist under the name *alpinus*). Thus, a notation for a footnote is given after "Arctic char" in the American Fisheries Society's list of common and scientific names. The footnote states that "Sunapee trout, blueback trout, and Quebec red trout are regarded by some authors as species distinct from the Arctic char." By revising three formerly recognized species of "trout" into the highly inclusive species *S. alpinus*, we transform three trout into one charr. If nothing else, this ambiguity of common names does illustrate the importance of scientific names for increased precision of definition and intent. The mention of Sunapee trout, blueback trout, and Quebec red trout offers an opportunity to get off an esoteric discourse on the peculiarities of fish names and get into the intended subject matter, the charrs of New England (I will only mention that I use the term "glacial relict"; to those who want to know when a relic is a relict, look it up).

Of the five species of charr native to North America, three are native to New England. The Dolly Varden and bull trout are restricted to the North Pacific basin. The lake trout has a broad distribution, essentially confined within the area covered by ice during the last glacial epoch, from Alaska, across Canada, the Great Lakes, to Quebec and New England. The Arctic charr (complex) has a great distribution in Arctic and subarctic waters of Europe, Asia, and North America. The Sunapee trout, blueback trout, and the Quebec red trout represent the southernmost worldwide distribution of the inclusive species *S. alpinus*.

The brook trout, the most ecologically plastic charr, has a native distribution from Hudson Bay, southward to the Great Lakes region, eastward throughout northeastern Canada and New England, and southward in Appalachian drainages all the way to northern Georgia and South Carolina (just about the southernmost distribution of the genus *Salvelinus*).

To understand the historical distribution of charrs in New England, both historical and ecological factors must be considered. Historical factors concern routes of dispersal used by ancestors. That is, an ancestor must have been able to reach a certain geographical area for the species to occur there today. Ecological factors concern the niche of a species and all of the environmental factors necessary for such a niche to persist. An ancestral species may have been in an area, but changing environmental conditions such as postglacial warming might have eliminated it.

In the past 100 years, man has enormously accelerated the influence of ecological factors such as introductions of nonnative species, reservoirs and river regulation, erosion, pollution, etc., to greatly increase the distribution of some species while contracting or eliminating the distribution of others.

The lake trout niche requires deep lakes with cold, well-oxygenated water. Also, lake trout are not capable of living in the salinity of marine environments. Thus, both historical factors (ancestor limited only to freshwater routes of dispersal) and ecological factors (freshwater route must contain a series of deep, cold lakes) affected lake trout distribution. With these limitations for dispersal and persistence, the native distribution of lake trout in New England was restricted to a few lakes of northern Vermont and New Hampshire and numerous lakes over a broad area of Maine (but many suitable Maine lakes lacked native lake trout). Of all the species of charr, the brook trout is the most "trout"-like. It can exist in a great range of stream and lake environments as long as temperatures are suitable. Brook trout utilize a broad range of food items in their diet. Also, brook trout can live in marine environments (ancestors could move from river to river via the ocean). This explains why the brook trout is the only charr native to all New England states and a species with a rather ubiquitous distribution throughout all of New England.

During the last glacial epoch, the ancestor of the Arctic charr, which gave rise to Sunapee, blueback, and Quebec red trout, may have persisted south of the maximum glacial front (south of New England) and/or in another glacier refugium. Although this ancestor undoubtedly used the marine environment for dispersal, similar to present Arctic charr in the Arctic Circle, its narrow niche in regards to water temperature, and its inability to coexist with lake trout, in most lakes, placed severe limitations on the persistence of Arctic charr as glacial relicts in New England.

About 15,000 to 20,000 years ago the glaciers began to retreat and the freshwaters of southern New England and the coastal regions of Maine became inhabitable for freshwater fishes (mainly species such as brook trout and Arctic charr that could move through marine waters). During this period it was likely that an Arctic charr was in a series of large lakes in the Connecticut River valley from where they eventually became established and persisted into historical times as the Sunapee trout in Sunapee Lake and Dan's Hole Pond, New Hampshire, and Averill Pond, Vermont (three suitably cold bodies of water where lake trout were not native). The introduction of lake trout in these three waters caused the extinction of all three populations of Sunapee trout—an example of man's acceleration of ecological factors. It was probably during this same glacial recession period that the same form of ancestral Arctic charr, via the ocean, entered coastal drainages of Maine where it

BROOK TROUT
Salvelinus fontinalis

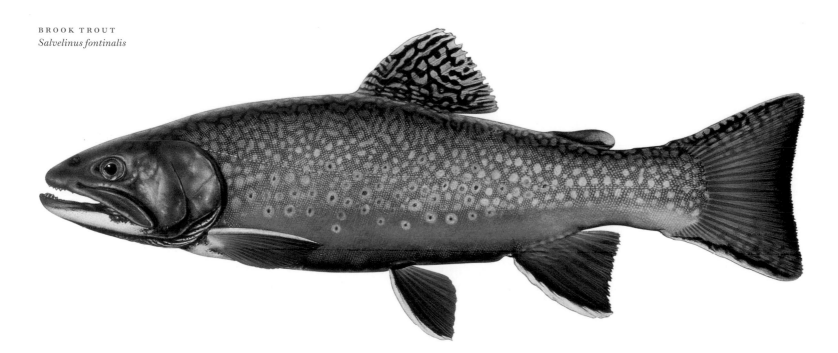

persists to present as the "Sunapee trout" of Floods Pond near Bangor, Maine. About 5,000 to 10,000 years later (5,000 to 10,000 years ago) the final glacier retreat allowed the possibility for freshwater fishes to disperse throughout all the drainages of Maine. During this period the lake trout's dispersal was limited to fresh-water routes with cold lakes but the brook trout ancestor dispersed ubiquitously. The Arctic charr ancestor, during this time, became established in the Rangeley Lakes and in 11 other smaller, deep, cold ponds (all sites where lake trout did not occur) in Maine. This charr is known as the blueback trout. The origin of the red trout of southern Quebec also occurred at this time.

In the nineteenth century, the discovery of these populations of Arctic charr stirred great interest and raised many questions. What species? From where did their ancestors come? How can they be caught by angling?

The blueback trout was named "*Salmo*" *oquassa* in 1854, the Sunapee as *Salvelinus aureolus* in 1887, and the red trout as "*Salmo*" *marstoni* in 1893. According to the scenario of origins given above, none of the populations, at the time of establishment, would have been separated from a common ancestral Arctic charr by more than about 10,000 years. This relatively short period of separation would not be expected to result in much evolutionary differentiation. All taxonomic and genetic comparisons of Sunapee, blueback, and red trout agree that all are very closely related to each other. As a group, however, they do differ from all other groups of *S. alpinus* to a degree that subspecies recognition is justified. Because the name *oquassa* is the oldest name, the Sunapee, blueback, and red trout together are classified as *Salvelinus alpinus oquassa*.

This is correct taxonomic procedure, but a highly significant point concerning intraspecific differentiation can be overlooked. This point concerns nontaxonomic traits such as life history differences and evolutionary specialization for niche diversity which are significant for fisheries management and for conservation of biodiversity. For example, most species of salmonid fishes have both anadromous and completely fresh-water populations (such as steelhead and rainbow trout, sockeye salmon and kokanee, Atlantic salmon and lake salmon, etc.) An understanding of this difference in life histories between anadromous and freshwater populations of the same species is obviously of great significance for management of such species. This life history-ecological difference, however, is not associated with taxonomic difference (the two life history forms are not recognized as different species or subspecies), nor can they be identified by even the most sophisticated genetic techniques.

To illustrate intraspecific (actually intrasubspecific) differences in life history-ecology of the subspecies *S. a. oquassa*, some comparisons can be made based on what is known about the extinct blueback trout of the Rangeley Lakes and the Sunapee trout of Sunapee Lake. The blueback of the Rangeley Lakes were extremely abundant, of small size (averaging 7 to 8 inches as mature adults), and not caught by anglers. They were only seen in October–November when they massed in great numbers for spawning. The brook trout (but not the lake trout) was also native to the Rangeleys. Evidently, over thousands of years a well-balanced predator-prey system evolved between brook trout (predator) and blueback (prey). The Rangeley Lakes were famous for large brook trout. Several fish of 10 pounds and a few of 12 pounds and slightly larger were recorded in the nineteenth century. This coevolution and coadaptation between the brook trout and blueback worked well; it created one of the most famous brook trout fisheries and supplied an abundance of food for the people who netted untold thousands of blueback during their annual spawning aggregations (bluebacks were so abundant that they were specifically exempted from fish protection laws). Thus a specialized "prey" form of Arctic charr and a specialized "predator" form of brook trout evolved in the Rangeley Lakes. It is likely that the Rangeley Lake brook trout differed from ordinary brook trout by an older age at maturity, a longer life span, and a special adaptation to feed on fish in deep water; all traits resulting in the attainment of a large maximum size. These life history traits are not taxonomic traits, nor can they be identified by modern techniques of genetics, yet they are real and they are important in considering the range of diversity expressed by a species.

In 1874, Atlantic salmon (both anadromous and lake salmon) were first stocked in the Rangeley Lakes. Subsequently, smelt were stocked for salmon forage. At the time there was no concept of niche theory. If there had been, the introduction of nonnative species would have been considered a benign addition (rather than a subtractive one) on the native fishes. By the 1890s, the blueback rapidly declined and was extinct in all the Rangeley Lakes by the early 1900s.

The increased predation by salmon and especially the intense competition from an abundant smelt population for zooplankton and other small invertebrates, so rapidly changed "ecological factors" that had allowed persistence of this glacial relict charr for thousands of years, that they became extinct in a very brief moment of evolutionary time. After the 1890s, the native brook trout of the Rangeleys never attained a size comparable to their former greatness.

In Sunapee Lake, the native Arctic charr, the Sunapee trout, was apparently the top predator, and the native brook trout were neither abundant nor of large size. Atlantic salmon and smelt were also stocked in Sunapee and the smelt became abundant. The Sunapee trout, in contrast to the Rangeley Lakes blueback, responded not by becoming extinct, but by increasing its abundance and size by utilizing smelt as a new food source. The demise of the Sunapee trout in Sunapee Lake came from introduction of lake trout. The lake trout posed a relentless triple threat for the Sunapee. It was a predator on the Sunapee, a competitor for forage fish, and a promiscuous hybridizer. The last few large "Sunapee" trout caught in the 1940s, including a "world record," were actually lake trout/Sunapee hybrids.

These examples illustrate the very real and important differences in life history and ecology among populations of the same subspecies. This is the type of biodiversity we should protect and preserve. For the "Sunapee" part of *oquassa* diversity, most has already been lost. Of the four historical populations, three became extinct after lake trout stocking. The population in Floods Pond is the only remaining Sunapee (the only population representing the first wave of Arctic charr invasion of New England waters as the glaciers receded). As such, should it receive special attention and priority in a conflict threatening its continued existence or should it be treated as only one of many populations of the subspecies *oquassa*? This question was faced by the Maine Fisheries and Wildlife Commission. Floods Pond is the source of water for the city of Bangor. As Bangor increased in population, water use increased and Floods Pond experienced fluctuations and lowering of surface level. The native charr spawns only on one gravel bed in shallow water. Lower lake levels during spawning had greatly reduced spawning success and in some years no reproduction occurred. Obviously, the native charr of Floods Pond cannot continue to exist without consistent reproduction. In 1989, the Maine legislature directed the Bangor Water District and the Fisheries and Wildlife Commission to develop a plan to ensure long-term survival of the charr while also having Floods Pond supply the water needs of Bangor (legislators are adept at coming up with win/win oxymorons). In response to this directive, a water management plan was devised for Floods Pond. The degree of protection for the charr was based on the charr's degree of quantitative differentiation. It was decided that if the charr of Floods Pond was unique at the species or subspecies level, then adequate lake levels for successful reproduction must be maintained 80 percent of the time (4 years out of 5). If they are unique at the population level, then reproduction needs to be ensured 50 percent of the time and if they "are shown to be no different from other populations of charr," 20 percent of the time would be enough.

When I see such statements I cringe at the ignorance displayed in seeking simplistic "scientific" solutions. A study on mitochondrial DNA (mtDNA) was performed at the University of Maine. As would be expected if a sufficient portion of the mtDNA is examined, distinctive sequences will show up (population markers) and the Floods Pond charr was declared to be a "distinct population" (which was already obvious—any population isolated from other populations of the same species must be "distinct" as they have no gene flow to another population). The resolution of the Floods Pond conflict probably improved the prospects for the continued existence of the native charr, but conservation biology was practiced "without a license."

Were the people who established the criteria for degrees of protection knowledgeable on such matters as what constitutes a species, a subspecies, or a "distinct" population? Did they understand what mtDNA is and its limitations for determining species, subspecies, and populations? The bottom-line fact on this matter is that the Floods Pond charr represents the last remaining population of the first wave of postglacial invasion of Arctic charr into New England waters. As such they deserve high priority for preservation irrespective of any genetic analysis. I believe a clever consultant to the Bangor Water District could have easily "shown them to be no different from other populations of charr." In this case would it be O.K. to let the charr become extinct? Modern technology can be a two-edged sword for good or for disaster fostered by well-meaning people ignorant of the technology and of evolutionary biology.

The tools of the trade for understanding charr diversity have much changed since William Converse Kendall published *The Charrs of New England* in 1914. Kendall witnessed the extinction of the bluebacks in the Rangeley Lakes and I think he would agree with me that the fate of the last of the Sunapees should not be decided solely on the base sequences of a tiny fragment of DNA—there's so much more to charr diversity than that. Try to recreate Shakespeare's writings or Beethoven's music by computer simulation of letter or note frequencies.

AUTHOR'S NOTE

Although char is the preferred or standard spelling, examination of the roots of the word would conclude that charr is more etymologically correct. Especially in Canadian publication, lake trout are now called lake charr and brook trout, brook charr. Take your pick. The spring 1984 column on Sunapee "trout," revealed that the native trout (or charr) from Sunapee Lake, New Hampshire, was transplanted into some high elevation lakes in Idaho in the 1920s. They still persist in one lake, many years after they became extinct in Sunapee Lake. The threat to the persistence of the last of the Sunapee-like charr, in Floods Pond Maine, is discussed. Since 1993, an artificial spawning bed was constructed in deeper water to allow for spawning when water withdrawal lowers the surface level to a point exposing the original spawning grounds.

COASTER BROOK TROUT

FALL 1994

WHAT IS A COASTER BROOK TROUT? What is an evolutionary significant unit? When the topic of coaster brook trout came up, I was in the midst of attempting to characterize an "evolutionary significant unit" applicable for defining what types of biological diversity should be eligible for protection under the Endangered Species Act. This was part of my participation in a symposium on evolutionary significant units sponsored by the American Fisheries Society.

Diversity of life can be divided into diversity between and among different species (interspecific diversity) and diversity within a species (intraspecific diversity). It is intraspecific diversity that has provoked most of the controversy surrounding the Endangered Species Act. Where can a line be drawn concerning eligibility for listing and protection under the ESA? Presently, species is defined in the ESA to include subspecies and "segments" (populations) of species of vertebrates. How can we sort out significant from insignificant "units," "segments," or populations of intraspecific diversity? Using trout and salmon as examples, my conclusions were that the most significant types of life history and ecological adaptations, the type of "significance" we want to preserve into the future, by and large, are not associated with whole species or subspecies, but are found at the population level—a small part or "segment" of a species. For example, the world's largest cutthroat trout and the world's largest rainbow trout came from populations that evolved in Pyramid Lake, Nevada, and Kootenay Lake, British Columbia, respectively, where their ancestors specialized to be the keystone predators of their ecosystems.

Admittedly, my ideas on "significance" to categorize diversity of fishes is colored by my interest in angling. Thus, the "segment" or population of the brook trout species, *Salvelinus fontinalis*, which produced the world record brook trout of 14½ pounds conforms to my idea of a significant evolutionary unit. And this introduces the coaster brook trout.

The coaster brook trout is a difficult fish to define. This particular unit of diversity has never been described as a species or subspecies. I know of no book or literature source that provides detailed life history or ecological data on coaster brook trout. George Becker, in his book *Fishes in Wisconsin*, defines "coasters" as a brook trout that spends part of its life in the Great Lakes. He wrote: "Coasters have an indefinable, perhaps sentimental attraction all their own." This does not give us much to go on to make a case for the coaster as a significant evolutionary unit.

Actually, there was not one origin of coasters in the Great Lakes. That is, coaster brook trout, like steelhead rainbow trout, had multiple origins from diverse brook trout populations which specialized to utilize the inshore resources of the Great Lakes. As the most significant population of coaster brook trout, I would select the coasters that spawned in or were associated with the Nipigon River on the north shore of Lake Superior. This was the population that produced the world record in 1915 which has not been surpassed for almost 80 years. How much, if any, of the genetic resource which produced the world record fish still exists is unknown, but the fact that the record has not been broken in almost 80 years is not a hopeful sign.

The great size of coaster brook trout of the north shore of Lake Superior was well known among anglers of the nineteenth century. Most were caught during their spawning run in the Nipigon River. In Charles Hallock's *Sportsman's Guide and General Gazetteer* (1877), one may read that the largest brook trout are found in the "Nepigon" River (to "17 pounds"). E. R. Hewitt devoted a chapter to the Nipigon River brook trout in his book, A Salmon and Trout Fisherman for Seventy-Five Years. Hewitt fished the Nipigon in 1877 and 1891. He wrote that "…one of 19 pounds is recorded by one of the early survey parties of which a friend of mine was a member. The fish was taken near where the river runs into Lake Superior." Hewitt came across an Indian catching brook trout in the Nipigon for his winter food supply. Hewitt claimed the largest fish caught by the Indian (fishing with a spoon) without head and viscera weighed "exactly 11 pounds." Although there is no documented record of a Nipigon brook trout larger than the 14½-pound record, perhaps by 1915 this population of coasters was already in decline. The decline (to extinction?) can be attributed to many causes: blockage or impairment of spawning runs, introductions of brown and rainbow trout or hatchery strains of brook trout which could hybridize and "dilute" pure coaster populations.

In 1853, Theodatus Garlick became the first person to artificially propagate trout in America. He made a 600-mile journey from Cleveland, Ohio to Saulte Ste. Marie, the outlet area of Lake Superior, to obtain his brood stock. He wanted the biggest and the best and Lake Superior coaster brook trout had that reputation. Since then, hatchery brook trout have gone downhill. Most subsequent hatchery stocks came from small stream, short lived populations and have been selectively bred to thrive under hatchery conditions but not in the wild.

Many years ago, the late Dwight Webster of Cornell University thought that among the range of intraspecific genetic diversity contained in *S. fontinalis*, some could be found that would be useful for fisheries management. Evidently, the world record coaster population of northern Lake Superior was gone so he turned to more virgin large lakes of the Hudson Bay drainage of Canada. Temiscamie and Assinica lakes were noted for long lived (9–10 years) and large (9–10 pounds) lake-adapted populations of brook trout and these populations supplied his brood stocks.

When stocked in numerous Adirondack lakes and compared with domesticated hatchery strains for many years, Webster and his associate Bill Flick demonstrated again and again, the longer life span, larger size, and much greater total return to angling from the wild, lake-adapted strains compared to standard hatchery strains.

Although the Temiscamie and Assinica brook trout have been propagated and stocked in other states, it has been only on a very limited scale. The concept of the significant evolutionary unit and the potential to utilize significant units of intraspecific diversity to increase the effectiveness of hatchery propagation and stocking, is simply not understood by most fish culturists. I don't expect that this situation will much change until a basic change occurs in the hatchery mentality from one of feedlot production technology to principles of wildlife management and conservation biology.

On May 19 and 20 in Denver, Colorado, a workshop was held: "Wild Trout and Planted Trout: Balancing the Scale." Unfortunately, I was in California at this time for the evolutionary significant unit symposium, but independent (non-agency) professional advocates of wild trout such as Ray White and me were not invited to participate. The workshop was designed to be a "win-win," feel good consensus;

it would not be appreciated to have someone raise hard, embarrassing points and questions that might jiggle the scale out of balance in favor of wild trout. During the workshop, the audience raised questions and issues to be addressed by a panel of experts (pro-hatchery or pro win-win, conciliatory experts). A questions raised was: "Is there real evidence of a difference between the survival of wild and hatchery trout due to genetic differences? Are hatchery reared fish really inferior from a genetic perspective?" The expert panel response was: "A non-issue. It is more important to create good stocking guidelines for where stocked fish will be used." So much for win-win workshops to provide brilliant insights for resolving conflicts between wild trout and hatchery trout. You bet it's an issue—a most significant issue. Is there evidence of survival differences? I have stacks of publications and reports from all over the country, covering several species, over the past 40 years to document these survival differences, which indeed reflect genetic based differences in survival in nature. Wild versus domesticated and genetic inferiority? Inferior for what? For a feedlot, the production of herefords would be much superior than trying to contain and fatten cattle of the wild ancestral species from which domestic cattle were derived.

Was the north shore Lake Superior–Nipigon coaster brook trout a significant part of the brook trout species? Was its loss a significant irreplaceable loss? Did hatcheries play a role in this loss? Could hatcheries have played a role in its prevention? These are the types of questions I would like to see addressed at a wild trout-hatchery trout workshop. Ray White and I should have been there, but we might have been ejected for disturbing the peace.

AUTHOR'S NOTE

In lakes Nipigon and Superior, brook trout evolved a migratory life history to utilize the inshore waters of these large lakes. I explained that because there is no single common ancestor for all coaster brook trout, it is futile to try to identify all coasters from all nonmigratory brook trout by genetic analysis. Despite my words of caution, genetic analysis, searching for the nonexistent holy grail of a coaster genetic marker, became a popular if fruitless endeavor; and, this quixotic quest has gone on and on.

DESERT TREASURES AT RISK

WINTER 1995

MORE THAN 35 YEARS AGO, my odyssey with native western trout began with a study of the trouts of the Great Basin. I was fascinated with trout that had evolved and survived for thousands of years in harsh habitats of arid lands. At the time, the native cutthroat trout of the Lahontan and Bonneville Basins were believed extinct. The species of trout native to the Oregon desert basins was unknown, the Gila trout had recently been described (1950) but was known to exist in only one small stream in New Mexico, and the Apache trout had not yet been described but was known to occur in a few small headwater streams in the White Mountains of Arizona.

The major cause of the rapid disappearance of the native trouts of the West were habitat destruction—largely caused by the cumulative impacts of more than 100 years of livestock grazing—and the introduction of nonnative trouts. During my travels and fieldwork throughout the arid lands region, a common pattern became apparent. Where there once were trout streams, I found horribly degraded watersheds stripped of riparian vegetation, unstable streambanks sloughing into stream channels, and braided watercourses carrying mere trickles of silt-laden flow.

Livestock grazing has been and continues to be the most ubiquitous and pervasive impact on western streams. The impact of livestock is exacerbated in arid land regions, because by mid-summer the only remaining palatable vegetation occurs near streams, and cattle concentrate there, doing tremendous damage. Watersheds in arid regions are particularly susceptible to livestock damage because, while there is often sufficient annual precipitation to sustain native grasslands, there is rarely enough for the vigorous growth needed to revegetate grazed land. After intensive grazing devegetates a watershed, the next major storm event triggers massive erosion and cutting of arroyos. In some Gila River tributaries, such as the San Pedro River, once downcutting begins, it can proceed 100 miles or more to the headwaters. The lowering of the water table results in dramatic changes in the landscape, commonly called "desertification."

The Gila River drainage of New Mexico and Arizona may have been especially vulnerable to livestock grazing impacts because bison were not native to this region. The native vegetation had evolved for many thousands of years without a large mammalian grazer, and so was not adapted for persistence under heavy grazing pressure.

The impacts of livestock grazing I observed during my first visits to the Southwest were nothing new. Conservationist Aldo Leopold described the ecological ramifications of destructive grazing practices in New Mexico more than 60 years ago. Ironically, on the Aldo Leopold Wilderness in the Gila National Forest (the first National Widerness Area), thousands of cattle continue to graze with devastating effect, while hikers and backpackers are instructed to "tread lightly" and respect the ecological integrity of the land.

The trouts native to arid lands have diverse origins and provide a natural laboratory for the study of evolutionary ecology—the evolution of life history strategies to cope with environmental extremes. Thermal adaptation is reflected in arid-lands redband trout, which I have taken on dry flies in 83° F water. Whitehorse Basin cutthroat trout show similar resistance to thermal stress. In the desert basins of southern Oregon and northern Nevada, redband trout regularly encounter water temperatures that kill other trout. Numerous experiments have demonstrated the obvious: brook, brown, rainbow and cutthroat trout are coldwater fish that typically experience stress when water temperatures rise above 72° F. With gradual increases in temperature, loss of equilibrium and death can be expected to occur at about 82° F–84° F. Nevertheless, I have found native redband trout in intermittent desert streams thriving in water of 83° F. They were actively feeding at this temperature, and those I caught on flies fought vigorously when hooked, indicating considerable energy reserves.

But despite their tolerance for high temperatures, all have been subjected to the basic problem that goes beyond their capacity to live in warm water. The ecological integrity of their watersheds is fragile, easily disrupted, and, as mentioned, the most ubiquitous and pervasive force for disruption and destruction is livestock grazing. The results have been predictable:

· The Alvord cutthroat trout is extinct as a pure form.

· Lahontan cutthroat are listed, and supposedly protected, under the Endangered Species Act, but in conflicts between livestock and Lahontan cutthroat habitat, livestock interests have consistently predominated.

· An active restoration program for the Bonneville cutthroat has restored several populations in Wyoming and Utah and has brought this subspecies back from the brink of extinction.

· Very few pure native redband populations still exist in the Oregon desert basins.

· The Gila trout is listed as endangered and the Apache trout as threatened under the Endangered Species Act.

Fortunately for the Apache trout, most of its surviving populations occurred in streams on the White Mountain Apache Reservation. Attempts or proposals to restore both Apache and Gila trout to streams on Forest Service lands often encounter conflicts with livestock.

During the last 20 years, I have served on the American Fisheries Society's riparian committee, participated in numerous livestock-riparian-fisheries symposia, and contributed to many proceedings that related the same horror stories over and over. All of the symposia sought solutions, provided hopeful examples of change and watershed restorations, and attempted to create an optimistic outlook for the future.

Has that hopeful "future" finally arrived with "ecosystem management" now practiced on federal lands by the Forest Service and Bureau of Land Management? Is the "ecological integrity" of watersheds being restored on a large scale?

In the fall of 1992, I attended a meeting of the Desert Fishes Council in Mesa, Arizona. There was a session on Apache trout restoration featuring the excellent work done by the Old Pueblo TU chapter in cooperation with Forest Service biologists to restore Apache trout to some small streams on Forest Service lands. One slide shown during the session depicted habitat improvement on a stream that had been transformed into little more than intermittent mud holes by cattle. Thirty-five years of deja vu swept over me. There is still a great chasm between the goals, missions, and stated intents of USFS and BLM policies and programs and guidelines and directives, and the realities of on-the-ground implementation of these goals when livestock conflicts are involved.

This is particularly ironic in arid land regions where livestock grazing on federal lands is a marginal but highly subsidized operation. A particularly high subsidy is devoted to grazing on arid lands, thereby promoting the continuing environmental degradation by livestock. Most of the native grasslands of the arid regions were destroyed 100 years ago, when the first waves of cattle hit the open range (the classic example of the "tragedy of the commons"). With erosion and lowering of water tables, grasses were largely replaced by more drought-tolerant vegetation such as sagebrush and greasewood. On such range,

100 acres or more are necessary to support one Hereford, and they are sorry looking beasts indeed. When you look at these scrawny cattle, it isn't hard to understand why the total contribution to the nation's beef supply resulting from cattle grazed on federal arid lands is quite insignificant—perhaps less than one percent. If vast areas could be restored to the native grasslands condition, benefits would accrue to all including the ranchers. Many more livestock could be produced on a sustainable basis if the stream were restored, and water levels raised to their natural levels.

The obvious question is: Why haven't meaningful grazing reforms been instituted by the Forest Service and BLM on a universal basis? Why the foot dragging? The answer was apparent last summer when Secretary of Interior Bruce Babbitt proposed grazing and mining reforms. Western congressmen reacted in a manner reminiscent of former

WHITEHORSE BASIN CUTTHROAT TROUT
Oncorhynchus clarki subspecies

congressional diatribes warning of the communist menace—cries of "war on the West," "genocide on the West," and "destruction of a way of life," echoed through Congress.

Who has the ear of these congressmen? Obviously not rational people. To be fair to Forest Service and BLM employees, put yourself in their shoes in a regional western office in the midst of sagebrush rebels and Wise Use Luddites with their threats and tactics of intimidation, determined to maintain the status quo. Also, you would be aware of what happened to the careers of former employees who courageously tried to implement goals and do the right thing in land management decisions. Thus, the cautious employee attempts compromise, but in so doing often incurs the wrath of both the ranchers and environmentalists. A common strategy is to seek delaying tactics. For example, grazing programs can't be changed, even when the habitat of an endangered species is involved, until more is known—"further research" is proposed on all sorts of nonsignificant and diversionary issues such as genetic analysis, habitat analysis, invertebrate analysis, etc.

When I hear a federal biologist call for "further research" in relation to impacts of livestock grazing, which is readily apparent to anyone with functional vision, a question is raised in my mind concerning their ecological competence. I also understand, however, that they have learned the rules of the game and are on the track to administrative advancement.

In the big perspective, it comes down to the type of stewardship we want our government to exercise in the management of our public lands. All commodity uses don't have to be shut down. There are highly competent and environmentally sensitive ranchers who do a good job and make livestock grazing compatible with goals of maintaining or restoring ecosystem integrity. With the entrenched political lobby, however, for resource exploitation which effectively networks through county commissioners, to state legislators, to state congressional delegations, it is the distorted extremist self-interest position that has gained political clout, rather than the rational voice of reasonable resource users.

Presently, the most rapid reforms in BLM and Forest Service land management programs are coming about because of legal action by such groups as the Environmental Defense Fund and the Sierra Club Legal Defense Fund. Typically, focus is on an endangered species issues where it can be demonstrated that an agency's resource programs such as timber or livestock are in violation of the Endangered Species Act. Drastic reforms or curtailment of programs are then ordered by a federal judge. This is an antagonistic and disruptive way of instituting reform, but in many areas of the West, it is the only feasible option to effect more rapid reform, and is welcomed by many frustrated federal agency employees. There should be better means to resolve our environmental conflicts. We live in a representative democracy. Note how your representatives and senators vote on public land issues such as livestock grazing, mining, and timber. Let them know your opinions, they're your representatives.

In this column I expressed my frustrations, accumulated over many years, concerning the policies of federal agencies that subsidized the destruction of native trout watersheds especially in arid regions of the West. There was indeed a large gap between the word and the deed. The noble goals expressed in the descriptions of multiple use management and restoration of ecological integrity on lands administered by the U.S. Forest Service and the Bureau of Land Management were not being implemented in any meaningful way. Legal action began to speed up the implementation process, especially in regards to livestock grazing.

My winter 1998 column (p. 201) described the improved conditions I observed in watersheds resulting from new livestock management programs. An example concerned gold mines in Nevada that purchased surrounding ranches. In cooperation with the BLM, new grazing management strategies designed to restore riparian vegetation were implemented. Several small streams that had been badly degraded greatly improved and the native Humboldt cutthroat trout rebounded from the brink of extinction. Large corporations accomplished what the Endangered Species Act had failed to do.

WILD SALMONID GENETICS:
AN IMPENDING CRISIS?

SUMMER 1995

IN 1991 THE AMERICAN FISHERIES SOCIETY published a list of 214 stocks of anadromous Pacific Coast salmonids that are already extinct or in various stages of endangerment. Since 1991, four races or stocks of Pacific salmon have been listed for protection under the Endangered Species Act. These include the winter run Chinook salmon of the Sacramento River, the spring-summer and fall Chinook of the Snake River, and the sockeye salmon of Redfish Lake, Idaho. The American Fisheries Society's publication warning of the precarious state of wild anadromous salmonids of the Pacific Coast stimulated a rash of petitions to list numerous races of Pacific salmon, steelhead, and coastal cutthroat trout for protection under the Endangered Species Act. The sheer number of petitions received contributed to an overload of the system. Many petitions are rejected for lack of information; others pile up in a backlog and will probably never receive adequate reviews.

The perceived urgency of the problem of conserving the genetic diversity of wild salmonid fishes is reflected in a list of priorities prepared by Trout Unlimited's Natural Resource Board at the 1994 annual meeting. Priority 4 is "wild salmonid genetics." This is certainly a worthy issue for TU involvement, but I would ask: If one million or ten million dollars were made available to address the issues and problems concerning "wild salmonid genetics," how would it be spent and would the expenditures have any real benefits for conserving the genetic diversity of wild salmonids?

"Genetic research" is a classic example of a nebulous term often resulting in large expenditures with no tangible results. This is because most fisheries biologists and administrators have no more understanding of the subject matter than they do of plasma physics. They lack the understanding necessary to phrase the right questions in need of answers and thus are vulnerable to diverting large amounts of funds to obtain precise answers to irrelevant or wrong questions. Thus, it is basic for the goal of maintaining the genetic diversity of wild salmonids to have credibility, to ask the right questions, and then understand the limitations of any method or technique to answer the question before any method or technique is chosen.

A most important question we must confront was asked in a recent newsletter of the Society for Conservation Biology: "Why do we want to conserve biodiversity, anyway?" The newsletter goes on to point out that conservationists have not been highly successful in getting out our message, such as, why is wild salmonid genetics important? We have a failure in communications at various levels of society. This lack of effective communications became obvious in the outcome of the November, 1994 Congressional elections. Helen Chenoweth was elected to represent Idaho in the new Congress. Ms. Chenoweth's environmental platform was essentially provided by the Wise Use Movement. To celebrate her victory, Ms. Chenoweth spoke at an "endangered salmon bake" in Stanley, Idaho (headwaters of the Salmon River, which contains three races of endangered salmon). She asked, "How can I take the salmon's endangered status seriously when you can buy a can at Albertson's?" Such a cute statement ignores the difference in values between meat in a can and live, wild salmon in a river, and also the fact that the dams that have made live, wild salmon so rare in Idaho export most of their benefits outside the state. Her statement does, however, emphasize our failure to communicate on the question, "Why do we want to preserve biodiversity anyway?"

To counter the anti-environmental message in relation to conservation of wild salmonid genetic diversity, two common fallacies should be understood concerning causes of extinction and the "adaptiveness" of intraspecific diversity (genetic diversity within a species). These fallacies were widely propagandized during the last election in one way or another. Their arguments generally follow these lines of reasoning: extinction is a natural process, it is a "built-in" attribute of species to become extinct, and man shouldn't interfere with the laws of nature; and, minor variation among populations and races of a species is nonadaptive, the different parts of a species are interchangeable; therefore, there is no need to save all the parts. The fallacious extinction theory is based on the outdated evolutionary theory of orthogenesis, which presumed a built-in mechanism causing extinction. Modern evolutionary theory has long rejected orthogenesis as lacking any valid basis. In the past, most species became extinct through evolutionary change. That is, they gave rise to new species through time. Their genes were modified and passed on to maintain evolutionary diversity. In contrast, man-induced accelerated extinctions result in termination of evolutionary lines before they can give rise to new species.

The argument against adaptiveness of intraspecific variation is based on the outdated evolutionary theory of early geneticists concerning evolution of new species by "saltation." Genetic mutations were thought of as "macromutations," which could result in a new species in one generation, and "micromutations," which caused the "minor variations" among populations and races of a species. In this theory, Darwinian natural selection, the basis for adaptiveness by slowly perfecting of survival, generation by generation, only played the role of accepting or rejecting the new species arising from a macromutation; "adaptiveness" played no role in the speciation process. Micromutations only supplied the "minor variations" observed within a species and were assumed to be nonadaptive. This theory has also been long rejected by most modern evolutionary geneticists. The fallaciousness of the "saltation" theory of evolution and its associated arguments against adaptiveness of intraspecific diversity has been clearly demonstrated in salmonid fishes. In the 1930s with the beginning of dam building on the Columbia River and blocking of salmon and steelhead runs, it was assumed that the abundance of salmon and steelhead could be maintained by substituting a few generic hatchery stocks for the great diversity of wild populations lost to dams under the mistaken notion of "interchangeable parts." We now realize, too late, that intraspecific diversity (the "minor variations") is indeed adaptive. The sockeye salmon spawning in Redfish Lake and the races of Chinook salmon spawning in the headwaters of the Salmon River, Idaho, may show only minor variation in genetic structure to other populations of their species which spawn in rivers near the ocean. The fact that the Redfish Lake sockeye and the Salmon River Chinook migrate almost 900 miles from the ocean (adults upstream, smolts downstream) means that they have very different life histories and physiologies compared to other populations of their species. These differences are "adaptive" for their specific spawning environments; they are not interchangeable.

Thus, a goal for the conservation of genetic diversity of wild salmonids would be to preserve the "range of adaptiveness" within a species.

For anglers and fisheries managers, prioritizing the types of adaptations we want to preserve and utilize might be based on "trophy" fish. What populations or races have adaptive specializations that result in exceptionally large fish? For example, the world's largest steelhead are produced by populations native to the Skeena River basin. The world's largest Chinook salmon are from the Kenai River, Alaska, populations. The world's largest rainbow trout is the Gerrard population of Kamloops rainbow of Kootenay Lake. The world's largest cutthroat trout is the Lahontan cutthroat trout native to Pyramid Lake. The world's largest brook trout was the coaster population of the Nipigon River. Most would agree that these are the types of intraspecific adaptiveness we want to preserve. Let us now return to the issue of wild salmonid genetics and the need to ask the right questions.

All of the examples of important types of adaptations found within species of trout and salmon mentioned above—the longest migrations, the largest size, etc.—have evolved during relatively recent evolutionary times, perhaps about 10,000 years. All of the most modern, state-of-the-art techniques of genetic analysis would find all of these important types of diversity to be quite "insignificant" in terms of their quantitative degree of divergence within their respective species because they have not been separated and isolated for a sufficiently long period of time. The important differences in life history and ecology, the "adaptiveness" of a particular form of trout or salmon, cannot be understood or predicted from the tiny fraction of hereditary material sampled and analyzed by modern genetic techniques. The most important attributes of adaptiveness lie within what is called the regulatory genome, which is not sampled. We can only understand these attributes from observing the life history of an organism.

Thus, I foresee the danger that research on wild salmonid genetics, although of the best intentions, can have a negative influence on the

CHINOOK SALMON
Oncorhynchus tshawytscha

conservation of the most important aspect of genetic diversity—preserving the range of adaptations. This danger will be manifested if people involved in decision-making substitute "data" and quantitative indices for knowledge and critical thinking and fail to ask the right questions.

There are analogies between evaluating and defining significant units of genetic diversity and critical assessment of significance in works of art, literature, and music. Just as artistic critiques require more than a quantitative assessment of colors, notes, and sequences of letters, understanding genetic diversity requires much more than a knowledge of DNA sequences.

AUTHOR'S NOTE

This column highlighted the naive embracement of "genetics" by biologists and the public to resolve all sorts of issues. I point out that an understanding of the subject matter is necessary to ask the right questions within the context of the limitations of genetic data to answer the questions. The problem concerns how the human mind is conditioned to function. We seek to transform uncertainty into certainty, shades of gray into black and white. Previously, the advent of computer modeling led many non-specialists astray to mistakenly believe, that somehow, computers could magically transform uncertainty (stochastic data) into certainty (deterministic data). Many years ago I wrote a paper, "The Illusion of Technique and Fisheries Management," explaining the uncertainties that limit models in regards to accurate predictions. The comments I made then also apply to genetic data.

The sophistication of modern technology has been commonly mistaken for factual representation of nature. Nature is not that simple. In politics, the manipulation and distortion of "science" by special interests became increasingly blatant after 2000. The new administration appointed "overseers" with decision-making power to direct policies of regulatory agencies dealing with environmental issues. The foxes appointed to supervise the hen houses had come from careers as anti-environmental lobbyists. An egregious misuse of "genetics" resulted in a policy recognizing hatchery salmon as the equivalent of wild salmon and resident rainbow trout as the equivalent of steelhead for interpretation of the Endangered Species Act. If the administration sought a genetic argument to justify the proposed action to remove many groups of salmon and steelhead from protection of the Endangered Species Act, they would have to invoke long rejected theories of the early twentieth century. In this view, a species, such as Chinook salmon, was a homogeneous entity and intraspecific diversity in life histories that are basic to maintaining abundance, is irrelevant and fully mitigated with hatcheries. The administrations policy to weaken the Endangered Species Act would appear to be based on ignorance but it was driven by political expediency that regarded the best scientific evidence as irrelevant.

THE TAILWATER TROUT PHENOMENON

SPRING 1996

HUMAN MANIPULATION OF RIVERS extends back into ancient history to the origins of irrigated agriculture. Tailwater trout fisheries in regions where trout never naturally occurred, however, are a relatively recent and largely unplanned phenomenon.

Such trout fisheries are associated with large volume storage reservoirs. The volume of stored cold winter flows are sufficient to maintain cold tailwaters when released from the depths of the reservoir during the following warm season. This is possible because of the properties of water. Colder water is heavier than warmer water (down to 39° F, then it becomes lighter than water colder than 39° F—that's why lakes and streams don't freeze from the bottom up).

As the weather warms in spring and summer, the colder water in the depths of a lake or reservoir (the hypolimnion) becomes sealed off from the warmer upper layer (the epilimnion) by a narrow layer (the thermocline) characterized by a rapid transition from warmer to colder water. Sediments settle out in the reservoir and nutrients concentrate in the hypolimnetic waters due to the decomposition of dead plants and animals settling on the bottom. Thus, tailwaters below high dams with a deep water releases should be clear, cold and enriched, creating ideal conditions for trout.

There can be severe problems with water quality in deep-water reservoirs, however. If the reservoir is productive, the rate of decomposition will be high. Aerobic decomposition uses oxygen and oxygen depletion occurs because oxygen produced by plants photosynthesizing in the epilimnion cannot penetrate through the thermocline into the depths of the hypolimnion. By late summer, the deepest waters may have no free oxygen. When waters become anoxic, anaerobic decomposition proceeds, releasing deadly hydrogen sulfide ("sewer gas") and ammonia. Also, toxic metal ions, such as iron, bound in bottom sediments, are released into the water under anoxic conditions.

Problems concerning water quality and quantity influencing the tailwater environment relate to the original purposes for which reservoirs were constructed—flood control, irrigation, water supply, and power generation. The conditions of the tailwaters are the result of reservoir operations and any tailwater fishery created, essentially, was a fortunate accident. Reservoirs designed for peak power generation can have wildly fluctuating flows in their tailwaters, from a trickle to a flood surge on a daily basis. The original purpose of reservoirs pretty much regulates the downstream flow regime and limits the degree of operational flexibility for improving a trout fishery, but the greater the popularity and economic value of a fishery, the greater the potential pressure which can be exerted to change reservoir operations for fishery benefits.

The first reservoirs creating cold tailwaters in regions where no trout nor any salmonid fish had previously existed, were Hoover Dam impounding Lake Mead on the lower Colorado River, completed in 1935, and Norris Dam impounding Norris Reservoir, a TVA project on the Clinch River, Tennessee, completed in 1936. Trout fisheries were not planned for these early tailwaters. Biologists noted that the warm-water sport fishes such as bass and catfish, which inhabited the river before dams, reservoirs, and cold tailwaters, failed to thrive or reproduce in the new environment. Trout were the obvious sport fish to occupy the fish niche in the new coldwater environments.

It was not until the 1950s and later that the fame of tailwater trout fisheries took off with Bureau of Reclamation dams in the West on the Colorado, Green, Gunnison, Bighorn, Frying Pan, and many other rivers, and Corps of Engineer dams, particularly in the White River drainage (Mississippi basin) of the Ozark region of northern Arkansas. Federal hatcheries were established to stock reservoirs and tailwaters and some of the resulting trout fisheries have been spectacular. The present world record angler-caught brown trout of 40-plus pounds was caught in the Greers Ferry tailwaters of Arkansas in 1992 and the unbelievable biomass of over 1,000 pounds per surface acre of brown and rainbow trout was attained in the Frying Pan River below Ruedi Dam in Colorado.

It is important to understand some basic differences in angler traditions and attitudes which affect management of tailwater fisheries, especially in relation to special angling regulations. In the West, angling has a long established tradition of fly-fishing for trout. In the Southeast, anglers grow up with bass, bluegills, crappie, and catfish. The fly-fishing ethic for trout places the greatest value on the experience of catching, or trying to catch trout, relative to the killing and eating of fish. The warm-water fishing tradition places more equal value on fish as sport and food, and less preference on any particular method of angling.

Because of these differences, the implementation of special regulations to take advantage of the productive Ozark tailwaters to grow large trout can encounter strong resistance. The Arkansas tailwaters are stocked with more than 10,000 catchable rainbow trout per mile—essentially, a put-and-take fishery. Virtually all the hatchery trout caught are taken soon after stocking before they have a chance to acclimate and grow. Brown trout mainly reproduce naturally, are more difficult to catch, and some persist for several years reaching enormous size. The conditions that produce 30- to 40-pound brown trout in Arkansas include enriched, cold water, and forage fish from the reservoir, such as gizzard shad, entrapped in the outlet flow and passing through turbines to feed the tailwater predators, supplemented with stocked catchable rainbow trout which are "bite size" items for the lunker brown trout. Many more trophy browns could be produced if angler kill could be significantly reduced. Some regulations of 18- or 20-inch minimum size for brown trout apply in some waters but without any gear restriction—bait fishing is allowed. Angler surveys in the late 1980s revealed that only 15 percent of anglers fishing Ozark tailwater trout fisheries fished with flies most of the time.

It won't be easy to convince most Ozark anglers that special regulations mandating flies or artificial lures can greatly benefit their tailwater fisheries, but I believe the tide is gradually turning in that direction. In the spring of 1994 I attended a trout conference in Missouri and met some of the growing number of fly-fishing enthusiasts of the region. I perceived excellent rapport between the leaders of the fly fishers and state biologists working to achieve a common goal of better trout fishing, especially for trophy trout.

Much of the progress in trout management in the Ozarks is due to the efforts and influence of Spencer Turner, longtime trout biologist with the Missouri Department of Conservation. Large volume cold springs are common in the Ozark region of Missouri, so the state had trout fishing long before the era of dams and tailwaters. In the early 1880s a federal fish hatchery was established at Neosho, Missouri, which stocked trout widely in the region, including the McCloud River rainbows which still persist in Crane Creek, a small, isolated spring creek. In the 1920s Missouri established their famous trout parks; pay-as-you-go, put-and-take fisheries where catchable trout are stocked on a daily basis for eager takers.

Spencer's goal was to put more "sport" in Missouri's trout program through special regulations designed to produce more larger trout and higher catch rates. In 1976, the trout parks were opened from November through mid-February for no-kill, flies and lures only angling. Some of the spring-fed rivers were managed as trophy waters with a 15-inch minimum size. In 1982, bait fishing was banned on the trophy waters. During this time, the numbers and influence of dedicated trout anglers, especially fly fishers, grew.

Missouri has initiated some special regulation waters without undue conflict because many tons of trout are annually supplied to anglers who want to catch and eat their fish. Besides the factory production at the trout parks, Lake Taneycomo, a 1,730-surface-acre reservoir impounding the tailwaters of Table Rock Reservoir, is one of the world's most intensive trout fisheries, supporting 600–700 angler-hours per acre per year of angling. Lake Taneycomo is, essentially, a put-and-take fishery, but a 20-inch minimum size limit for brown trout (without bait restrictions) has resulted in longer survival of stocked browns to take advantage of the natural productivity of the water to grow. Missouri's aim is to develop a put-grow-and-take brown trout fishery, under intense fishing pressure.

For many fly fishers who have the opportunity to fish for trout in the Ozarks this summer, it will be a new experience. Meet some of the local experts and seek advice on regional fly patterns for trophy trout—some White River streamer patterns may appear to be more appropriate for tarpon, but some of the brown trout in Arkansas are as *big* as tarpon. We may optimistically hope that catch-and-release trout fishing will become a more significant part of the Ozark angling tradition. Catch-and-release fishing regulations have the potential to improve fishing for everyone, whatever his choice of tackle.

AUTHOR'S NOTE

During the depression era, construction of large dams and their reservoirs for irrigation, power generation, and flood control, became a politically popular program to stimulate the economy and create jobs. A depression era song by Woody Guthrie, "Roll on Columbia," extolled the benefits of transforming the Columbia River into an economic engine created by dams and river regulation.

Consideration of fish and aquatic environments were not part of the original intent of the dams and river regulation of the time. The best of the tailwater fisheries were incidental to dam operations. The best tailwaters are those that resulted from a fortunate combination of flows, temperatures, and oxygen creating optimal environments for trout, often in areas where no trout are native, such as the southeastern U.S.

These popular tailwater and reservoir fisheries created unintended economic benefits that were not considered in the original calculations of cost-benefits. A problem was that the political popularity of dam building created a momentum whereby large dams continued to be built that could not be justified by impartial critique of costs versus benefits. Examples include the TVA's Tellico dam (and the famous snail darter), and, especially, the four dams on the Snake River, completed in 1976, to make Lewiston, Idaho, an inland "port." The Snake River was the greatest producer of Chinook salmon and steelhead in the Columbia River basin. By the time the Snake River dams were proposed, fisheries values could not be ignored. The simplistic solution was to build hatcheries that were predicted to maintain salmon and steelhead abundance. Of course, this proved to be an expensive failure. A considerable body of evidence now argues that the only way to, at least, begin to restore Snake River salmon and steelhead and conform to the Endangered Species Act is to remove the Snake River dams. These dams would not have been built if they were subjected to an unbiased and critical analysis of the project when it was proposed. In relation to tailwater trout fisheries and salmon and steelhead, dams can be categorized as the good, the bad, and the ugly.

WERE FISH REALLY BIGGER
IN THE OLD DAYS?

⌃

SUMMER 1997

AROUND 200 A.D., Aelian recorded the first known account of fishing with an artificial fly—for brown trout in the Macedonian region of Greece. It is not difficult to imagine a conversation between Aelian and the anglers of his time to the effect that fishing is "nothing like it was in the old days," meaning, the trout were much larger then. And so it continues through the history of angling into modern times.

An in-depth look at several case histories in which a decline in the size of fish can be well-documented provides useful insights for modern fisheries management and illustrates the importance, to anglers at least, of preserving evolutionarily significant units of fish biodiversity that have the hereditary basis to attain large sizes and the necessity for maintaining all components of an environment required by fish to reach that size. (For more information on preserving fish biodiversity, see "Wild Salmonid Genetics: An Impending Crisis?", p. 185.)

The most common, popular explanation for why fish don't attain the size they did "in the old days" is overfishing. This is particularly true when fishing pressure increases without more restrictive regulations. Most trophy size trout are older fish of 6 to 10 years of age. Under high angling pressure, total mortality can reach 75 to 80 percent annually, and essentially no fish will live more than five years. Regulations that reduce mortality due to angling can correct the negative effects of overfishing, as exemplified by the cutthroat trout of Yellowstone Lake and the Yellowstone River. Other causes of decline in growth are not so easily treated. Environmental changes, including pollution, dams and the introduction of nonnative species of fish and invertebrates, can drastically alter an ecosystem so that a fish species that once produced a trophy fishery no longer attains trophy size.

Another, more elusive explanation for fish not reaching a size comparable to that of the old days is genetic change—that is, the original population has been replaced or hybridized so that the original genetic or hereditary basis for large size has been lost or diluted. Such an example is well-documented for the cutthroat trout of Pyramid Lake in Nevada. Following is a brief review of the facts, which leaves no reasonable doubt that the population of Lahontan cutthroat trout native to Pyramid Lake was distinguished by its genetics to attain a great maximum size.

A 41-pound Pyramid Lake cutthroat caught in 1925 is still recognized as the world record for the species. In 1938 the last spawning cutthroat run from Pyramid Lake contained numerous 20- to 30-plus pound fish. All were lost when an upstream irrigation dam, located approximately 30 miles from the mouth of Pyramid Lake, diverted the entire flow of the Truckee River and destroyed Lahontan spawning habitat. For more than 40 years since then, millions of Lahontan cutthroats, of the same subspecies as the original Pyramid Lake population, have been stocked into Pyramid Lake to sustain a "trophy" fishery, but none have attained a maximum size that equals even half the maximum size of the original population. Adequate food sources are not a problem: The main forage fish of Pyramid Lake, the chub, is still exceedingly abundant, probably much more so now then when a million pounds or more of the native cutthroat population was consuming it at a great rate. Although the Pyramid Lake "replacements" are populations of the same subspecies of the original cutthroat population, they lack the genetic basis to produce world-record fish "like the old days."

In large lakes, where trout or salmon populations can fraction into separate races, each race may have different life histories with differences in growth and maximum size. Lake Vänern, Sweden, once contained several races of both brown trout and landlocked salmon. They maintained their genetic distinctions by homing to different rivers for spawning. Many races were lost to hydroelectric dams that eliminated spawning, including the race of brown trout attaining the oldest age (16–17 years) and largest size (35 pounds or more). Presently, two rivers still support salmon populations—the Klar River and the Gullspångs River. The Klar River salmon typically spend three years in the river and three years in the lake before returning to spawn at about six to seven pounds. The Gullspångs salmon typically spend one or two years in the river and four or five years in the lake before spawning when females weigh in at 13–14 pounds and males at 18–20 pounds.

A similar situation is found in Kootenay Lake, British Columbia. Most rainbow trout of Kootenay Lake are rather "ordinary," but one population spawning in the river at the north end of the lake, is known as the Gerrard race of giant Kamloops rainbow. Compared to the "ordinary" rainbow, the Gerrard race spawns at an older age, has a longer life span, and has specialized as a predator on kokanee salmon.

The Fisherman's Encyclopedia (Stackpole, 1954) contains a photo of a 52-pound Gerrard race Kamloops caught in Jewel Lake, British Columbia, where they had been stocked eight or nine years before. The caption states that descendants of this trout are now taken in Lake Pend Oreille, Idaho. In 1942 Gerrard Kamloops trout of Kootenay Lake were stocked in Pend Oreille, which had an abundance of kokanee salmon. Four years later, in 1946, a 32-pound Kamloops was caught and in 1947, a 37-pounder was caught. No larger trout has since been caught, and growth rate and maximum size have declined.

Neither kokanee salmon nor rainbow trout are native to Pend Oreille. Various forms of hatchery rainbows had been introduced and established in the drainage long before 1942 when the Kamloops were stocked. But these "ordinary" rainbows never established a population of large fish in the lake. This was accomplished only by the Kamloops rainbow from Kootenay Lake, which were preadapted to capitalize on the abundant kokanee of Pend Oreille. When the Kamloops trout went up tributaries to spawn, it would encounter "ordinary" rainbow trout. Hybridization with the rainbows diluted the Kamloops' hereditary basis to attain an extremely large size. The decline in kokanee abundance has also limited growth potential. In the late 1970s, *Mysis* shrimp, another nonnative species, became established in Pend Oreille. *Mysis* directly competes with kokanee fry for zooplankton. By the 1980s, kokanee abundance declined to only about 10 percent of their former abundance. The introduction of nonnative species has been called a game of chance—you win some and you lose some.

The state of Maine offers two more examples of fish not reaching the size they did in the old days, namely, the salmon of Sebago Lake and the brook trout of the Rangeley Lakes. Similar to the coevolved, predator-prey relationships of the Pyramid Lake cutthroat trout-chub and the Kootenay Lake Kamloops-kokanee combinations that resulted in record-size trout, the brook trout of the Rangeley Lakes evolved a similar predator-prey relationship with the blueback trout (relict Arctic char) and were renowned for their large size. Many brook trout of

10–12 pounds (up to 12 pounds) brought fame to the Rangeley Lakes in the nineteenth century. Introduction of Atlantic salmon in 1875 (both landlocked salmon and anadromous salmon) and of smelt in 1891 led to the rapid extinction of the blueback trout (the last specimen seen was in 1904). Although smelt is a good forage fish for both trout and salmon, the brook trout must compete with the salmon for smelt, and the salmon is a more specialized (preadapted) predator on smelt. After the early 1900s, the 10–12 pound brookies of the Rangeleys were not seen again.

J.V.C. Smith's book, *Fishes of Massachusetts*, published in 1833, mentions the "Sebago Trout," but Smith was not impressed by their large size. He wrote: "…they have degenerated not only in size, but numbers, owing to various causes unnecessary to detail." Little of Smith's accounts of New England fishes is authentic, but I wish he had detailed the causes he believed resulted in the degeneration of size of the Sebago Lake salmon. In any event, they must have recovered from the effects of the degeneracy perceived in 1833 by the early 1900s, but then "degenerated" again.

On August 1, 1907, a 22-pound Sebago salmon was caught by an angler that was long recognized as the world record for landlocked salmon. On this same day, W.C. Kendall, author of a 1935 monograph on New England salmon, caught a 16-pound salmon in Sebago Lake. Kendall cited salmon of 31¼ and 35½ pounds taken during fish culture operations on the lake in 1908.

Hatchery records dating from 1916 to 1930 of spawn-taking operations at Sebago, show a steady decline in the maximum size of salmon from 18 pounds (1916–17) to 8 pounds (1928–30). Data on age and growth of Sebago salmon during 1957 to 1981 show salmon at age seven (about the maximum age attained during this period) ranged from 15¾

LAHONTAN CUTTHROAT TROUT
Oncorhynchus clarki henshawi

to 23½ inches in different years (reflecting cycles of smelt abundance, the salmon's principal food).

What happened to the former world-record size of Sebago salmon? Clear-cut conclusions can't be made, but I strongly suspect that the original genetic basis for attaining a great size and a long maximum life span that characterized the salmon native to Sebago Lake, has been thoroughly diluted and replaced by a homogenized "generic" Maine landlocked salmon, analogous to the case of the Pyramid Lake cutthroats.

Landlocked salmon are native to only a relatively few lakes of four river drainages of Maine, but their popularity as a sport fish led to their artificial propagation and widespread stocking around the state (as mentioned above, the Rangeley Lakes were stocked with salmon by 1875). Artificial propagation of Maine landlocked salmon began in 1867 at Grand Lake, where the maximum size of salmon was about six to seven pounds. Egg-taking operations were soon started at Sebago Lake and at many other lakes where salmon had been established from stocking, including the Rangeley Lakes. No attempts were made to maintain pure lines; rather, eggs from different sources were mixed into a "common pot" at central hatcheries, and the young fish of mixed parentage were stocked back into many lakes. After many years, a homogenized, generic stock of Maine landlocked salmon would be the expected result.

The only way the original Sebago salmon population could have maintained its genetic integrity would have been if the salmon population in the lake was maintained entirely by natural reproduction of the native fish (that is, all generic hatchery fish stocked perished before reaching sexual maturity). That this is not true can be seen in data collected at Sebago Lake from 1963 to 1974. During those years, of all salmon caught by anglers, only 4 to 28 percent were from natural reproduction and 72 to 96 percent were from hatchery fish. Even this natural reproduction can be assumed to be from the homogenized generic stock previously stocked in Sebago. The rapid decline in maximum size from 18 to 8 pounds recorded during the 1916–1930 period indicates that the true native Sebago race of salmon was lost a long time ago.

A review of the above case histories demonstrates that, in some instances, it is indeed true that present fish populations do not attain the sizes formerly reached. A major reason for this is that "in the old days," a species was thought of as a homogeneous whole—all parts (populations) being equal, identical and interchangeable. With current knowledge, we know that each population of a species has unique attributes that are not interchangeable with other populations of the same species. A goal of conservation is to "preserve biodiversity," meaning the preservation of a range of adaptations found in the most "significant evolutionary units" of a species. A problem concerns identifying and defining "significant." For anglers and fisheries managers, the hereditary basis for attaining a great size in a given species would certainly qualify as an evolutionarily significant unit to be protected before those fish go the way of the Sebago salmon.

AUTHOR'S NOTE

The Lahontan cutthroat trout of Pyramid Lake is an example where the relative influences of nature (heredity) versus nurture (environmental factors) can be tested. Comparing maximum sizes attained by the original Pyramid Lake cutthroat to sizes of nonnative cutthroat of the same subspecies stocked into the same lake is revealing. Diversity within a species or subspecies represents adaptations to specific environments—that must be understood for proper management.

ECOLOGICAL INTEGRITY
& THE ANGLER

→

FALL 1997

IN MAY 1997, THE LARGEST RAINBOW TROUT ever caught in Colorado was caught and released in the Taylor River in a no-kill regulation section below Taylor Reservoir. Based on length and girth measurements, this trout was estimated to weigh 22 pounds. What might be surprising is that everything about this state record rainbow violates and contradicts the scientific principles of ecological integrity. The rainbow trout is a nonnative species to Colorado and was stocked from a hatchery; Taylor Reservoir is an artificial impoundment; the controlled flow regime from the reservoir is quite unnatural; and the Mysis shrimp from the reservoir that supply most of the food for the fast-growing and abundant nonnative trout living in the river, is also a nonnative species.

It could be considered an innate desire of humans to exert dominance and control over nature—to bring order out of chaos by modification and regulation of nature for perceived human benefit. In the United States, the control, alteration and regulation of rivers as dictated by public policy at the local, state and federal levels can be traced to Colonial times, and has now been implemented on such a grand scale that the natural flow and temperature regimes and the composition of native species of plants and animals in virtually every major river and its watershed in the U.S. have been dramatically altered.

The history of river modification in this country extends back to the mid-seventeenth century when the earliest settlers in New England began building dams to power mills. This resulted in the loss of Atlantic salmon in most New England rivers by the mid-nineteenth century.

In 1824 Congress created the Army Corps of Engineers, whose primary purpose was to make rivers navigable by channelization, later expanded to include flood control. The Reclamation Act of 1902 established the Bureau of Reclamation, to "reclaim" arid lands by building dams and diverting water from rivers for irrigated agriculture. The very first Bureau of Reclamation project, the Newlands Project, on the Truckee River, California, led to the demise of the world's largest cutthroat trout, the giants of Pyramid Lake.

By the same token, agencies such as the Bonneville Power Administration and the Tennessee Valley Authority were created to harness rivers to generate electricity from hydropower.

Large rivers such as the Missouri and Mississippi were channelized, straightened and confined by levees. Such confinement breaks the connection between a river and its flood plain and disrupts the efficient functioning of a river. Fishes and other aquatic life lose vast spawning and nursery areas. Plants and animals dependent on wetlands disappear. Wetlands' natural water filtering and purifying process is diminished. Until relatively recent times the federal government funded large-scale eradication of riparian vegetation in the West (phreatophyte control) with the sole purpose of increasing flows in rivers (for irrigation) by reducing plant transpiration. Another common practice was the removal of fallen trees from stream channels to speed flow and enhance navigation. Today, we know better, and there is considerable activity to restore and protect riparian vegetation and to put large woody debris back into streams to create high quality fish habitat.

Presently, with a better scientific understanding of how streams and watersheds function, a more holistic perspective reveals that our former single purpose actions for managing water were truly not in the public interest. For example, most of the earlier flood control projects sponsored by the Corps of Engineers and the Soil Conservation Service channelized streams to accelerate flows from upper parts of a watershed to downstream areas. Subsequently, when floods occur, they are of a greater magnitude than under pristine, natural conditions. When these structurally-enhanced floods breech levees, enormous economic damage and human suffering results. The tremendous power of a flooding river can make a mockery out of all human attempts to control, confine, and regulate.

Based on past mistakes and a vast body of knowledge on rivers, watersheds and aquatic biology, a new paradigm for river management has started to emerge. Essentially, it is that nature knows best: Natural flow regimes are critical to the restoration of the ecological integrity of rivers. In reality, however, there are severe constraints for completely restoring "natural flow" regimes on most rivers. It is beyond the realm of reason to believe that many dams will be dismantled, even if it were technically feasible. And, if it could be done, would it always be in the "public good" to do so? For example, I might prefer the Taylor River in its pristine condition, when the beautiful Colorado River cutthroat trout inhabited its waters. Many of the anglers currently fishing the Taylor River below the reservoir for the large and numerous nonnative trout, I suspect, would strongly disagree. Further, reservoirs and tailwaters have recreational and economic values of their own. As such, there are advocacy groups that would challenge tampering with the status quo. Plans to restore a natural flow regime to a river for the sake of restoring ecological integrity would meet strong opposition in such situations where river regulation and reservoirs are popularly conceived to be in the best interests of society. Trout Unlimited as a salmon and trout conservation organization (without reference to native or nonnative species) stands to catch flak from both sides of the issue.

Political compromises for river regulation might occur, but mostly these would be what I'd call the Band-Aid or aspirin effect. A highly publicized event occurred in March 1996 when Secretary of Interior Bruce Babbitt pushed a button to release a torrent of water from Lake Powell at Glen Canyon dam on the Colorado River, ostensibly to restore ecosystem health to the Grand Canyon. For about two weeks, the artificial flood, peaking at 45,000 cubic feet per second (cfs), roared through the Grand Canyon, at a cost of about $3 million in lost electrical generation. This artificial flood flow, however, was hardly a ripple compared to the flow of the pre-dam Colorado River, whose average flood flow in the Grand Canyon was about 100,000 cfs and could exceed 300,000 cfs.

A flow of 40,000 to 45,000 cfs for a few days is sufficient to suspend sand from the river bottom and deposit it along shorelines. I suspect, however, that most of the beaches created by last year's artificial flood have already eroded back into the river. Some anglers and angling businesses were outraged; they feared ruination of the trout fishery at Lee's Ferry below Glen Canyon dam (for non-native trout—no salmonid species inhabited the lower Colorado River before Glen Canyon dam changed the flow and temperature regime). I doubt there was much to fear. Although

45,000 cfs might look like a torrential flow, the turbulence beneath the surface creates low velocity microhabitats where fish find refuge.

Even if the pristine natural flow of the Colorado River in the Grand Canyon could be restored, would it be in society's interest, the public good, to do so? Besides the irrigation water, the electricity and the recreational benefits derived from Glen Canyon dam, the great reduction of historical flood flows has dramatically changed the terrestrial environment along the Colorado River through the Grand Canyon compared to what John Wesley Powell encountered in 1869. An annual flood of 100,000 cfs or greater scoured the banks of vegetation, and virtually no animal or plant life occurred there. After dams eliminated the annual scouring flows, vegetation became established, mostly the exotic salt cedar tree. The plants attracted insects and other invertebrates. Birds and mammals soon followed and now inhabit the formerly barren riparian zone with 214 species of birds recorded, including the endangered Southwestern willow flycatcher and peregrine falcon. The diversity of life along the Colorado River is certainly much greater than it was under pristine conditions, but it is dependent on river regulation and nonnative vegetation. On the other hand, the native fishes, including the endangered Colorado squawfish, razorback sucker, and bonytail chub, are gone. Their marvelous adaptations evolved to cope with the extreme conditions of the natural flow regime of the Colorado River, but place them at a great disadvantage in the new, controlled environment in competition with nonnative fishes.

The "public good" is a synthesis of values held by individuals in society. There's the economic side (electrical generation, recreation, etc.), as well as the environmental side, which is subject to change over time as scientific understanding increases and as things become rarer in nature. We didn't value Atlantic salmon runs in pioneer days when salmon were abundant, but today we expend great efforts to restore them. It's the same with endangered species: The public has decided it is worthwhile to spend a lot of money to save species from extinction. By modifying natural flows, we lose uniquely adapted species and replace them with widespread generalized species (take the Grand Canyon, for example). We now are beginning to understand that the best way to ensure long-term survival of species is to have high ecological integrity and natural ecosystems. Letting rivers run more naturally is a good way to accomplish that.

A flow regime can be broken into five components: Magnitude, frequency, duration, timing, and rate of change of flow conditions. Natural flows occur in rivers with little or no watershed alterations. Natural flow regimes can't be completely restored on heavily regulated rivers; however, incremental steps to help ecosystems and salmonids can be taken. We know enough about the benefits provided by flows to restore certain aspects of flow regimes to help improve ecological integrity. The licensing of many dams is contingent upon maintaining favorable environmental conditions, and reasonable efforts to restore aspects of the natural flow regime should be pursued. For example, TU chapters across the country are involved in modifying hydroelectric practices that cause frequent and rapid fluctuations in flow below dams, which are highly unnatural and harm benthic insects and fish, including trout. The altered timing of high flows can harm anadromous salmonids by slowing down the time it takes smolts to reach the ocean. In the Columbia River Basin, a major recommendation of an independent scientific review community is to restore some of the seasonal high flows to recover Pacific salmon. In regulated rivers that severely dampen high flows, fine silt can accumulate in downstream gravel beds. Occasional high flows can flush the silt away, enhancing benthic insect production and improving spawning habitat for salmonids.

There is a danger that anglers voicing outrage at any attempt to modify flows in regulated rivers to benefit ecological integrity or endangered species will come across as selfish and environmentally insensitive. However, anglers should have input into the process for any plans to change a flow regime of a popular fishery. To be effective, they should be knowledgeable about all of the issues and should not automatically assume that any tampering with established flows will be disastrous to trout. As a whole, I believe efforts to restore some semblance of natural flows to regulated rivers will do trout more good than harm: Helping the ecosystem function more naturally will benefit salmonids, which, after all, exist in an ecosystem context.

AUTHOR'S NOTE

The moral of this story is you can't please all of the people all of the time. Conflicting interests often become polarized in relation to how water and land is managed. A few years ago, more than 30,000 Chinook salmon perished in the lower Klamath River because agricultural interests influenced the Department of Interior to favor water diversion for irrigation over water in the river for salmon. When river flows are manipulated for endangered species of minnows and suckers, the modified flows can be too high or too low, depending on time of the year, for anglers fishing tailwaters for nonnative trout. Anglers, however, lack the political clout of agricultural interests when it comes to influencing federal agencies to ignore the Endangered Species Act. A purist philosophy of ecological integrity will frequently encounter internal contradictions. Terms such as ecological integrity and ecosystem management are open to interpretation from different points of view. In reality, most environmental changes caused by a rapidly expanding human population are essentially irreversible. These ecosystems cannot be returned to their pristine states. Nature, however, is resilient. When a river is regulated by dams and regulated flows a tailwater trout fishery can occur changing the system from native warm-water species habitat of minnows and suckers to nonnative species of trout. The aquatic ecosystem undergoes dramatic change, but the basic energy-flow functions of an ecosystem from primary production to consumers and detritivores continue to operate. Only that many new species are now filling the niches necessary to maintain functioning. It's similar to a Shakespeare play, whereby, the theme is the same, but different actors fill the same roles over time.

GOING HOME AGAIN:
REVISITING NATIVE TROUT WATERSHEDS
OF THE WEST

❧

WINTER 1998

IN 1957 I JOURNEYED FROM CONNECTICUT to Berkeley, California, full of wonder in anticipation of participating in a fishing expedition from California to Alaska. This was the initiation of a study of the native trout of western North America that has lasted much of my lifetime.

Forty years ago it generally was known that there was a species of rainbow trout and a species of cutthroat trout, but not much more than that. The geographically distinct races could be called subspecies, but their distributions, or, even if they still existed, were unknown. Federal and state fishery agencies were concerned mainly with the propagation and stocking of hatchery trout (mostly nonnative species in relation to the waters stocked). Such management policies were particularly hard on native cutthroat trout; they ranged from benign neglect to outright extermination.

I decided to do my master's graduate study on the cutthroat trout of the Great Basin—the internal basins that have no outlet to the sea. This should have been a relatively simple thesis because the only basins known to have cutthroat at the time were the Lahontan basin of Nevada, California and Oregon, and the Bonneville basin of Utah, Wyoming, Idaho, and Nevada. The published literature available in 1957 declared both the Lahontan and Bonneville cutthroat trout extinct, so my thesis could have consisted of an obituary for two cutthroat trout subspecies.

In view of the large areas of the Lahontan and Bonneville basins and the myriad drainage networks, many remote and isolated, I thought there was a good probability that some populations of native cutthroat still existed, waiting to be discovered. I began annual summer collecting trips, which were later expanded to include the northern parts of the Great Basin (the Oregon desert basins) where the primitive interior form of rainbow trout (redband trout) is the native species.

I discovered native populations of both subspecies of cutthroat trout and redband trout, but the conditions of the watersheds where I found most of them were shocking. A long history of livestock overgrazing denuded the watersheds, initiating massive erosion. Riparian vegetation was long gone; small streams commonly were trenched down into arroyos, with trout barely surviving in pools maintained by small seeps. I found the Humboldt River form of Lahontan cutthroat to exist in 80° F water, and redband trout in temperatures up to 83° F. Those trout were surviving in habitats where no trout should have survived. I became fascinated with their adaptations. They had evolved over thousands of years to survive the harshest environmental conditions. For some populations, however, no amount of adaptiveness could ensure survial under conditions of continued watershed degradation. Despite supposed protection under the Endangered Species Act, 5 of the 10 known populations of Lahontan cutthroats in tiny tributaries in the Quinn River drainage were lost by 1990. The irony of native trout extinctions is that they were occurring in watersheds on federal lands—notably, those managed by the U.S. Forest Service and the Bureau of Land Management (BLM). Why couldn't federal agencies at least obey the Endangered Species Act and protect and restore watersheds by better livestock management practices? The conflict between resource stewardship and unregulated resource exploitation has been a matter of tradition and precedent in federal lands management as influenced by politics.

In 1905 Teddy Roosevelt and Gifford Pinchot, the first U.S. Forest Service chief, became aware of uncontrolled exploitation of natural resources, especially of the effects on watersheds from livestock overgrazing. They set aside large tracts of land as federal forest reserves (later national forests) to protect watersheds. The forest reserves were to be managed according to Pinchot's definition of conservation: The greatest good for the greatest number for the longest time. That is, in modern terms, resource sustainability.

Grazing allotments were assigned to family ranches and designed to avoid overgrazing and protect watershed integrity. How did things go wrong? Both cattle and sheep grazed on the lands of the U.S. forest reserves. Entrepreneurs bought up numerous sheep operations to form conglomerates. They didn't want to be fettered by federal regulations. They understood that it was more profitable to make money while the getting's good—make a fast buck and sell out. The devastation of the land was of no concern to them. They used their money and influence to elect members of Congress sympathetic to their interests. When William Howard Taft succeeded Roosevelt in 1909, Pinchot's days were numbered. The special interests profiting from federal lands were out to get him. The first attempt to manage federal lands on a sustainable

basis was short lived. In 1910, at the annual meeting of wool growers at Ogden, Utah, Idaho's Senator Heyburn beamed as he announced to the gathering: "When the sun rolled over the eastern mountains this morning, it marked a new epic in the history of the West; Czar Pinchot has been dethroned and the western stockman is now free." Sound familiar? Do we as individuals or as agencies learn from history? I believe we do, to some extent, but it's a slow and inconsistent process.

Although the Forest Service and the BLM now operate under more environmentally enlightened guidelines of ecosystem management with a goal of restoring ecosystem health, the results are far from uniform. Large differences can be observed among areas and regions of federal lands in the success (or lack thereof) in managing livestock to restore watersheds. There are hopeful signs, however. In the fall of 1996, I had the opportunity to fish for native redband trout in the Donner and Blitzen River drainage of the Malheur Basin, Oregon. After comparing watershed conditions with what I remembered 25 years before, I was delighted to find the colorful and feisty redbands still there, and even more delighted to find them in greater abundance than 25 years earlier. The watershed had improved: grasses and other forage vegetation were still present in upland areas; willows and aspen were vigorously growing in the riparian zone; eroded banks were healing; and fish habitat had greatly improved. This was the result of the BLM's revised grazing management. By properly controlling livestock numbers and the grazing season, grazing can become sustainable and watersheds can be restored.

In the summer of 1997, I made several trips to Nevada to examine many of the same streams where I first found the Humboldt cutthroat trout 35 to 40 years ago. Again, I was heartened to find greatly improved conditions in the streams and their watersheds. Willows were coming back to stabilize banks and shade the streams. Native cutthroat trout still occurred in all of the streams where I found them many years ago, and their continued existence appears bright. How some of those populations survived for the past 40 to 50 years or more in such severely degraded habitat seems almost beyond belief and is testimony to their tenacity. The improvements on the Nevada watersheds I observed are due to "corporate ranching." Generally, this term has negative connotations, but in this case the corporations are large gold mines that purchased large ranches and want to demonstrate that "multiple use" can be a reality. Professional range managers cooperate with the BLM to design specific grazing strategies (prescriptive grazing) for watershed restoration, especially the restoration of riparian vegetation and cutthroat trout habitat.

Historical negative experiences regarding livestock impacts on watersheds and trout habitat raised doubts in my mind on the compatibility between livestock and trout, but I've seen examples of new techniques of grazing management, and they work—if done properly.

Will the "new" grazing strategies catch on and rapidly spread throughout the country? Can we learn from history? An analogous situation would be a public school that ranked at the bottom in test scores and percent of students graduating. A new principal initiates new teaching techniques and instills discipline, raising test scores and graduation rates. Although the school is now highly rated with benefits to all its students, a few obstinate students rebel against the principal's "tyranny." They complain to their parents who have influence with members of the school board because they contributed to election campaigns. The school board fires the principal and the school soon reverts to its former condition.

Members of Congress who loudly proclaim slogans such as "genocide on the West" or "freeing stockmen" from tyrannical federal controls are ignorant of—or choose to ignore—the history of natural resource exploitation.

POISON CREEK REDBAND TROUT
Oncorhynchus mykiss newberrii

In 2006, I made a tour of the Northern Great Basin of Oregon and found restoration of stream habitat; riparian and upland vegetation has continued and has been expanded to large areas of BLM lands. During the past 50 years, changing attitudes on conservation resulted in federal laws to guide the actions of federal agencies as a basis for implementation of improved multiple use management. Bureaucracies have built-in inertia to change, however, and much of the improvements I observed were forced on the agencies by legal action from environmental organizations.

The period associated with increasing influence of environmental organizations to bring about needed change for proper management of federal lands, is roughly that of the history of TU. Trout Unlimited progressed from a small, dedicated group of fly fishers promoting wild trout fisheries, to a major player involved in larger issues on a national scale. It's a win-win situation. Agitation and legal actions that restore watersheds benefit wild trout much more than any angling regulations could accomplish (regulations are meaningless if the habitat is destroyed). And, the benefits of environmental restoration extend well beyond trout populations. Vegetation and wildlife flourish again when the causes of environmental degradation are corrected.

LIMIT YOUR KILL

SUMMER 1999

THE PHRASE "LIMIT YOUR KILL, don't kill your limit," has perhaps been Trout Unlimited's most enduring slogan. It really wasn't a new idea upon TU's founding 40 years ago: Dame Juliana Berners (or her ghost writers) had given similar advice to anglers about 500 years earlier by urging them not to be greedy, as in, "don't take too many at one time."

During Trout Unlimited's early years, the organization's leaders faced a dilemma. They intuitively believed that limiting the kill would result in increased abundance of older and larger trout in a population exploited by anglers. They also believed in science and research as a basis for fisheries management and fishing regulations. But what they heard about the results of research on restrictive angling regulations that greatly reduced or eliminated the kill was discouraging.

Several studies on small stream populations of brook trout in Wisconsin and Michigan in the 1950s and '60s showed that population abundance and size-age structure were unaffected by any type of regulation that limited or even eliminated the kill. Reducing mortality due to angling during the fishing season only resulted in a proportionate increase in natural mortality, especially during the winter, so that the total annual mortality remained unchanged. A classic example was Lawrence Creek in Wisconsin, where a one-mile section of stream was closed to angling for five years and the trout population was closely monitored. At the end of five years, with no angler kill of trout, there were fewer trout than before the experiment when this section was open to statewide fishing regulations.

Forty years ago the fisheries profession followed the now rejected paradigm of "maximum sustained yield" (MSY). MSY sought to keep "surplus" fish from going to "waste" by designing regulations so that fishing mortality largely replaced natural mortality.

What scientists were telling the early TU leaders was not good news. According to their research, if an angler caught and released a trout, it would only die a natural death before the next year, thus going to "waste."

TU's first conservation policy statement, announced in 1960, stated in part that TU would "promote and support continuing research programs to determine the basic biology and ecology of trout populations." The statement continued: "The causes of the high annual winter mortality of all trout in streams are a primary concern of Trout Unlimited and we encourage investigations and research in this regard."

No doubt the Michigan and Wisconsin brook trout populations under study exhibited very high mortality from one year to the next, mainly during winter. Typically, there is high mortality within a few weeks after young trout hatch and emerge from redds. If they survive to the end of their first growing season (age 0), there can be relatively good (about 40 to 50 percent) overwinter survival to the next year (age 1). Most brook trout populations in small streams attain sexual maturity and spawn in the fall of their second growing season (still age 1, but two years after their parents spawned). Overwinter mortality can be very high after spawning. In the Michigan and Wisconsin populations, mortality between age 1 and 2 (after spawning) often ranged from 80–95 percent. From age 2 to 3, mortality ranged from 95 to 98 percent despite any angling regulations to limit the kill. There were very few fish living to age 3 (i.e., the fourth year of life).

The first well-documented examples of highly successful special regulations that "limited the kill" and greatly increased abundance came in the '70s and concerned cutthroat trout in Idaho (the St. Joe River and Kelly Creek) and in Yellowstone National Park (the Yellowstone Lake and Yellowstone River).

In my autumn 1989 *Trout* article, "We're Putting Them Back Alive," (p. 117) I reviewed the history of special angling regulations and the conditions that favor success, as with cutthroat trout, and those that cause failure, as with the small stream, short-lived Wisconsin and Michigan brook trout populations. The important determinants of success for any regulation designed to limit or eliminate angling mortality are:

- rates of recruitment (the success of natural reproduction);

- production (the percent of biomass increase of population in one year); and

- age-growth dynamics (annual survival rates and the increase in size, i.e., the number of years to attain 12 inches, 16, 20, and so forth).

Another accurate predictor of success is the species of trout, and how vulnerable it is to being caught by angling. For example, how many hours of angling does it take, per surface acre of water, to catch (and release) each catchable-size trout, on average, once per year? For a brown trout population, it may take 500 to 1,000 hours or more of angling per acre to catch, on average, each fish once. For a cutthroat trout population, this level of exploitation can be achieved in 10 to 12 hours of angling per acre.

In the 1960s, the cutthroat trout of Yellowstone Lake were managed for "maximum sustained yield." The population was severely overexploited at no more than five to six hours of angling per acre per year. After a 13-inch maximum size limit went into effect (i.e., all trout larger than 13 inches must be released), the numbers of adult trout of 5, 6, 7, and 8 years of age on spawning runs increased by several fold. The no-kill regulation protecting the cutthroat trout in the Yellowstone River now supports much greater angler use than in the old days, and maintains a much more abundant population of older, larger fish than before the no-kill regulations. It has been calculated that, on average, each cutthroat trout in the Yellowstone River population is caught and released 9.7 times during the fishing season.

This vulnerability to being caught, and caught again and again, has been a boon for the popularity of several rare subspecies of cutthroat trout. They are stocked in lakes for restoration purposes and provide a high catch rate as they are "recycled" over and over. No other species of trout can sustain such a high catch rate as cutthroat trout.

To illustrate the significance to anglers and the economic importance of catching the same fish several times, data from the "Miracle Mile," a six-mile segment of Wyoming's North Platte River, can be cited. Electrofishing sampling in the Miracle Mile in 1996 estimated that there were a total of 20,795 catchable-size brown trout (all from natural reproduction) and 5,777 rainbow trout (with 4,197 hatchery trout stocked a year or two before and 1,580 wild, naturally reproduced rainbows). The ratio of brown trout to rainbow trout was 78:22.

About 115,000 hours of angling occurred during the year (about 700 hours per acre) to catch an estimated 70,138 trout (with a catch rate of 0.62 per hour). The catch consisted of 24,519 brown trout, averaging about 16 inches and 45,303 rainbow trout averaging about 17 inches. On average, each of the 20,795 brown trout was caught 1.2 times during the year to give a total catch of 24,519. Rainbow trout, which made up only 22 percent of the total trout numbers (versus the 78 percent made up by brown trout) made up 65 percent of the angler catch. That means that each of the 5,777 rainbows available to be caught, had to be caught (and released) several times to provide a catch of 45,303. On average, each wild rainbow was caught 6.3 times and each hatchery rainbow was caught 8.3 times. The new paradigm of fisheries management should be "maximum sustained catch (and release)." There's no other alternative for maintaining an acceptable catch rate of older, larger fish under intense fishing pressure.

I think the famous fishery of the Miracle Mile is what the early TU leaders had in mind in regard to what could be accomplished by limiting your kill, and not killing your limit. Surprisingly, there are no gear restrictions on the Miracle Mile—flies, lures, bait, single, double, treble, barbed, and barbless hooks can be used, and two trout per day can be harvested. About 90 percent of all trout caught are released. For each pound of hatchery rainbow trout stocked, about 15 pounds are caught, of which 1.7 pounds are harvested. There are reservoirs, well stocked with trout (and walleye), above and below the Miracle Mile where anglers can harvest fish to eat. Thus, most anglers seeking fish to catch, kill and eat, go to the reservoirs. The Miracle Mile is much preferred by anglers practicing catch-and-release.

Although limited-kill (typically one or two trout per day), wild trout management programs have been expanded in recent years, it is common to face strong opposition when a new wild trout regulation is proposed. Most opposition focuses on the theme of "elitist" anglers versus the "common" angler who wants to keep and eat fish. You can bet that state legislators will take up the cause of protecting the "common" angler if an intense controversy develops. The less restrictive the regulations in regard to gear and methods, the more likely new wild trout management waters will find acceptance. Also, the availability of fish for catching and eating in nearby waters enhances the chances of gaining more limited-kill fisheries for wild trout.

A more philosophically-based opposition to catch-and-release angling is based on the European tradition of hunting and fishing as "blood sports," whereby the hunter stalks and kills the prey. This is what makes hunting a "sport." The line of reasoning of this philosophy concludes that catching and releasing a fish demeans the sport, reducing angling to a trivial, cruel game whereby humans obtain pleasure by inflicting unnecessary pain on animals. However, there is strong circumstantial evidence that "pain" in fishes is not comparable to that of higher vertebrates, nor is catching a fish a very traumatic experience for the fish (otherwise catch-and-release regulations wouldn't work).

A new philosophy of American sportfishing should argue that fishing is not a "blood sport" comparable to hunting. From the earliest literature of Dame Juliana, followed by Izaak Walton, the descriptive words associated with fishing are gentle, contemplative and therapeutic. Fishing is more spiritual, hunting more worldly.

Considering Yellowstone National Park as an example, the hundreds of thousands of trout that are caught and released to meet a natural death, are not "wasted," but instead provide a large food supply to fish-eating birds and animals, and recycle nutrients—the trout's natural role in ecological processes. As such, catch-and-release angling is environmentally correct, and not a "trivial" pursuit.

The early years of Trout Unlimited must have been disappointing for many members embracing the stated goal of TU to "limit your kill, don't kill your limit." The results of studies on short-lived and slow growing brook trout revealed that annual mortality was so high, none of the trout survived beyond age 3, and if they were caught-and-released they would die of natural causes before the next year. During this period it was common to read about the failures of catch-and-release fisheries and how it was a ploy by elitist fly fishers to monopolize the best trout waters for their selfish interests. In reality, this was a classic case demonstrating the errors of inductive reasoning. Because special regulations designed to recycle the catch in typical brook trout populations in small streams, didn't work, therefore such regulations would also fail with all species of trout in all environments. My thinking on this matter was influenced by experience with cutthroat trout populations that, compared to small stream brook trout, had longer life spans, faster growth, and lower annual natural mortality rates and could be caught-and-released again and again. My 1989 article, "We're Putting Them Back Alive," (p. 117) explained the factors that must be understood to make special regulations successful. The factors that determine success are not difficult to comprehend; so why did it take so long before biological-based special regulations were widely implemented?

RUMMAGING THROUGH THE BASEMENT
FINDING PISCATORIAL AUDUBONS

SUMMER 2001

TWENTY-FIVE YEARS AGO the College of Veterinary Medicine at Colorado State University vacated a WPA-era building on campus and it was turned over to our expanding Department of Fishery and Wildlife Biology, where I was teaching. At the time, I needed space for my collection of trout specimens and a great volume of books, journals, literature, notes, and files I had accumulated over many years. I was allotted a large area of the basement where I unloaded my goods and set up shop.

Over the years the Fishery and Wildlife Department continued to grow; today, faculty and graduate students need even more space. With the university's decision to tear down and reconstruct the old basement, all my possessions must be removed. A large part of my time in recent months has been devoted to sorting through boxes, shelves and file cabinets to decide what to save and what to discard—separating wheat from chaff. Sorting through the files has turned up some interesting bits of historical miscellany that I'd like to share with *Trout's* readers.

A review of some of the miscellany illustrates two points of importance for anglers and conservationists. First, despite modern, cutting-edge technology and the most sophisticated computer models, predictions on components of natural systems such as fish population abundance are often far off the mark. This is because most natural systems,

in contrast to the stability of the motions of the solar system, are highly variable—they lack any consistent pattern of regularity on which accurate predictions depend. Second, amateurs, with a love and enthusiasm for their subject matter, can make significant contributions to promote the understanding and appreciation of native trout.

A 1974 newspaper clipping reported that the first Atlantic salmon had returned to the Connecticut River. The story included a prediction that 30,000 salmon would return to the Connecticut River in 30 years. Along with the clipping is a copy of a special supplement to the Greenfield, Massachusetts *Recorder* of June 8, 1990, announcing the upcoming dedication of a new $17 million anadromous fish research laboratory on the Connecticut River at Turners Falls, Massachusetts. The U.S. Fish and Wildlife Service would operate the lab with an annual budget of $1.7 million. The main emphasis of research would be Atlantic salmon, especially salmon restoration in the Connecticut River. A sophisticated computer model predicted that by 2021, returns of Atlantic salmon to the Connecticut River would reach 38,000.

The greatest number of Atlantic salmon counted in the Connecticut River since the first one was recorded in 1974 was 529 in 1981, followed by 70 in 1982, and 39 in 1983. Since then, despite great increases in hatchery production and stocking, salmon returns to the Connecticut River have run between 100 and 300 in most years. These figures remind me of what I have written about the "illusion of technique" where sophisticated but simplistic models are often a poor substitute for knowledge and a deeper understanding of the subject matter, in this case, fish ecology.

Sometimes we can learn real-life lessons from the research of dedicated amateurs who seek to document the most obscure pieces of a larger salmonid biodiversity puzzle. My files contain correspondence, notes and photos covering many years of communicating with some of these people who developed a passion, or sometimes a near obsession, to find and learn about rare and vanishing forms of trout. One such person was Bob Smith, whom I first met in 1975. At that time Bob was a recently retired waterfowl biologist with the U.S. Fish and Wildlife Service. He was an avid angler who had attained a stage of angling satisfaction whereby his greatest pleasure was derived from catching

and photographing all of the species, subspecies and distinct races of North American trout. This passion for wild, native trout culminated in his book, *Native Trout of North America* (Frank Amato Publications, revised 1994).

Bob did an excellent job of interpreting my publications on trout evolution, which until then were largely confined to the scientific literature, and making them available to the angling public. He became an effective crusader for the preservation of wild, native trout.

Bob's book encouraged others to develop a similar interest in native trout. Kyle McNeilly of Calgary, Alberta made contact with both Bob and me to further his interests in putting together a museum—a quality exhibit of realistic taxidermy models of all the forms of trout covered in Bob's book. In return, Kyle helped Bob find and catch the "Sunapee golden trout" from an Idaho lake.

The "golden trout" of Sunapee Lake, New Hampshire, was an Arctic char left over from the last glacial retreat. It has been long extinct in

COLORADO RIVER CUTTHROAT TROUT
Oncorhynchus clarki pleuriticus

Sunapee Lake, but some eggs had been shipped to Idaho in the 1920s and stocked into a few cold, mountain lakes. Bob was elated to learn that he now had an opportunity to catch a Sunapee trout to add to his life list of rare trout and to include it in the second edition of his book. By the time Bob had arranged his Idaho trip in search of the Sunapee trout, Kyle had already been there and found the fish. Later, Kyle made a return trip, meeting Bob at the lake where he caught, photographed and released the Sunapee trout to fulfill his dream.

I had the opportunity to see Kyle's exhibition of trout replicas at a 1999 trout conference in Alberta. It's an amazing one-of-a-kind exhibit. Truly a labor of love.

Glen McFaul of Arizona is another angler with a deep fascination for rare, native trout. Glen carries a portable aquarium to photograph live fish. He has traveled throughout much of the Western United States, checking on sites where I found rare trout from 25 to 40 years ago. His photographs and observations on the current status of many rare trout have assisted me in keeping up-to-date on extinction threats. Page 142 of my 1992 monograph on Western trout (*Native Trout of Western North America*, American Fisheries Society) mentions that the known natural distribution of the rare Colorado River subspecies of cutthroat trout was extended to the Escalante River drainage based on Glen's finding a population there in 1991.

Perhaps the most unusual of the modern day trout Audubons is Johannes Shöffmann of Austria. Although Johannes is not an angler, he lives out his obsession for rare trout in his far-flung travels from China to North Africa. He dons a wet suit and enters the fish's domain. He makes observations and captures specimens for further study with a hand net.

In the Winter 1986 *Trout* (p. 45), I wrote about brown trout. I mentioned a relative of the brown trout that I named as a new species, *Salmo platycephalus*. This species was known only from three specimens collected from a river in Turkey in 1966. I also discussed a peculiar trout described in 1924 as *Salmo pallaryi* from Lake Algueman, Morocco.

I made a request for anyone who might have any information on the status of *S. platycephalus* or *S. pallaryi* to contact me.

Johannes went to Turkey and sent me photographs and detailed notes on platycephalus that he found in a spring stream. Its distribution is restricted to a small area of the river drainage and its continued existence is threatened by sediment loading from agriculture and road building. Johannes went to Morocco and verified that *pallaryi* is extinct, but found that the diversity of the native brown trout of North Africa has its origins in at least two separate invasions of two distinct ancestors. (Johannes preserved tissue samples from the trout he collected for use in molecular genetic research.)

Johannes also made surveys and collections to determine the status of some peculiar trouts of Adriatic drainages: the marble trout, *S. marmoratus*, and the "soft mouth" trout of the genus *Salmothymus*. He found both are now very rare; their original distributions have been greatly reduced.

After returning home from his expeditions, Johannes writes up a report of his findings, including detailed taxonomic descriptions, life history observations and an analysis of the threats to continued existence of the rare forms of trout. He publishes the reports in an Austrian fisheries journal. When I read Johannes scientific papers, the range and depth of knowledge displayed indicate formal training in ichthyology. When I later learned that Johannes is a baker by profession and an amateur ichthyologist, his level of expertise all the more impressed me.

In 1995 I received a letter from a Yale student, James Prosek. James was then putting together a text to accompany his paintings of trout in what was to become a highly popular book, *Trout, An Illustrated History* (Alfred A. Knopf, 1996).

James inquired about trout in the Tigres-Euphrates basin (did a trout stream run through the Garden of Eden?). Johannes had recently sent me a paper on his expedition to record the characteristics of trout native to the Tigres drainage of Turkey (this was the first description of Tigres trout in the world literature).

James was planning a trip to Europe and I suggested he contact Johannes. With two such passionate trout aficionados getting together, wonderful adventures should be forthcoming. In the first two trips, James and Johannes sampled the historical trout waters of Slovenia, Serbia, Bosnia, Croatia, Greece, and Turkey. James wrote the story of their adventures, including his portraits of the diverse forms of trout they encountered, and published it in *Audubon*.

In the Summer 1992 *Trout* (p. 157), I wrote about grayling. I mentioned a specimen of a grayling-like fish in the fish collection of the British Museum. St. George Littledale brought this specimen back to England in 1897. The specimen was considered so distinct that a new genus and species was described for it. The collection locality is stated to be "South slopes Altai Mountains on Chinese territory" (Mongolia). This species has not been found since and there is no other record of a salmonid fish in south slope Altai drainages in China (drainages toward the Gobi Desert).

The mystery of the south slope Altai grayling set the stage for the next wonderful adventure of Johannes and James in search of the mystery fish. The two met in Ulan Bator, Mongolia, rented a Russian jeep and began their quest. I received a postcard from Mongolia relating that the jeep had four flat tires in the Gobi Desert. They failed to find the south slope grayling but encountered a known species of Mongolian grayling, *Thymallus brevirostris*, in north slop Altai drainages, part of a large internal basin. No other salmonid fish exists in the internal basin and the Mongolian grayling evolved as a predator on the several species of minnows it lives with. It attains the largest size of any species of grayling but is so little known that there is no official world record for Mongolian grayling. The most up-to-date account of the Mongolian grayling can be found in a paper authored by Johannes in the Austrian fisheries journal.

Last summer, James and Johannes traveled to Kyrgyzstan to find the easternmost natural distribution of brown trout—*Salmo trutta oxianus* of the Aral Sea basin. Their trout adventures continue.

The small fraternity of piscatorial Audubons is composed of a disparate group whose common interest is their passion for learning about trout—a passion that goes well beyond the ordinary. How many potential new members might there be? Is there anyone out there interested in taking another look at the south side of the Altai Mountains?

WHAT MAKES TROUT
& SALMON RUN?

SUMMER 2002

IN REGARD TO TROUT AND SALMON, the word "run" has two meanings. One refers to the migratory behavior whereby smolts of anadromous species "run" to sea; the other refers to spawning adults that "run" from the ocean into rivers. Anadromous species, such as Chinook salmon and steelhead, spawning in one river basin often consist of populations with several distinct times of spawning runs from the ocean, such as spring, summer, and fall "runs." The questions of what makes some part of a species have an anadromous life history, such as steelhead, while other members of the same species remain in freshwater for their entire life, such as rainbow trout, and what makes for segregation of anadromous runs by different timings of runs, concern the genetic or hereditary basis governing differences in migratory behavior.

The year 2001 produced "record" runs of salmon and steelhead in the Pacific Northwest, especially in the Columbia River. More than three million salmon and steelhead came into the Columbia on spawning runs during 2001, compared to fewer than one million about five years before. The runs consisted of 1.3 million Chinook, 1.1 million coho, and more than 700,000 steelhead. A run of about 10,000 chum salmon was the largest in almost 50 years (however, chum runs once numbered in the millions).

The year 1999 saw above normal precipitation and higher than normal flows, which increased survival of salmon and steelhead smolts during their migration to the ocean. During the past few years, conditions in the North Pacific Ocean have improved. Cooling and upwelling of nutrients increased the food supply for salmon and steelhead. Favorable freshwater conditions coinciding with favorable ocean conditions produce boom years in runs of salmon and steelhead. If we have learned from past boom-and-bust cycles of salmon and steelhead, the abundance of the 2001 runs in the Columbia River should not have been completely unexpected. It's important to bear in mind, however, that about 75 percent of the Chinook and steelhead runs and about 95 percent of the coho run in the Columbia in 2001, were hatchery, not wild, fish.

Last year the Transactions of the American Fisheries Society published an article about a steelhead run in a river in Argentina. In the early 1900s, eggs from resident rainbow trout and anadromous steelhead were shipped to Argentina. Both resident rainbow trout and steelhead have become established in the Rio Santa Cruz. The authors of the article performed state-of-the-art genetic analysis on the rainbow trout and steelhead of the Rio Santa Cruz and found no statistical differences. They concluded there was no genetic or hereditary difference between rainbow trout and steelhead; they were a single population. They extrapolated this opinion to include all rainbow and steelhead throughout their entire native range from California to Alaska. The logical extension of this opinion is that there are also no hereditary distinctions governing the timings of spring, summer, and fall runs of steelhead and salmon.

Such an opinion is a classic example of forgetting or not understanding history—the history of the late nineteenth and early twentieth century when government policies and programs determining the future of salmon and steelhead management were set in motion. The goal was to maintain and increase salmon abundance despite overfishing, dams, and pollution. It was thought this could be accomplished with hatcheries. To be successful, however, a species such as Chinook salmon must be homogeneous, i.e., not consisting of separate adaptive races, on which abundance depended. If the species is homogeneous, then Chinook salmon from many different areas could be mixed together for propagation.

We now know this belief system was wrong. In the late nineteenth century, little was known of the life history of salmon and steelhead. By 1875, concern was expressed that Chinook salmon in the Columbia River were being commercially overfished. The solution to overfishing, dams, and pollution was a technological fix. Hatcheries would make salmon so abundant, there would be no need for regulations or environmental protection. To make salmon hatcheries efficient and economical, they had to be large. In 1909, the Central Hatchery on the Columbia River was constructed to handle 60 million eggs. To keep the hatchery

COHO SALMON
Oncorhynchus kisutch

operating at full capacity, eggs from Chinook salmon were taken from all parts of the Columbia River basin and from many other rivers. Eggs from spring, summer, and fall runs were mixed together, hatched, and stocked into the Columbia and other rivers.

The breaking-down of distinct races of Chinook salmon by artificial propagation was well underway in the early 1900s. The commercial fishers on the Columbia River were well aware that Chinook salmon ran into the Columbia on successive waves of peak abundance known as the spring, summer, and fall runs. If there is a hereditary basis for the different run times, and, by implication, the abundance of the different runs, then a management program should strive to maintain each run or race intact and avoid mixing. But management programs to protect and preserve hereditary distinctions of different races would be diametrically opposed to the operation of large-scale "central hatcheries" that deliberately mixed different races.

By the early 1900s, a naive faith in technology had created an entrenched bureaucracy devoted to an ever-expanding hatchery system. The theoretical basis justifying the way artificial propagation was conducted was to assume that a species is essentially uniform—that there is no genetic or hereditary basis determining different times of spawning runs and different life histories. A uniform species can be viewed as so many equal and interchangeable parts that could be indiscriminately mixed together for artificial propagation. If the different runs or races of Chinook salmon were genetically determined, a homing instinct would be necessary to ensure segregation of the different races; otherwise, all spawners would indiscriminately mix (as was being done in hatcheries). Thus, it was expedient to deny that salmon and steelhead possessed a homing instinct. It seemed incredible that an organism with such a primitive brain as a fish could possess an innate navigational system to roam the ocean, return to its home river, and precisely locate its natal spawning tributary.

This belief system was not based on science. In the early 1900s, studies were initiated to interpret life history differences from the scales

of salmon and homing: juveniles were marked and recaptured as returning adults. These studies left no reasonable doubt that salmon and steelhead possessed a homing instinct that maintained hereditary differences among different races of a species. The findings challenged the conventional wisdom of the hatchery establishment. They were largely ignored. In the 1920s, despite all factual evidence to the contrary, a spokesperson for the U.S. Bureau of Fisheries declared there was no hereditary basis for different life histories; the status quo could continue. Only in recent years, under the influence of the Endangered Species Act, have serious reforms in hatchery propagation of salmon and steelhead been initiated to protect the remnant diversity that still remains.

In rivers where steelhead and rainbow trout exist together occasional hybridization is likely to occur unless the fish are completely isolated from one another by time or place of spawning. Where a slight amount of genetic interchange occurs, genetic analysis will not show clear-cut distinction between rainbow trout and steelhead. This could lead to the wrong conclusion that there is no hereditary basis for anadromous and resident life histories. In such instances, the question that cannot be answered by genetic analysis is: Does like give rise to like? Do steelhead give rise to steelhead and do rainbow trout give rise to rainbow trout, at least in the overwhelming majority of cases?

To answer this, non-genetic techniques are called for. One of these is determination of the strontium-calcium ratio in the nucleus of an otolith (inner ear "bone"). The developing eggs of a female steelhead have a strontium-calcium ratio denoting life in a marine environment that differs from that of the eggs of a rainbow trout that lived her whole life in freshwater. The strontium-calcium ratio of the egg is retained in the otolith of the offspring. It can now be determined if the mother of a particular fish was a steelhead or a resident rainbow trout. When this technique was applied to rainbow trout and steelhead from the Deschutes River, Oregon, it was found that all of the 20 steelhead tested came from steelhead mothers and all of the 38 resident rainbow trout had rainbow trout mothers. In the Babine River of British Columbia,

1 of 24 steelhead trout had a rainbow trout mother and two of nine rainbow trout had a steelhead mother (one or both might have been "residual" steelhead). Evidently, the degree of reproductive isolation between steelhead and rainbow trout is greater in the Deschutes River than in the Babine. The Babine is part of the Skeena River basin, the home of the world's largest steelhead. To me, it is inconceivable that there is no hereditary basis for the largest of all steelhead.

I'm all for applying the most modern techniques to fisheries problems, but let us not forget history and the past mistakes that created today's problems.

AUTHOR'S NOTE

It's ironic that modern genetic analyses has been used by special interest groups seeking to weaken protection of many groups of salmon and steelhead listed under the Endangered Species Act. This denial of a hereditary basis for life history differences that determine anadromy and the times and places of spawning, is similar to the misguided federal policies of 100 years ago. These policies caused a loss of adaptive intraspecific diversity and resulted in many of the present problems confronting salmon and steelhead restoration.

A FISHY "WHODUNIT?"

SPRING 2003

THE IDENTITY OF THE FIRST PERSON in America to artificially fertilize, hatch, and raise trout, and the date when it occurred, is established beyond reasonable doubt. However, the rest of the story concerning contending claims and why it took more than 50 years to conclusively decide the issue is an interesting, little known aspect of the history of fish culture.

My involvement in the matter began five years ago when Cleveland attorney Peter Krembs invited me speak at a banquet of the Trout Club of the Cleveland Museum. I brought along *A Treatise on the Artificial Propagation of Fish*, published in 1857, and authored by Dr. Theodatus Garlick. In the book, Garlick describes how, in 1853, holding ponds and a spawning raceway were constructed in a ravine fed by several large springs on the 100-acre farm of his associate, Dr. Horace Ackley, "two miles" from Cleveland. Garlick had traveled to Saulte Sainte Marie, the outlet of Lake Superior and an area noted for its large brook trout, now known as "coasters." About 150 live trout were brought back to Cleveland and stocked in the ponds on Ackley's farm. On November 21, a male and female were seen on the spawning grounds. These were netted out and the eggs and sperm were manually expressed into a container. The fertilized eggs developed and hatching began in late January 1854. Garlick named the female trout, "Naiad Queen" and the male, "Triton."

Beginning in January 1854, Garlick presented papers and exhibits at meetings of the Cleveland Academy of Natural Science. He also wrote articles describing his experiments in fish culture for the *Ohio Farmer*. These articles were combined in his 1857 book.

I wanted to visit the site of Ackley's farm. We made inquiries about its location, to no avail. Curators at the Dittrick Medical Museum showed us their collection of Garlick's personal papers, which included his autobiography written on his deathbed (Garlick, 79, died in 1884). Garlick grumbled that Ackley, who has often been co-credited with him as America's first fish culturists, really did very little and "never hatched a single ova." It was also obvious from Garlick's papers that he had long been outraged at the claim of Rev. John Bachman that Bachman artificially propagated brook trout in New York State in 1804, at the age of 14. Bachman made his claim in 1855, after reading Garlick's paper reprinted from the *Ohio Farmer*. In the appendix of Garlick's 1857 book, he critiques Bachman's claim, showing it would have been impossible to fertilize brook trout eggs when the sperm and ova are immature. (Bachman wrote that he did this on August 31, about two months before brook trout would have naturally spawned in the vicinity of Bachman's home in Duchess County.) Garlick believed his exposure of Bachman's claim as fraudulent would end the matter on who was the first to artificially propagate fish in America. He was wrong.

In the first report of the U.S. Fish Commissioner for 1872–73, Spencer Baird, the Commissioner of Fisheries, wrote: "On the authority of the Southern Cultivator, the Rev. John Bachman of Charleston, South Carolina, as early as 1804, at the age of fourteen, impregnated and hatched the eggs of trout and other fishes. This has been questioned by some, but Dr. Slack in his work on trout culture, well remarks that Dr. Bachman's reputation as a Christian and naturalist is too well established to permit us to doubt his word."

Infuriated, Garlick began writing Baird, restating and elaborating on his refutation of Bachman's claim. Garlick had these letters published in various sources, such as *Forest and Stream*. His petitions to Baird were finally rewarded. The Dittrick Museum's holdings include a February 20, 1880 letter to Garlick from Baird, acknowledging that Garlick was the first person in America to artificially propagate fish.

Garlick published a second edition of his book in 1880. There was no substantial change from the 1857 edition except that the new one contained a copy of Baird's letter. Garlick hoped the matter of the first culturist was settled for all time. But he was wrong again. The Rev. Bachman's reputation was all-powerful. I'll come back to his reputation later, but let us return to my quest with Peter Krembs to find the site of Ackley's farm.

Ackley's residence still stands in an old part of Cleveland. For some time it has housed the Rowfant Club, whose members have compiled much biographical material on Horace Ackley; however, no one had the slightest idea on the whereabouts of Ackley's farm. After I left Cleveland, Peter continued searching for the farm. He turned up wonderful historical data on Ackley and Garlick, but we "lost the farm." A copy of land ownership in Cuyahoga County (the county containing Cleveland) for 1852 lists several Ackleys but no H. A. Ackley. Perhaps Ackley did

not purchase his farm until 1853. In any event, the mystery concerning the site of America's first fish hatchery is yet to be solved.

In seeking to understand the basis of John Bachman's powerful reputation as a "Christian and naturalist," I turned to Bill Wiltzius, who authored a 1985 work on the history of fish culture in Colorado. Bill, who has compiled a storehouse of files on the early history of American fish culture, lent me two folders on John Bachman and the Bachman/Garlick controversy.

Born in 1790, Bachman was raised in Rheinbeck, New York. He developed an early interest in natural history, which he attributed to George, a family servant. Bachman was ordained as a Lutheran minister and in 1815, became rector of St. John's Lutheran church in Charleston, South Carolina, a position he held until his death in 1874. He was influential in expanding and developing the Lutheran church in the South. He also continued his studies in zoology, botany, and horticulture. He published many papers and monographs and became widely recognized as one of America's leading naturalists.

In 1831, Bachman met John J. Audubon and they became lifelong friends and collaborators. A monumental work on mammals, "The Quadrupeds of North America," with text by Bachman and illustrations by Audubon, was published in three volumes during 1845–1849. Two of Bachman's daughters married two of Audubon's sons. Audubon named new species from specimens collected by Bachman, including two rare species of birds, which he named the Bachman and Swainson's warblers (Bachman's warbler has not been seen since 1962, and is presumed extinct).

By the mid-nineteenth century, Bachman's reputation as a naturalist was firmly established. From all accounts of his life, he was a paragon of virtue and industry. Why would a man of such credentials claim that he was the first in America to artificially propagate fish with an obviously fabricated story? Perhaps he believed his fanciful story of boyhood fish culture would not extend beyond the local region and his circle of friends and devotees. In his 1855–56 accounts, however, Bachman stated that he presented a paper on his early fish culture work in 1838, at the Royal Society of London. Garlick had Spencer Baird review all issues of the Proceedings of the Royal Society from 1835 to 1840. There is no paper by Bachman, nor any paper on fish culture.

An 1888 tribute to Bachman has a "list of published works" that includes: "On the introduction and propagation of fresh-water fish, published about 1848." Bill Wiltzius queried the libraries at the University of South Carolina and the South Carolina Historical Society, requesting a search for any such "about 1848" publication by Bachman. Nothing could be found.

Bachman's reputation kept him in contention for the title of America's first fish culturist for many years after his death. Although Baird, in his 1880 letter, acknowledged that Garlick was first, he never published a correction to the 1872–73 Fish Commission Report. The "official" USFC view on America's first fish culturist remained ambivalent. No one wanted to sully Bachman's reputation.

Fortunately, Garlick's many friends relentlessly continued his quest for official recognition long after his death. The files of the Western Reserve Historical Society contain letters and notes detailing the efforts to validate Garlick's claim and reject Bachman's. A March 9, 1907 letter from the Acting Director of the then U.S. Bureau of Fisheries to the Historical Society is astounding in its ignorance of all that had gone on before. The letter cited Bachman's 1855 publication to the effect that he propagated trout in 1804; therefore, Bachman must have been first. The letter elicited an immediate response with documentation that irrefutably established Garlick as first. In a return letter of March 25, 1907, the Acting Director somewhat apologetically admitted Garlick was right and Bachman, wrong. Since that time no one has defended Bachman's claim based on his reputation. Theodatus Garlick could finally rest in peace. He is unquestionably recognized as America's first fish culturist.

One final mystery: Garlick claimed to have been the first person in America to make plaster casts of fish. When he discovered that a mink had killed "Triton" (it weighed 6 pounds, 3 ounces), he made a cast of Triton that he kept in his room. If this cast still exists, it should have a special place of honor as the "true father" of American fish culture.

AUTHOR'S NOTE

In 1998 during a visit to Cleveland, Peter Krembs, a member of the Trout Club of the Cleveland Museum of Natural History and I failed in our attempt to find the site of "Ackley's farm," where Theodatus Garlick artificially propagated brook trout in 1853. During a return visit to Cleveland in 2004, we were successful in finding the site where Ackley's farm and America's first fish hatchery had once existed. In the meantime, we accumulated a substantial amount of historical information on Garlick. He was a skillful plastic surgeon and well known for his diverse endeavors. I returned to Cleveland in March 2005 for the Trout Club's 27TH annual banquet and the opening of the Theodatus Garlick Exhibit at the Cleveland Museum of Natural History. It was the 200TH anniversary of Garlick's birth. I was told that Garlick had the documents that testified to the fact that he was America's first fish culturist sealed in his tombstone. Perhaps he believed he might confront the Reverend Bachman in an afterlife and force Bachman to recant his fraudulent claims on who was really first.

AMERICA'S FIRST BROWN TROUT

>

SUMMER 2003

IN MY LAST COLUMN (P. 217), I RELATED THE STORY of the first artificial propagation of trout in America and the controversy surrounding it. Another "first" that has long fascinated me concerns the when and where of the first American propagation of brown trout. I have written about this at various times and in various places, but I was never able to tie up all of the loose ends of the story. In March, my book editor George Scott arranged a visit to Connetquot State Park and Preserve, near Islip, Long Island, where we would meet with Gil Bergen, the park's superintendent. Gil possesses a vast knowledge of the preserve's history. I had met him a few years ago and we agreed that I must come to this historic site to see where, I believe, newly hatched brown trout and Atlantic salmon were being raised in 1865. Until then the brook trout was the only species propagated in America.

My quest for documentation on the first brown trout in America began when I was researching the Garlick-Bachman controversy on who was the first to artificially propagate trout in America. I consulted Thadeus Norris' 1868 book, *American Fish Culture*. Norris, like most others at the time, evidently, did not want to challenge the reputation of the distinguished Rev. Bachman and avoided the question on who was first. On page 114, I was captivated by the following:

"The first attempt at breeding salmon artificially in the Unites States, as far as I have been able to ascertain, was by James B. Johnson, Esq., of New York City. Four years since he imported the ova of salmon, salmon of the Danube, trout, and charr. A part of these were hatched out at the studio building on Tenth St., New York in troughs similar to those at the College of France, but the Croton water was fatal to most of them. The fry which Mr. Johnson removed to Long Island were promising in confinement, he says, but died of preventable causes when liberated."

From this, it can be concluded that about December 1864 or January 1865, when fertilized eggs would be available, James B. (Bowman) Johnson received eggs of Atlantic salmon, "salmon of the Danube" (huchen, *Hucho hucho*), "trout" (brown trout), and char (European char, *Salvelinus alpinus*). Were the "part" of the eggs not hatched at the studio building also sent to Long Island? Where on Long Island? Who was the fish culturist in charge of this first attempt to propagate brown trout in America?

As with the Theodatus Garlick story, I consulted Bill Wiltzius, a veritable Sherlock Holmes of fish culture. Bill located two *New York Tribune* articles on "Propagation of Trout." One dated September 30, the other October 7, 1865. The articles tell us that James B. Johnson employed Robert Ramsbottom, a fish culturist from England, and that they were propagating "salmon, trout, and black bass" on the Snedecor Preserve, which was owned by Johnson. "Snedecor" is the older name for the Connetquot Preserve. The Snedecor family had long lived in the area and operated a tavern, hotel, and grist mill on the Connetquot River. For anglers, the Connetquot and Carmans rivers were the most famous of the many rivers on Long Island and were fished by notables of the time, such as Daniel Webster and Martin Van Buren.

The present Long Island was the site of the maximum extent of glacial front during the last glacial period. About 11,000 years ago, the glacial front began its retreat. A terminal moraine deposited its fine sediment of sand, gravel, and topsoil scraped off the surface of New England, and Long Island came into existence. The substrate of Long Island acts like a sponge with numerous cold springs and rivers providing ideal habitat for the brook trout ancestor arriving after the glacier's retreat. Many Long Island rivers have long estuarine areas where trout can become "salters" (sea-run brook trout). From Colonial times, well into the nineteenth century, Long Island was the center of American brook trout angling. The *Tribune* articles mention a farmer in Maspeth, "only a mile east of Brooklyn," who leased fishing rights to a group of gentlemen for $2,500 per year. Fishing was restricted to fly-fishing only. In 1865, he enlarged a pond and charged $5,000 per year. Long Island trout sold for fifty cents per pound in the city. By the 1860s, wealthy men began to purchase large parcels on the best trout streams for private preserves. In 1865, James B. Johnson bought a large part of the Connetquot River watershed. He employed Ramsbottom to propagate trout and salmon to stock the preserve.

BROWN TROUT
Salmo trutta

What happened to the brown trout and Atlantic salmon that were being raised on the Connetquot Preserve according to the 1865 *Tribune* articles? Johnson had told Thaddeus Norris that most of the "part" of the eggs hatched at the studio building perished, but I could find no mention in any of my sources as to the approximate number of salmon and trout fry being raised by Ramsbottom on the Connetquot Preserve in 1865. The *Tribune* story relates that: "Although many persons contend that the pair turned into South Bay will never return to Mr. Johnson's preserve. I doubt it." ("Pair" is most likely a typo for "parr.") By September, salmon or trout fingerlings or parr hatched in late winter or early spring would be no more than three inches long. Were these parr stocked into "South Bay"? The Connetquot River is a tributary to South Bay and it a more likely scenario is that Ramsbottom released them below the mill dam, hoping they would migrate to the bay to grow and return as large adults. None of the parr released was ever seen again. Unfortunately, neither Johnson nor Ramsbottom left any written account of their attempt to stock the Connetquot Preserve with Atlantic salmon and brown trout in 1865, or what happened to the eggs of the Danube huchen and European char.

Ramsbottom's brother, William, had previously gone to Tasmania to prepare a hatchery for the introduction of Atlantic salmon to Australia and New Zealand. In 1864, the first successful transoceanic shipment of salmon and trout eggs was made. Brown trout eggs were added to the 1864 shipment of salmon eggs to fill out the space in an ice house constructed on a ship to transport the eggs. The salmon did not become established, but the brown trout did, and William Ramsbottom gained some fame from this. What happened to his brother Robert?

Nick Karas' book, *Brook Trout* (The Lyons Press, revised and up-dated, 2002), contains a wealth of historical information on Long Island brook trout fishing. Karas mentions that in January 1866, James Johnson sold the Connetquot Preserve to a group who founded the Southside Sportsmen's Club. Evidently the new owners did not employ Robert Ramsbottom. Keith Harwood of Clitheroe, England, who is a biographer of the Ramsbottom family, contacted me. He told me that Robert Ramsbottom returned to England and joined his father, Robert Sr., in the manufacture and sale of fishing tackle in Clitheroe. Gil Bergen, while perusing the old log books of the Southside Sportsmen's Club, came across a brief statement that, "the trial of Mr. Ramsbottom was not successful," which I interpret to mean that none of the salmon and brown trout held at the Connetquot Preserve in 1865 was ever seen again. It wasn't until 1883, when the first shipment of *Salmo trutta* eggs arrived in New York, that brown trout were established in North America.

In 1963, the Southside Sportsmen's Club property was sold to New York State and became the Connetquot River State Park. Amidst a sprawling metropolitan area, the park is a wonderful oasis of what the Long Island landscape looked like in Colonial times. Anglers pay a fee and are assigned a beat to fish for four hours with catch-and-release, fly-fishing-only regulations. Fishing is excellent with a high catch rate. But now, nonnative brown and rainbow trout occur with the native brook trout. Occasionally, large brown trout are caught in the lower Connetquot River that have fed in the tidal waters of South Bay—just as envisioned by James Johnson and Robert Ramsbottom so long ago. Most anglers today have some awareness of the Connetquot Preserve's historical significance as they fish its waters. Now there is additional significance associated with the Preserve as the site of the first attempt to artificially propagate brown trout and Atlantic salmon in America.

Three successive columns in 2003 deal with historical research. They were the culminations of a reawakening of my interests in history that had been in a semi-dormant state while I pursued my career. I began to come up with bits and pieces of historical information in regards to fish culture when I was putting together material for my monograph on western trout, published by the American Fisheries Society in 1992. For example, I learned that the first hatchery rainbow trout did not come from the McCloud River as commonly believed. In subsequent years, I continued to accumulate more bits and pieces until they could be put together to tell a whole story. I am reminded of my early interest in history by *Inside U.S.A.* John Gunther (Harper Brothers; 2ND edition). An inscription reads: "Robert Behnke for excellence in American History Stamford High School June 18, 1947." Has it really been that long? I think my history teacher, Mrs. Bohn, would have enjoyed my continuing interest in historical research.

SAMUEL LATHAM MITCHILL
& THE BROOK TROUT

FALL 2003

THE LEGACY OF SAMUEL LATHAM MITCHILL, the first ichthyologist born in America (in 1764), is associated with names of fish species he described in the early nineteenth century. For example, taxonomic listings cite the brook trout, *Salvelinus fontinalis* (Mitchill 1814). This means that Mitchill named *fontinalis* in 1814, but described it in a different genus as denoted by the ( ) around his name. The genus *Salvelinus* was not officially described until 1836, and was not generally used in the literature for another 60 years or so. Most of the nineteenth century fisheries literature continued to use Mitchill's original designation "*Salmo fontinalis*." Mitchill described many other species of fish that are recognized today. In truth, however, his ichthyologic publications are not of high quality and contain some egregious errors. But this is understandable, considering the state of knowledge of his time and, particularly, his prodigious activities in science and politics.

My fascination for Mitchill began when fisheries historian Bill Wiltzius and I attempted to find the original description of the muskellunge, *Esox masquinongy*, credited to an 1824 description by Mitchill in "the Mirror" (a New York journal). No one has ever found this original description, but James De Kaye reprinted it in his 1842 work, *Fishes of New York*. Evidently Mitchill had written a description of the muskellunge—which was never published—and De Kaye obtained a copy for his book. Wiltzius and I accumulated a great deal of information on Mitchill in the course of verifying that his description of the muskellunge is actually found in De Kaye (1842), not "the Mirror." My fascination for Mitchill grew, and I wondered why the legacy of a man so influential in American politics and science had virtually vanished from history except for an association with the fish species he named. This same question was addressed in a tribute to Mitchill in the April 1870 issue of *Harper's* magazine that began:

> "It is unfortunate for the memory of the late Samuel Latham Mitchill that no complete biography of him has ever been published. To the current generation his talents, learning, and public services are almost unknown. Yet sixty years ago few citizens of this country held so prominent a place in the literary and scientific world as did this remarkable man."

In 1891, another admirer wrote a "Sketch of Samuel Latham Mitchill" in volume 38 of *Popular Science Monthly*, with a similar theme. A man, who during the first quarter of the nineteenth century was "…one of the most conspicuous figures in the literary and scientific life of the United States," but virtually unknown by the late nineteenth century.

Mitchill was born in Hempstead, Long Island. In 1796, he graduated with an M.D. from the University of Edinburgh. Instead of practicing medicine on his return home, he obtained a law degree as an entrée into politics and public service. In 1790, he was appointed Professor of Natural History, Chemistry, and Philosophy at Columbia College. He produced such a great output on such a broad range of subjects that his knowledge was regarded as encyclopedic. From 1804 to 1813, he served in Congress in both the House of Representatives and the Senate. He was a friend and admirer of President Thomas Jefferson, sharing Jefferson's views on science and enlightenment.

In the early nineteenth century, what little was known of American fishes depended entirely on European publications. Mitchill set out to produce the first American publication devoted to fish. In 1814, he privately published a small number of copies of *Fishes of New York*. Although full of blunders made in his attempt to align American species with known European species, the 1814 work contains the first published description of brook trout, "*Salmo fontinalis*" (Mitchill mistakenly described the brook trout as having no scales). The 1814 publication had faded into obscurity until Theodore Gill, an eminent American ichthyologist, reprinted Mitchill's text. Gill commented that he knew of only three copies of the original work still in existence. Gill critiqued all of Mitchill's mistakes, such as how Mitchill listed the smelt *Osmerus eperlanus* (European smelt) on one page while on the next page he describes the smelt of New York as a new species, *Atherina mordax*. *Atherina* is a genus in the silverside family and quite unrelated to smelts of the genus *Osmerus*. Mitchill somehow mistook the adipose fin of smelt as a second dorsal fin and classified it as a species of silverside. Nevertheless, the species name *mordax* was the first name given to the American rainbow smelt that is now known as *Osmerus mordax* (Mitchill 1814). Gill remarked that the species named by Mitchill that

were still recognized are more the result of "lucky hits," rather than critical comparative study. Although Gill was critical of Mitchill's ichthyologic competence, he recognized the significance of his efforts to initiate study on American fishes.

With influential friends, Mitchill founded the Literary and Philosophical Society of New York (later the New York Lyceum of Natural History, and, finally, the New York Academy of Sciences). In 1815, in the Transactions of the Literary and Philosophical Society, Mitchill published a revised and expanded version of *Fishes of New York*. He must have recognized the errors and inadequacies of his 1814 publication as he made no mention of them in the 1815 version. This version expanded discussion of the brook trout to include Long Island catches reported in the newspapers during 1814 and part of 1815.

It took some time for the stimulus provided by Mitchill for more critical study of American fishes to take hold. This is apparent in J.V.C. Smith's book, *Fishes of Massachusetts* (1833). Smith's book is the first American work that is well known to angling historians because of its firsthand accounts of angling and the tackle used at the time. Smith's knowledge of ichthyology, however, was essentially nonexistent. Gill's critique of Smith's book accused Smith of being a charlatan who would write about any subject he deemed salable. Smith's understanding of trout classification was derived from English books. Evidently, Smith was unaware of Mitchill's *Fishes of New York* or that Mitchill had described the American brook trout as *Salmo fontinalis* to distinguish it from the European "brook trout," *Salmo trutta* (or more commonly, *S. fario* at the time). In Smith's classification of New England trout, his "brook and pond trout" was *Salmo fario*, and the sea-run or salter brook trout of Cape Cod was a "sea trout," *Salmo trutta*. Smith also believed that the Danube huchen, *Hucho hucho*, occurred in New Hampshire and Maine (most likely lake trout were confused with huchen). Thus, Smith's 1833 book was a giant step backward as a contribution to American ichthyology.

With so many of Mitchill's publications available to me, I thought some light might be shed on the origins of the folklore surrounding the legendary trout of 14 pounds (plus or minus) reputedly caught by Daniel Webster from the Carmans River, Long Island, in 1827 or thereabouts. How did this story, in its numerous variations, get started? Frank Forester's book, *Fish and Fishing* (1849, U.S. edition 1850), states that many years ago, a trout of 11 pounds was caught at Fireplace and a rough sketch of this fish is on the wall of the tavern (Fireplace was the tavern and hotel on the Carmans River frequented by anglers). Although no one has ever found any newspaper or any verifiably published account of a brook trout of legendary size caught on Long Island or anywhere in New York, such a fish would not have escaped Mitchill's

attention. In his 1815 work containing catch records of Long Island brook trout, the largest specimen listed was caught by a Mr. Purvis. It was 24 inches, 4 pounds. It was mentioned that "a drawing of this fish remains at Fireside near where it was caught." De Kaye's 1842 book on the fishes of New York also gives 4 pounds as the largest brook trout ever caught in New York State, of which he had knowledge.

A microfilm copy of Mitchill's 1815 *Fishes of New York* that Wiltzius and I received evidently was reproduced from Mitchill's personal copy. There are handwritten notes in the margin. One note dated May 17, 1825, is about a trout specimen he received that weighed 10 pounds. Mitchill noted that it was "in agreement with *fontinalis*" (which, until

BROOK TROUT
Salvelinus fontinalis

then, he believed was restricted in distribution to Long Island). The locality given for this large trout was "the Hudson River 100 miles north of Albany." I doubt that a brook trout of 10 pounds was ever caught in the Hudson River, or anywhere else in New York State. Mitchill, nor anyone else that I am aware of, ever published a record or further details of this reputed 10-pound brook trout. One might assume that some of Mitchill's associates were aware of it. Perhaps its dubious catch locality was transferred to "Fireside" and an enlarged paper sketch placed on the tavern wall. Add Webster to this scenario and one of American angling's most enduring legends might be born.

This is only wild speculation, of course, and I don't wish to play the role of an iconoclast. The story of Webster and his great trout is a wonderful part of American folklore, but I would like to know how it got started.

The virtual disappearance of Samuel Mitchill from American history can, in part, be attributed to a lack of a complete biography. Mitchill died in 1831. He entrusted his papers and correspondence with his brother-in-law, Samuel Ackley, who was to write Mitchill's biography. Ackley claimed to have made some beginnings at producing a biography, but the house where Mitchill's material was kept was lost in a fire. Although probably not the type or magnitude of legacy Mitchill would have desired, his name is at least properly honored by its association with *fontinalis*, the name he endowed upon our beautiful brook trout.

AUTHOR'S NOTE

Both Theodatus Garlick and Samuel Latham Mitchill were prominent figures of their time. Now, if they have any name recognition at all, it is associated with brook trout. Garlick was the first to artificially propagate and Mitchill was the first to name the species *fontinalis*. The column mentions Mitchill's hand-written notations found on his 1815 publication. Besides his note about a reputed 10-pound brook trout, he also noted that Atlantic salmon is not native to the Hudson River.

Henry Hudson's seventeenth century observation of "salmon" in his namesake river must have been based on a school of shad or striped bass. Yet, for about 200 years since Mitchill's time, the southernmost distribution of Atlantic salmon has been commonly assigned to the Hudson River. Old myths die hard.

PROSPECTING FOR NATIVE TROUT

SPRING 2005

WHEN I LEFT CONNECTICUT for California to begin graduate studies at Berkeley in 1957, I had a fascination for fish in general and trout in particular, but I perceived no real distinction between hatchery trout and wild trout or between wild trout and native trout. I was simply captivated by this wondrous fish and by the environments in which they live.

Soon after arriving in Berkeley, Professor Paul Needham and I loaded a pickup truck and departed on a trip to collect specimens of native rainbow and cutthroat trout from California to Alaska. It was a glorious experience for me. In 1953, while serving in the Army in Japan, I caught "yamame," a landlocked masu salmon, in mountain streams. Except for this angling experience, my personal contact with trout had been fishing for newly stocked put-and-take hatchery fish.

The first stop on the trip was at the University of California's Sagehen Creek Research Station in the Sierras north of the town of Truckee, California. The Sagehen Creek station was founded by Needham for a long-term study on wild trout and their habitat. In the nearby Little Truckee River, I caught my first wild rainbow and brown trout. I knew, however, that we were in the Lahontan basin, where the only native trout was the Lahontan cutthroat trout (subspecies *henshawi*). At the time the Lahontan cutthroat was believed to be extinct as pure, unhybridized poulations.

During the summer of 1957, we collected and preserved more than 1,000 specimens from different geographical areas, from California to Alaska. Back in Berkeley, the plan was for me to examine the specimens and record their morphological data in an attempt to detect patterns of diversity and interpret these patterns for a more firmly based system of classification.

At the time, trout classification mainly was based on the 1896 work of D.S. Jordan and B.W. Evermann. In 1902 Jordan and Evermann summarized their previous publication in their book, *American Food and Game Fishes*. Although about 35 species presently attributed to rainbow trout (now *Oncorhynchus mykiss*) and cutthroat trout (*O. clarki*) had been described in the literature, it was not known how many of these described "species" might represent distinctive groups that could be recognized as subspecies in a revised modern classification.

Another problem concerned subspecies presumed to be extinct. If some pure populations still persisted and were found, how could they be positively identified? For this, museum specimens collected in the nineteenth century, before widespread introductions of nonnative trout occurred, were necessary. I struck gold with the fish collection at Stanford University. In 1890 Jordan became president of the newly founded Leland Stanford Jr. University in Palo Alto. His associate, B.W. Evermann, became associated with the California Academy of Sciences in San Francisco. Stanford received the bulk of the trout collections, but some went to the ichthyology collection at the Academy of Sciences. Both were within an hour's drive from Berkeley (in the late 1950s that is; it takes longer today to negotiate the traffic).

What I did was basically simple and straightforward. To diagnose Lahontan cutthroat trout so I could recognize them if found, I examined many museum specimens collected around the Lahontan basin before hybridization with introduced rainbow trout had occurred. In comparison to cutthroat trout from other regions, the subspecies *henshawi*, in its pure form, could be clearly distinguished by the number of gill rakers (typically 23–25 versus 18–20 on first left gill arch), counts of pyloric caeca, the appendages on the intestine (typically more than 50 versus 30 to 40), and by the spotting pattern on the body; relatively large, rounded spots all over the sides of the body (versus smaller spots and/or spots concentrated on the rear of body).

Now that I knew the key characteristics of the subspecies *henshawi*, I could positively identify extant populations if they could be found. I decided I would write a master's thesis on the Lahontan and Bonneville cutthroat—the trout of the Great Basin—and I set out to find some. I made inquiries with biologists, game wardens and anglers. Did they know of or had they heard of any "peculiar" trout in some remote area?

Following leads, in 1959 I made a backpack trip into the headwaters of the East Carson River, California, and found pure populations of Lahontan cutthroat trout in two small creeks, isolated by falls. Another lead took me to Pine Valley, a small town in southern Utah. Two other Berkeley students came along on the trip, but we were disappointed

BONNEVILLE CUTTHROAT TROUT
Oncorhynchus clarki utah

to find the "peculiar" trout of Reservoir Canyon to be a rainbow/cutthroat hybrid.

Ultimately, a friendly rancher saved the day. He said his grandfather had transplanted some of the original native cutthroat to the headwaters above impassable falls in 1905 and they were still there. He loaned us horses and his two sons as guides. We found our pure Bonneville cutthroat, the descendents of the 1905 transplant. And I had something important to say in my thesis.

In 1960, after completing my thesis, I had no doubts about future plans. I would pursue doctoral studies on the family Salmonidae, following the methods used in my study of Western trout. I continued to make field trips in the West to fill in gaps for a better understanding of the evolutionary history of Western trout. During completion of my doctorate, I was also accepted for a 10-month postdoctoral exchange program with the old Soviet Union. In 1960, I made brief visits to evaluate ichthyology collections in museums in Leningrad and Moscow. In the few weeks available, I could barely scratch the surface of the vast collections that began to accumulate in the 1700s. Then I arranged a ten month program to return. I was married by this time, and my wife Sally and I lived in Leningrad from the winter of 1964 to the autumn of 1965 while I could more thoroughly examine specimens in the museum of the Academy of Sciences.

I came to Colorado State University in 1966. Now I could have my own graduate students to assist in filling in the gaps of knowledge of Western trout. In 1967, I went to the Apache Reservation in the White Mountains of Arizona to study the yet unnamed Apache trout. I understood that historically Apaches did not eat fish. The tribe, however, took great pride in its native trout and set aside Ord Creek, one of the few streams that still held Apache trout, as a protected refuge. In 1968, with graduate students, I initiated further study on California golden trout and redband trout of northern California and southern Oregon. In the 1970s and '80s, data from genetic studies were available to supplement my morphological data and to test and modify my former assumptions.

Finally, in 1992, almost 30 years after I wrote my first unpublished manuscript on Western trout, the American Fisheries Society published AFS monograph 6, *Native Trout of Western North America*. New information continually becomes available, and I updated some of the 1992 monograph in the text accompanying the magnificent illustrations of Joe Tomelleri in the 2002 book, *Trout and Salmon of North America* (Free Press).

The quest for native trout has resulted in a great life with wonderful memories. One of the best was the discovery of bull trout, then called Dolly Varden, in the Upper Klamath Lake basin in 1968. The fish hadn't been recorded since 1873. After several days of futile searching, the lead to finding "Dolly Varden" came from a taxi driver after my car broke down in Klamath Falls. In 1969 I found pure greenback cutthroat in Colorado, a trout that was declared to be extinct by 1938; and in 1979, the world's largest cutthroat trout, the Lahontan cutthroat native to Pyramid Lake, assumed to be extinct after its last spawning run up the Truckee River was lost in 1938, was discovered in a small stream on the Nevada–Utah border where it had been transplanted many years before.

The quest for native trout and for more knowledge of salmonid fishes is never ending. There's always more yet to be learned, but I hope to remain actively engaged as long as I can. The joy of life is in the quest.

I had no epiphany that led to my acquiring a passion for wild, native trout. I had no innate sense of "biophilia" that made me "see the light." My value system about trout developed gradually, as I continued to study and learn. In view of this, I am tolerant of the values of other anglers who do not share my views. During the ontogeny of an angler, the transformation from an attitude of "Wild trout, hatchery trout, who cares?" to a distinct preference for wild trout, with the highest value placed on native trout, is a learning process. Many anglers have no desire to complete the process. During the past 50 years, however, a continually increasing number of anglers have experienced this transformation.

NEW TOOLS & OLD MYSTERIES:
ON THE TRAIL OF THE ALTAI GRAYLING

➤

SUMMER 2005

THIS SPRING, I RECEIVED A REQUEST for information on grayling, especially about a specimen in the British Museum collected by St. George Littledale in 1897. Littledale claimed that specimen, which was named a new genus and species in 1898, came from the "south slope Altai Mountains on Chinese territory." This location is an unsolved mystery. I've often wished that there was some way to know the route Littledale had followed in 1897, as we would then at least know the general area where he obtained his grayling.

When I received the recent query, I recalled how Joe Tomelleri, the illustrator for my book *Trout and Salmon of North America* (Free Press, 2002) had uncovered new information on Mexican trout on the Internet. (The first thought that came into my technologically challenged brain when he told me about the Google search engine was *what's that? How can such an array of information be available at the touch of a button—or a mouse?*) I thought: St. George Littledale and search engine!

I enlisted the help of Mike Douglas, senior research scientist at the Department of Fishery and Wildlife Biology at Colorado State University, who had been most helpful in finding literature on the Internet for me. (Mike's wife, Marlis, a molecular geneticist, also keeps me abreast on what's new in genetic research.) Mike punched in St. George Littledale and all sorts of bits of information appeared.

Littledale was characterized as a sportsman, explorer and eccentric. His passion was hunting wild sheep in the mountains of Asia. We noted that a 2002 issue of the journal *Sibirica* contained an article on a sheep hunting trip Littledale made in the Altai Mountains in 1897 with a Russian nobleman, Elim Demidov. An interlibrary loan of the article was arranged.

When I read it, I realized I had been mistaken to have assumed that Littledale's locality of "south slope Altai" most likely was from a stream draining to the Gobi Desert. He was nowhere near the Gobi basin in 1897. But just what route did they follow? The article mentions that Demidov wrote a book (in English), *After Wild Sheep in the Altai and Mongolia*. Another interlibrary loan was arranged.

Demidov's book gives a day-by-day account of the expedition, whose primary purpose was to hunt argali, the largest species of wild sheep. Demidov and Littledale, and their wives, brought along fly-fishing tackle and caught hundreds of grayling, which were used to feed their camp. Besides the Littledales and Demidovs, the camp included a cook, translator, doctor, valets and servants who rode on 10 horses. There were 16 native men from the Russian Altai region with 40 pack horses to transport tons of supplies and guide the hunters. Obviously Littledale and Demidov were not your average tourist sportsmen.

Some elaboration on Mongolian drainage relationships is necessary to put Littledale's grayling locality in its proper perspective. He says the fish comes from "Chinese territory," which in 1897 would have included Mongolia (the Autonomous Peoples Republic of Mongolia came into existence in 1921). About 60 percent of Mongolia consists of internal drainages with no outlet to the sea; comparable to the Great Basin of the Western United States. The largest of the internal basins is the Kobdo (or Hovd) basin, also referred to as the West Mongolian Great Lakes Valley.

The Kobdo basin is the only basin known to be inhabited by the Mongolian grayling *Thymallus brevirostris*. The Arctic grayling, *T. arcticus*, has also been reported from the upper Kobdo basin. This species must have made a headwater transfer from an Arctic basin. Only two other fish species are known from the Kobdo basin, a loach genus *Noemacheilus* and a minnow of the genus *Oreoleuciscus* commonly known as osman.

A 1972 Russian paper on Mongolian grayling discussed a former connection between the Kobdo basin and the Gobi basin. The presence of the loach and osman in the Gobi basin verifies such a former connection to the Kobdo basin. If the loach and osman utilized this former connection from the Kobdo basin to become established in the Gobi basin, the grayling also should have come with the other two species. The Gobi drainages begin at between 9,000- to 11,000-foot elevations, and should have considerable habitat for salmonid fishes. Perhaps the Mongolian grayling does exist in remote headwaters of the Gobi basin, but considering problems for travel, they would be difficult to find.

The Demidov-Littledale expedition in the summer of 1897 was confined to the Westernmost headwaters of the Kobdo basin in Mongolia. Although many of the mountain headwater streams begin in a southerly direction, the general direction of flow toward the valley floor is easterly, then northeasterly. Thus, I have no doubts that the specimen obtained by Littledale was *T. brevirostris*, but it does have some distinctions such as fin ray counts compared to the few museum specimens of *brevirostris* I have examined. The Kobdo basin, like the basins in the American Great Basin, is not a network of continuously interconnected drainages, but contains many isolated waters where fish populations can differentiate. Some differentiated populations might be recognized as subspecies.

Although Demidov's book does not mention the site from which Littledale obtained his specimen, it does give the localities where they fished. The expedition followed the headwaters of the Irtysh River into the Altai Mountains. They crossed a pass over the Russian-Mongolian border into the Kobdo basin. They followed the Souk River (Sagoo River on my map of Mongolia) down to its confluence with the Kobdo river (or Hovd River on Mongolian map). Mrs. Demidov caught grayling in the Souk River. They followed the Kobdo River upstream and crossed its tributary, the Tsagaan River. They found "capital fishing" in the Kobdo, and the grayling they caught supplied food for the camp—60 grayling were taken in two hours and they rose to any fly. They averaged three-quarters of a pound. A day or two later "over 100" grayling were taken. The camp was moved upstream to the river flowing between the Kobdo Lakes (Lakes Hoton and Hungan on Mongolian map, which are reputed to have the largest grayling, up to 3–4 kilograms). Here they caught enough grayling, averaging 1½ pounds, to feed the camp.

The last mention of fishing is on the return trip to the Russian border. They crossed the headwaters of the Tsagaan River and camped in a wide valley at 8,200-foot elevation. The weather turned bad for hunting, so Littledale and Demidov fished a small lake below their camp (near Nam Duba Pass). I suspect Littledale may have caught his British Museum specimen in this small lake—a last-minute afterthought on their last day in Mongolia. With the grayling specimen, the skulls of 32 sheep, 1 ibex and 5 antelope were packed out.

In my Summer 2001 *Trout* column (p. 209), I wrote about the odd couple of James Prosek and Johannes Schöffmann, who make annual expeditions in search of rare salmonids. In 2000, James and Johannes went to Mongolia in search of the "south slope" grayling. They were misled by my mistaken theory that Littledale's grayling came from the Gobi basin. They found only a loach there. James did catch a Mongolian grayling from the Kobdo basin later in the trip. I apologize to James and Johnnnes for leading them on a wild grayling chase. But James Prosek's book, *Fly-Fishing the 41st Parallel* (HarperCollins), published in 2003, contains an entertaining chapter on their Mongolian trip and problems they encountered with travel in regions lacking an infrastructure to accommodate tourists. I find some consolation in that without being misled by my wrong directions, there would be no Mongolian section in James's book.

If a 3 kilogram (6.6 pounds) Mongolian grayling could be caught by an angler and duly verified, it would be a world record for any species of grayling. The International Game Fish Association's world record Arctic grayling (*T. arcticus*) is 5 pounds, 15 ounces. The world record European grayling (*T. thymallus*) is 3 pounds, 11 ounces. The IGFA has yet to receive an entry for the Mongolian grayling, so the first submission would be the IGFA world record. Following the lead of Littledale and Demidov, hunters after sheep in the Mongolian Altai should bring along their fly rods. They could return with a world record grayling.

ARCTIC GRAYLING
Thymallus arcticus

The story of his Littledale's Altai Mountain sheep hunt in Mongolia really captivated my imagination. I had to see this country for myself. My trip to Mongolia occurred later in 2005 as I recount in the next selection.

A MONGOLIAN ADVENTURE

WINTER 2006

I'VE NEVER LOST MY CHILDHOOD FANTASIES about what adventure might lie beyond the horizon. I loved to watch trains come and go. In reality, the trains were probably headed for Bridgeport or New Haven, but I would fantasize their destination to be some magical wonderland such as the "North Woods" where wild animals roamed the wilderness and remote waters held great fish. Sometimes I would indulge such fantasies while fishing for sunfish in the neighborhood mill pond. When sitting at my desk in grammar school, many times I would be scolded by the teacher for daydreaming.

I've been fortunate that I have been able to transform some of my fantasies into reality during the development of my career, with many trips to distant lands to observe exotic fishes. Thus, it was essentially predetermined that I would accept an offer to go on a fishing trip to the Darhat Valley, a remote, roadless area of northwestern Mongolia. My body gave off signals that this would be a foolhardy thing to do, but my mind said "let's go."

I learned through a friend about Mongofly Tours, arranged by Peter Mullett and an educated Mongolian native by the name of Chinbat, who studied violin and classical music in Bulgaria and is the conductor of the Mongolian Symphony Orchestra. I would characterize Chinbat as

erudite, but that might detract from his skills and resourcefulness as an outdoorsman learned from growing up in the country.

Chinbat does only one angling tour a year, and when I started pondering the trip scheduled for late August through mid September 2005, the old fantasy area of the brain kicked in—I'm going to board the train for the North Woods. The reality area of my brain went through a worst case scenario. In the Darhat Valley I would be hundreds of miles from a medical center. I checked on an insurance policy that would rescue an emergency case by helicopter or plane and transport them for treatment. It seemed reasonably priced until I read all the stipulations. First, at my age, the premium increased five fold. Second, it would not cover pre-existing conditions. Among other things, I've been treated for more than a year for osteoporosis, so broken bones would be excluded. As it turned out, while exercising extreme caution, I had no problems; the only negative part of the trip was the travel time on airlines. I had a wonderful experience while in Mongolia, especially in the beautiful and remote Darhat Valley. The valley has an elevation of some 5,000 feet and is ringed by snow-capped mountains and sparsely inhabited by herdsmen and their array of sheep, goats, yaks, cows, Mongolian horses and an occasional Bactrian camel (two humps) used to transport heavy gear. Most families lived in gers, which are essentially Mongolian yurts. It would appear that the herdsmen way of life hadn't much changed since the time of Mongolian hero Ghengis (or Chinggiss) Khan and the Golden Horde, although occasional motorized vehicles, solar panels and satellite dishes were reminders that we were in the twenty-first, not the twelfth century.

The Darhat Valley receives almost 100 inches of annual precipitation. With virtual continual snow melt from surrounding mountains, the valley is abundantly laced with streams, ponds and lakes. A diversity of waterfowl includes majestic swans (a beautiful, but bad-tempered bird) along with numerous terrestrial birds; particularly impressive is the giant eagle. The valley drains to the north to the Yenesei River. Just to the south, the drainages are tributary to the Selenge River, the main tributary to Lake Baical. The outlet of Baical, the Angara River, joins the Yenesei in its course to the Arctic Ocean, about 1,500 miles due north from its source at the Darhat Valley divide. Most taimen fishing in Mongolia is in the Selenge drainage, especially the Uur and Eg rivers.

Only a few species of fish inhabit the headwaters of the Yenesei basin of Mongolia. The most important from an angling—and ecotourism— perspective species is the taimen. The lenok, another salmonid species, is commonly caught while fishing for taimen. The lenok, although obviously very different from taimen, is closely related to taimen, and from a classification based on evolutionary relationships, should be placed in the same genus, *Hucho*. The arctic grayling is common in all rivers with taimen and lenok.

Taimen fishing in Mongolia has rapidly expanded, and there is some scientific interest in the fish as well. Two nonprofits, the Taimen Conservation Fund and the Tributary Fund, have received considerable funding from international development grants. Five scientists from American universities are employed in taimen research. A native Mongolian fisheries biologist, Manchin Erdenebat, has also been employed for tracking taimen movement by radio tags. Erdenebat received his fisheries education at a college in Kalingrad, Russia, before the collapse of communist governments in the old Soviet Union and in Mongolia. He works for the Institute of Geoecology of the Mongolian Academy of Sciences.

When I was in Ulan Bator, Erdenebat and I discussed his research on taimen and the fishes of the Great Central internal basins of Mongolia. We also talked about the dire need for students in the fields of natural resource management and development to replace the few native biologists and natural resource scientists when the present generation educated in the old Soviet Union retires.

The need for trained scientists and adequate budgets for their work becomes apparent when one considers the explosive development of the mining industry, which has seen great increases in the annual production of gold, copper, zinc, uranium and fluorspar. On one hand, 60 percent of the country's export revenue and 25 percent of the national budget comes from mining. On the other, the impact on watersheds with the great excavations and the widespread use of mercury to extract gold is occurring on a vast scale with virtually no oversight, monitoring or enforcement of reclamation laws. A photo in a tourist guide depicts an enormous gold dredge reaming its way up a river channel. With such threats, the protection of taimen by catch-and-release fishing with barbless hooks seems to pale into insignificance.

Such were the thoughts going through my head while I pursued my own Mongolian fishing adventure. I had caught taimen during a 1991 Siberian trip, so felt no need to add it to my "life list." I mainly practiced low-energy, contemplative dry-fly-fishing for large grayling (up to about 3 pounds) on 3 or 5 weight tackle. One day, however, our vehicle was parked at a river bank and I picked up one of the taimen outfits, took a few casts and caught a taimen in the 8 to 10 pound range. It was a rather small taimen, but quite satisfactory. This led to a camp joke that I had the best cast per taimen ratio. Our group of anglers did catch many taimen; the larger ones were in the 20 to 25 pound range.

Perhaps it's part of the process of ontogenetic development (in plain English, getting to be an old gaffer), but I believe the degree of satisfaction derived from a foreign fishing trip can be more influenced by the learning experience than by the quality of the fishing. On the last evening in Ulan Batar before departure for home, Chinbat wanted to be sure I attended a performance of a cultural revival of traditional Mongolian music. The tones coaxed from the bizarre array of instruments and the sounds produced by "throat singers" (something like humming multiple tunes while gargling) had to be seen to be believed.

It was a most memorable experience. I would highly recommend to all tourists that they make this performance a "must" part of their trip. The theater is easy to find. It's next to Ulan Batar's most popular restaurant, "The Great Khan's Irish Pub." One can go to the pub next door and hear modern Mongolian rock music (not so memorable) and have a Guinness—but Chinggis beer is half the price.

AUTHOR'S NOTE

My trip to Mongolia fulfilled my expectations. I recognized that risks associated with advanced age are involved when one indulges their fantasies to go on a camping trip to a remote part of the earth. It was a wonderful experience to meet nomadic Mongolians and learn about their way of life, history, and culture, while enjoying some fishing.

Just ten years ago, sport fishing for taimen was a relatively new phenomenon. Catering to foreign anglers in Mongolia is now a major enterprise. A scan of websites advertising taimen fishing trips will indicate its magnitude. A note of caution concerning information on taimen websites: the claims of maximum size (250 pounds) and age (to 100 years or more) are based on myths and folklore rather than factual documentation. Taimen can attain a great size but don't believe everything you read.

GHOST TROUT
OF THE RIO CONCHOS

SUMMER 2006

IN A PREVIOUS COLUMN, I TALKED ABOUT "ghost fish," species that are so rare and elusive as to be presumed extinct or on the verge of extinction. The newly discovered Rio Conchos trout is just such a fish.

The first suggestion of ghost trout in the Rio Conchos appeared in a short note published in 1886 by E. D. Cope. Cope wrote that he received two small specimens of trout from Mexico sent by Professor Lupton. Cope identified the specimens as cutthroat trout, but the river drainage where the specimens were collected was not given. The specimens were lost and their identification as cutthroat trout was never verified. All of the trout subsequently known to be native to the Mexican mainland occur in tributaries to the Gulf of California. Although they are obviously divergent from typical rainbow trout, a genetic analysis connects them to the evolutionary line leading to rainbow trout after the separation of the rainbow and cutthroat lines from a common ancestor. The Rio Conchos drains eastward to the Rio Grande but its mountainous headwaters intertwine with drainages flowing westward to the Gulf of California. If the specimens collected by Professor Lupton were cutthroat trout, they must have come from the Conchos drainage. Cutthroat trout should have occurred in the Rio Grande at least as far downstream as the confluence of the Conchos and Rio Grande during the last glacial period. The fish fauna of the Rio Conchos are typical Rio Grande species, including the longnose dace and mountain sucker, species commonly found with Rio Grande cutthroat trout in New Mexico. Joe Tomelleri conducted in-depth historical research on Professor Lupton who was a mining engineer. In the 1880s, Lupton did indeed travel through the headwaters of the Rio Conchos at elevations between 6,500 and 9,000 feet. The circumstantial evidence supported the belief that Rio Grande cutthroat trout once occurred in high elevation headwaters of the Rio Conchos. As typical of other mountainous regions of Mexico, roads for mines and logging opened the door for human habitation, and the subsequent agriculture, livestock grazing and pollution resulted in severe watershed degradation, which has only accelerated in recent years. Also, nonnative hatchery rainbow trout have been widely propagated and dispersed. If native trout still existed in the Conchos drainage, it would be a race against time to find them before they were lost. This year, a small population was found in a short section of a tiny creek. They are barely hanging on and unless protected, they will truly become ghost trout in a short time. Joe sent a photo of the Conchos trout and although very distinct from hatchery rainbows, it is not a cutthroat trout. Its ancestors most likely came from the southern headwaters of the Rio Yaqui via a headwater transfer into the Conchos headwaters. If Rio Grande cutthroat made it to Rio Conchos headwaters, they are long gone. Unless the two specimens sent by Lupton to Cope in the 1880s miraculously turn up in some museum, we will never know the true identity of these fish.

In addition to verifying a native trout in the Rio Conchos drainage, I will summarize new information on Mexican trout discovered since the publication of my 2002 book, *Trout and Salmon in North America* (Fress Press). Trout have been found in the headwaters of the Rio Acaponeta and Rio Baluarte. The Rio Presidio had been thought to be the southernmost natural distribution of Mexican trout and also the southernmost natural occurrence of any species of the family Salmonidae. The Rio Baluarte and Rio Acaponeta drain to the Gulf of California

just south of the mouth of the Rio Presidio (which enters the Gulf near Mazatlan). An ancestor gaining access to the Rio Presidio should also have made it up the Baluarte and Acaponeta. The headwaters of all three drainages are in close proximity, suggesting natural headwater transfers could have occurred. Also, humans could have transplanted trout from one drainage to another. Further research is needed on the Baluarte and Acaponeta trout. They appear to be similar to Presidio trout and, as a group, represent the most recent establishment of trout in the Sierra Madre Occidental in evolutionary time. North of the Rio Presidio, native trout were found in the Rio Piaxtla drainage. These trout were previously unknown. They appear to be derived from the same ancestor that gave rise to trout native to the upper San Lorenzo drainage, immediately to the north of the Rio Piaxtla.

An interesting discovery of a peculiar trout was made in the Rio

RIO CONCHOS TROUT
Oncorhynchus mykiss subspecies

Sidra, a tributary to the lower San Lorenzo. The Rio Sidra trout was found above a barrier falls that isolates them from a hatchery raising nonnative rainbow trout below the falls. The Rio Sidra trout are quite distinct from the trout native to the upper San Lorenzo. I assume the Sidra trout are derived from an ancestor different from the one that became established in the upper San Lorenzo. Their high number of vertebrae suggests a relationship to the trout of the Presidio, Baluarte and Acaponeta. The Rio Yaqui is the largest and northernmost drainage basin tributary to the Gulf of California with native trout. The trout of its northern tributaries have been long separated from trout of the southern tributaries. Genetic analysis reveals two distinct groups associated with northern and southern segments of the drainage. The southern Yaqui trout gave rise to the Rio Mayo trout immediately south of the Yaqui, and, evidently, to the newly discovered Conchos trout.

A better understanding of distribution and patterns of differentiation of Mexican trout raises questions on their classification. In my book, I recognized the Mexican golden trout, native to the Rios Fuerte, Sinaloa and Culiacan, as a full species *Oncorhynchus chrysogaster* because of its extreme degree of differentiation from any form of rainbow trout *O. mykiss*. I considered the differentiation expressed by Yaqui-Mayo, San Lorenzo and Presidio trout to represent undescribed subspecies of *O. mykiss*. There is no generally accepted standard of criteria to recognize species and subspecies. Philosophies and belief systems of classifications can be found to conform to anyone's personal preference. Recognition of the undescribed Mexican trout as new species, rather than subspecies, should have a greater positive impact for their conservation, and the native trout of Mexico will need all the help they can get.

AUTHOR'S NOTE

My notes for the "Rio Grande Cutthroat Trout" column (p. 107) tell of another native Conchos trout discovered in April 2007. Photographs of the new trout sent to me by Joe Tomelleri reveal distinct differences from the "ghost trout" featured in this present column. I tentatively identify the trout in the photos as a Mexican golden trout. Although the mystery of Professor Lupton's specimens has not been solved, the recent discoveries of two new forms of trout native to the Rio Conchos basin are exciting news. They indicate how much is yet to be learned about the native trout of Mexico, which all began with Professor Lupton's 1883 "ghost" specimens.

ROBERT J. BEHNKE, PH.D. is professor emeritus of Fisheries Conservation and Wildlife Biology at Colorado State University in Fort Collins, Colorado. He is the author of more than 200 articles and papers regarding fish and fisheries and has served on numerous advisory boards for state and federal agencies. He is the author of several books including *Native Trout of Western North America* (AFS, 1992) and *Trout of North America* (Free Press, 2002). He began writing the quarterly "About Trout" column for Trout Unlimited's *Trout* magazine in 1983. He lives in Fort Collins, Colorado with his wife, Sally.

JOSEPH R. TOMELLERI graduated with an M.S. in biology and pursued research in botany before becoming a full-time artist in 1986. Since then, he has traveled extensively around North America collecting specimens and photographing native fishes to create his illustrations. His work has appeared in dozens of magazines and journals and many books including, *Trout and Salmon of North America* (Free Press, 2002) and *Fishes of Alabama* (Smithsonian, 2004). He lives in Leawood, Kansas with his wife Susan and his two young sons.

INDEX

This book is set in $^{9.25}/_{14}$ point *Monticello*,
a typeface designed by Matthew Carter.

The heads are set in 20 point *Monotype Baskerville*.

It was printed on 140 gsm White A matt art paper
by Max Production Printing Limited in China.

The design is by Jason Ramirez,
with art direction from Charles Nix.